TO A SAFER PLACE

Known locations to where the Isle of Thanet, Canterbury and Ashford evacuees were sent during World War II. It should be noted that Staffordshire was the destination of school children from the Isle of Thanet under the Government Evacuation Scheme.

1. **Staffordshire**
Abbots Bromley
Adbaston
Betley
Boney Hay
Denstone
Draycott in the Clay
Eccleshall
Gayton
Gnosall
Great Wysley
High Offley
Hints
Hopwas
Kingstone
Lichfield
Madeley
Norbury
Rocester
Rugeley
Seighford
Stafford
Stonall
Tamworth
Uttoxeter
Wall
Willstock
Wootton

2. **Northants.**
Courteenhall

3. **Rhondda Valley.**
Gilfach Goch

4. **Gloucester.**

5. **Oxford.**

6. **Wantage.**

7. **Reading.**

8. **East Grinstead.**

9. **Seaford.**

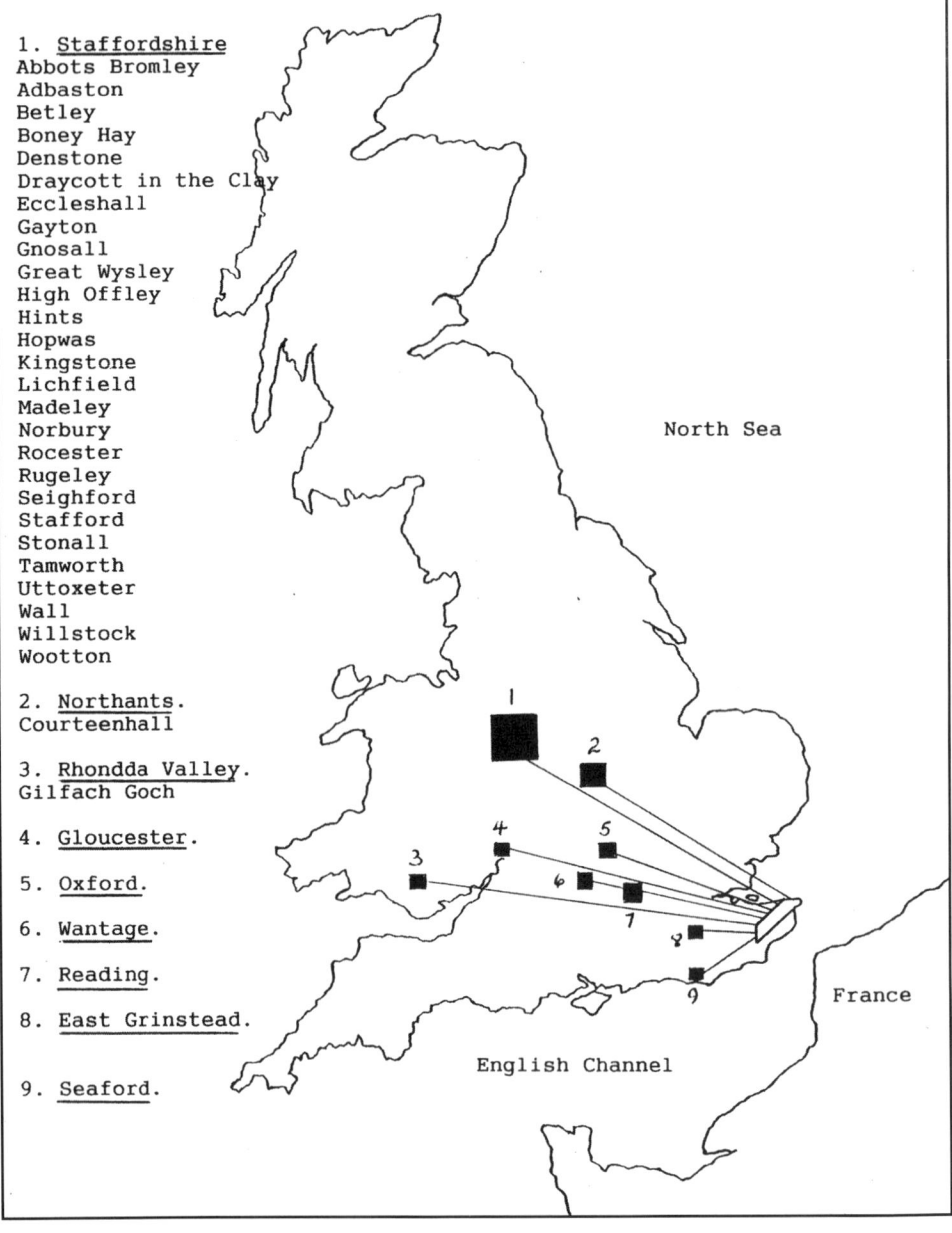

TO A SAFER PLACE

Peter Hayward

Buckland Publications Ltd
Barwick Road, Dover

THIS BOOK IS DEDICATED

TO THE MEMORIES OF

DON WRIGHT, PETER HOAD,

JANICE PRENTICE, JAN BARBER

AND BOB SYMONS

This book is a companion volume to
Children in Exile
and
For the Sake of the Children
– the story of the evacuation of children
in the Second World War
from Hellfire Corner
and the Medway Towns
respectively

© Copyright Peter Hayward 2000

Published in 2000 by Buckland Publications Ltd
Barwick Road, Dover, Kent CT17 0LG

ISBN 07212 0937 8

Printed in England by Buckland Press Ltd, Barwick Road, Dover CT17 0LG

CONTENTS

		Page
Introduction		9
Chapter		
1	In the Beginning	13
2	To a Safer Place	29
3	Memories of Staffordshire	64
4	More Memories from the Midlands	87
5	Unhappy Billets and Tragic Memories	104
6	Private Evacuation	115
7	The Schools' Perspective	120
8	The Canterbury Chapter	138
9	The Ashford Chapter	171
10	The Home Front	191
11	Epilogue	205
Maps		215
Acknowledgements		221
Personal Name Index		223

ILLUSTRATIONS

Where the evacuees went	Frontispiece
Young evacuees leave	8
Government encouragement to take evacuees	14
A royal certificate for taking in evacuees	17
A means of exploding magnetic mines	18
Some allied troops en route from Dunkirk	19
German aircraft in silhouette	20
British soldiers saved from Dunkirk	22
Routes from Dunkirk	24
Commemorative tablet at Margate	25
Identity Card	26
Children in gas masks	28
Lifebuoy soap and evacuees	29
Children leave by bus	30
A graveyard of road signs	34
Evacuation advice	38
Irene Thompson, aged 5	49
Irene Thompson's mother and Uncle Jim	50
Wood Bridge, Hopwas	50
'Don't waste food!'	51
The church at Hopwas	52
Friday was Home Guard night	52
'Miss Margate'	53
Irene Thompson, aged 10	53
Clarendon House Grammar School	54
A postcard from Sergeant Collison	61
Hostess Gertie Oliver and Audrey Collison	62
Chatham House Grammar School, Ramsgate	63
Foster father Mr Bradbury	65
Peggy Horn and Mary Bradbury	66
Salmestone Primary School	66
Drapers Mills Primary School	70
The Bisto kids were evacuated too	71
An appeal for aluminium	72
A railway ticket to evacuation	73
Arthur Campany and Bertie Clayton	73
Arthur Campany's school report	74
'Dig for Victory'	76
Eileen and Tony Walker	79
St Mildred's Primary School	80

A reunion with Mrs Milly Jackson	80
Children of St Laurence School, Ramsgate	82
Ray Doherty's first billet	83
The only tap in Drayton-in-the-Clay	84
Douglas and Patrick Knight	85
Joan and Hazel Knight	85
Laurie Johnson	86
Ramsgate evacuees returned to Staffordshire in 1995	86
June Edwards	89
The emblem of Chatham House Grammar School	90
Barbara Tilbrook, aged 6	92
Barbara Tilbrook in school uniform	93
Ramsgate evacuees at Ellastone	93
The four Cox sisters	94
Fees for accommodating evacuees	95
'Please don't return home!'	96
The Holland family about to be evacuated	101
Edna and Peggy Tipping	104
Broadstairs railway station bombed	110
Peter Rogers and Christopher Fright	115
Dame Janet Junior School, Ramsgate	124
The motif of Clarendon House School	135
Lorries in Canterbury Cathedral!	137
Tons of earth in the Cathedral nave	140
Running to an air-raid shelter	148
The BEF trapped	149
Canterbury Home Guard	150
A Battle of Britain sky	151
The Dean's narrow escape	152
Old shops badly damaged	153
The blitz comes to Canterbury	154
Women, grow vegetables!	155
National Savings	156
Women, come into the factories	159
Old Simon Langton's Boys' School	161
Canterbury evacuees about to depart	163
Devastation in the High Street	164
Simon Langton's Boys' School gutted	167
St Augustine's College gateway	168
A bomb map of Canterbury	169
Fifty years on – a plaque unveiled	170
Ashford girls evacuated to Oxford	183
The chapel of Lady Margaret Hall, Oxford	185
Girls of South Central School, Ashford, in Oxford	187
South Central School, Ashford...	187
Mary Cramp in steel helmet	188
'Don't do it, mother!'	189
Erecting an Anderson shelter	191
A Morrison shelter	192
How to put on a child's gas mask	193

A Wills' cigarette card	193
Recruiting for the ARP	193
Appreciation for Home Guard Service	194
Advertisements supporting wartime efforts	195
'Your new Ration Book'	196
A German propaganda leaflet	197
Rationing of clothing	198
Ploughing is as vital as arms	199
Thanet War Weapons Week	200
After a raid on High Street, Margate	201
The *Dunbar Castle* sunk	202
Holy Trinity Church, Margate, damaged by a bouncing bomb	203
The two hats of Winston Churchill	204
Victory in Europe	205
Ramsgate's deep shelters	215
Bomb map of Margate and Cliftonville	216
Bomb map of Broadstairs	217
Bomb maps of Ramsgate	218
A royal message to all children at school	219
The doodlebug map of Kent	220

*Young evacuees leave with their teachers –
escorted by local police!*

INTRODUCTION

IMAGINE, IF YOU CAN, a very organised but lonely looking crocodile of children, each laden with a haversack or small case containing a few items of clothing and enough food for the day, making its way to your local railway station; a station already packed with hundreds of children, each with luggage label attached and a gas mask slung over a shoulder. Imagine also, the feelings of all those children, not knowing where they were going and not knowing for how long they would be away. Not knowing when, or if, they would see their parents again. Parents, who, with the gathering threat of invasion ever nearer, had had to make the most heart-searching decisions for their children's safety.

Some of the children who had never been on a train before were excited and thought it was a big adventure. Some thought they were going away for a fortnight's holiday in the country. Others were frightened and confused and some were crying for their mothers.

This then was the scene, duplicated at many railway stations throughout the South-East of England at the time of evacuation.

On the 2nd June 1940, at just three years old, I was one of those children, who, together with my three elder sisters, stood on the station platform waiting to be evacuated from East Kent.

Fifty-four years later I attended an evacuees' reunion and on that day the idea to record the experience of evacuation was born. At the reunion, the camaraderie, excited chatter, fond and less happy reminiscences inspired the feeling that these personal memories ought to be recorded for future generations – before they were lost for ever. I launched into a campaign to contact as many Kent ex-evacuees as possible and the response was so overwhelming and the volume of memories so great that they evolved into not one, but three books. Hence the trilogy: *Children into Exile, For the Sake of the Children* and *To a Safer Place*.

These three books try to give the reader as thorough an insight as possible into the experience of evacuation, particularly the experiences of Kent evacuees.

I feel it would be helpful if I now include a little bit of background information leading up to the largest movement of civilian population this country has ever seen. Evacuation during the Second World War affected millions of British people: children, young mothers with babies, pregnant women, those with sight and limb disabilities, the aged and infirm. What prompted the Government to organise this vast movement of population? Well, its roots can be traced back to the First World War, when, in 1915, London was bombed by German Zeppelins and later by aeroplanes. 1,117 civilians lost their lives.

After the First World War rapid development in both bomb and aircraft power fuelled fears about the effects of bombing on densely-populated areas. The intervention of the German Luftwaffe in the Spanish Civil War (1937-1939) added to the British Government's concern. In 1938 Sir John Anderson chaired a committee to review the situation and it soon reported that in the event of war, evacuation would be a necessity. Meanwhile, the London County Council, under its energetic leader, Herbert Morrison, actually started an evacuation when, following the German invasion of Czechoslovakia, it sent 4,300 nursery and physically-handicapped children to the country in September 1938. It soon brought them back!

A Home Office directive dated 24th September 1938, gave some information concerning evacuation procedures:

From Home Office

General description of evacuation scheme

Billeting will be under compulsory powers. Householders are required to provide shelter.

Payment to householders: 5/- for each adult and 3/- for each child, but for this, food is not required to be provided. Later, persons who can afford to contribute towards the cost of their billets will be expected to do so.

Refugees in need of financial assistance will be able to receive payments on application through the Employment Exchange.

Refugees will be brought to detraining station by main line trains, if possible to run during daylight hours, 6am to 6pm. Necessary arrangements for transport will be made by Traffic Commissioners, or by London Passenger Transport Board.

A Traffic Officer, appointed by a transport authority, will be at each railhead, to divert and control transport required for the transportation of refugees from railheads.

County clerks should immediately arrange with Traffic Commissions for appointment of Co-ordinating Traffic Officers, who can ensure that transport at railheads, in areas of which County clerks are responsible, will be provided.

Refugees will be asked to bring a day's supply of rations and a blanket, but many will not, and some hot food should be provided under local arrangements. W.V.S. no doubt will be of assistance.

Powers to requisition unoccupied buildings will be given to clerks of County Councils, Town Clerks etc.

Lists of persons to be given to billeting officers in reception areas.

* * *

By the beginning of 1939, a clear Government Evacuation Scheme had been formulated under the general direction of Sir John Anderson and the Ministry of Health. The country was divided into three zones – evacuation, reception and neutral, and it was estimated that around 3,500,000 people in England and Wales and 400,000 in Scotland would need to be evacuated.

On 31st August 1939, Hitler's troops invaded Poland. On the same day, the British government ordered the evacuation to start. The evacuation proceeded swiftly and during the first three days of September 1939 a total of 1,473,391 persons were evacuated under the official scheme, made up of 826,959 unaccompanied school children; 523,670 children with mothers; 12,705 expectant mothers; 7,057 blind and other handicapped persons; 103,000 teachers and helpers. In addition, between June and September 1939, about two million other people evacuated themselves privately.

Most evacuees were conveyed by train. The stations were crammed full with children, with labels attached, carrying haversacks or small cases and the inevitable gas masks in cardboard boxes.

Some of these children included those who came from south London and the Medway Towns and were evacuated to other parts of Kent. This book will cover the journey and reception of these evacuees to places like Ashford, Canterbury and other locations in East Kent, but the bulk of the book will deal mainly with the evacuation of Kent children from the Isle of Thanet, who, on Sunday, the 2nd June, 1940, were whisked away to the rural areas of Staffordshire, at a time when enemy invasion seemed imminent.

The story of the Thanet evacuees is told mainly in personal accounts which are varied in the extreme, from good billets and loving foster parents to abuse and neglect.

Readers may find the following *Kentish Express* article for 8th September 1939 interesting. It lists in chronological order, the main events leading up to and including the outbreak of the Second World War:

1939

31 March	The Premier told Parliament that if Poland were threatened and had to resist, Britain would support her.
27 April	Conscription.
28 April	Hitler denounces Anglo-German Naval Agreement, and Treaty of Non-Aggression with Poland.
5 May	Poland willing to join in conversations with Germany if latter were prepared to proceed by peaceable methods.
28 May	First serious reports of military preparations in Danzig.
10 June	Reaffirmation of British pledge to Poland.
18 August	German Press outburst against Poland.
21 August	German-Russian non-aggression pact announced.
23 August	Britain reaffirms to Hitler our determination to stand by Poland.
24 August	Herr Forster proclaims himself head of the Danzig State. Poland accepts President Roosevelt's appeal to Germany and Poland to submit dispute to peaceful negotiation.
25 August	Hitler gives British Ambassador communication emphasising demands on Poland and mentioning prospects of Anglo-German co-operation.
26 August	British Ambassador attends Government meeting. France stands by Poland.
28 August	British Ambassador gives Hitler reply, again reaffirming pledge to Poland.
29 August	Parliament reaffirms national unity. Hitler sends note which, it is

	claimed in Berlin, accepted a British proposal for direct negotiation between Germany and Poland if a Polish plenipotentiary reached Berlin within 24 hours.
30 August	Poles decline to send such representative under menace. British Ambassador visits Hitler and von Ribbentrop, and is told German terms. Hitler sets up defence council.
31 August	Full mobilisation of British Fleet. Polish Ambassador in Berlin informed at 8pm of German terms. Two hours later these terms are announced by German wireless, and that Germany regards them as having been rejected.
1 September	Germany invades Poland and Poland tells Britain and France that this is direct aggression. Britain and France tell von Ribbentrop that unless German forces are promptly withdrawn, obligations would be fulfilled. Von Ribbentrop says he must consult Hitler. Full mobilization in Britain and France. (Government Civilian Evacuation Scheme starts in Britain).
2 September	No reply from Germany. Mussolini proposes 5-power conference, but we say we cannot attend conference while Germans are on Polish soil.
3 September	Our Ambassador tells Germany that if her troops have not begun to withdraw from Poland in two hours he is to ask for passports. No reply by time stipulated, and we were at war. Similar ultimatum by France expired, and France and Germany were at war. Reported sinking by German submarine of liner *Athenia* without warning. R.A.F. planes attacked German warships at entrance to Kiel Canal.
5 September	Poles stated that over 30 of their aircraft flew over Berlin and returned.
6 September	The French began to advance against the Siegfried Line.
7 September	The French made slight advances. German machine gun nests were captured. Warsaw was within reach of German guns and is soon expected to fall. Germany is putting immense forces into Poland – no less than 1,600,000 troops and guns and tanks and aeroplanes.

Chapter One

IN THE BEGINNING . . .

The progression to war increased during the month of August 1939, so did the activity in that part of Kent known as the Isle of Thanet, made famous by its main holiday resorts of Margate, Broadstairs and Ramsgate.

It was at the height of the holiday season as war approached, with thousands of holiday-makers enjoying the fine weather. The following personal account gives a glimpse into the life in Ramsgate during that time. **Anthony Cinderey** *was a young Welsh boy from Abertillery who came to Kent before the Second World War to stay with an aunt and uncle:*

As a child, I was very delicate and, having had lots of illnesses, the family doctor advised my parents that, if they could, they should send me away to get plenty of sunshine. This would have been impossible had it not been for the fact that an uncle and aunt had moved to Dover in the early 1920s. My uncle was a collier, and had moved to Kent to work in the Kent Coalfield.

Eventually, my aunt and uncle moved from Dover to the then brand new mining village of Aylesham where my uncle, Albert Coles, an amateur wrestler, helped start up a gymnastic club in nearby Snowdown village. I was about six when a relative took me to Aylesham to stay with my uncle and aunt. The climate seemed to agree with me so my family decided to let me stay in Kent and I enrolled at Aylesham Primary School. Unfortunately, sometime later I became ill again and returned to Wales. Meanwhile, my aunt and uncle had moved from Aylesham to Ramsgate to run a boarding house in Augusta Road.

My family now agreed to send me to Ramsgate for 6 to 8 months of each year. I therefore had a unique life – a sort of 'Tom Sawyer' existence where I would spend my summer months wandering around Ramsgate – the funfair, the beach or just dangling my feet from the harbour wall. My aunt had even bought me a little dog, which I called Tony.

As August 1939 approached, Ramsgate was put on a war footing. Sandbags were being filled on the beach to be placed around the public buildings in the town – and gas masks were being issued! I remember my cousin and myself queueing for our gas masks – which gave me some claim to fame when I was sent back to Abertillery. For a while I was the only boy in school with a gas mask and I had to stand in front of the assembly and demonstrate to the rest of the school how quickly I could put my gas mask on.

One of the many advertisements placed by the Ministry of Health in local newspapers to encourage householders to take in evacuees

I remember extra trains were put on during the last few weeks of August 1939. Ramsgate, as with other seaside towns, was, as usual, full of holiday-makers, and these special trains were needed to cope with the people who had cut short their holiday because of the possibility of war. A brand new word had suddenly appeared on people's lips – evacuation!

My last pre-war memory of Kent was two days before the outbreak. I was 11 years old by this time and helping to fill the sand bags on the beach at Ramsgate. I was dragged away from the beach and the next day, much to my annoyance, I was put on a train for the journey back to Wales and my family. The trains were so crowded that we stood all the way from Paddington to Newport. Meanwhile, my aunt and uncle stayed on in Ramsgate as shells and bombs rained down on Kent.

One day I answered a knock on the door to find my aunt, with Tony the dog and a bird cage in each hand. She had evacuated herself from Ramsgate – and stayed with us for the duration! About a year later, Uncle Albert, who had been a full-time air raid warden in Ramsgate, also arrived. He had suffered a mental breakdown due to the air raids. They both eventually went to work at the munitions factory at Usk.

When the war finally came

to an end, my uncle and aunt returned to Ramsgate and bought a large house in Wellington Crescent to continue with their guest house business, and their son, Jack Coles, became deputy headmaster at a local Thanet school. Shortly after the war I met my wife Maureen and took her to Ramsgate for a holiday. She fell in love with Kent and it is still one of our favourite places.

Ironically, as thousands of holiday-makers were streaming home with the thought of imminent war on their minds, the Isle of Thanet was preparing to receive an influx of evacuees from London and elsewhere, as the extract from the Isle of Thanet Gazette for 2nd September, 1939 shows:

THANET REFUGE
FIVE HUNDRED CHILDREN COMING TO MINSTER AND MONKTON

Over five hundred children from evacuated areas are arriving at Minster and Monkton today (Friday) and tomorrow, and are to be billeted with village families. Others are expected in the Sandwich district.

'I am going to take in as many as I can. I had five boys killed in the last war and I know what it is like,' one elderly Minster woman told a *Gazette* reporter yesterday. 'I am taking two, but I would not close my door if two more turned up,' said another. This is typical of the spirit in which the country folk have met the urgency of the situation. Nearly everyone has been willing to help and seldom have the billeting officers had to call upon their powers of compulsion.

VICAR WILL TAKE THREE

The Vicar of Minster (the Revd A. MacMichael), who has agreed to take three children, said he felt sure that every public-spirited member of the community would do his best to comfortably accommodate any adults or children the Government saw fit to evacuate. 'It is unbelievable,' declared the Vicar, 'that anyone who has room would hesitate one moment about doing all he could to help in this way to serve his country in these troubled times.'

Arriving at Minster today (Friday) would be 200 children of school age together with their teachers. Two hundred mothers and babies will be billeted the following day in addition to fifty adults on National Service. Accommodation has been found for the majority of these, but Mr J. Simpson, chief billeting officer, has expressed the hope that anyone with accommodation still available will come forward. The chief officer and his deputy Mrs Simpson have a hard-working team of eleven, consisting of Mrs F. K. Horn, Miss E. Wellard, the Misses Markham, Mrs H. J. Card, Mrs P. Golder, Mrs Fuller, Mrs Blair, Mrs Madge, Miss Simpkin and Miss Pearson.

The thirty-nine children and their teachers coming to Monkton today and the forty mothers and children coming tomorrow will be provided with accommodation sought out for them by Mrs Simpson and Mr N. H. Kennett.

*   *   *

By January 1940, rumours had started to circulate in East Kent about the possibility of school children being evacuated from the area. The following small article appeared in the Isle of Thanet Gazette *for 19th January 1940:*

NOT EVACUATING
THANET RUMOUR DISPELLED

There is a rumour prevalent in Thanet that school children are to be evacuated. Fortunately, like so many war-time rumours, there is no truth in it.

Mr E. F. Owen, clerk to Broadstairs and St Peter's Urban District Council, told the *Gazette* yesterday (Thursday) that he wished the rumour to be denied. It was absolutely without foundation.

He added that such a rumour was doing a considerable amount of damage in Broadstairs and the other Thanet towns. He had made enquiries and found out that there was no truth at all in the statement.

(Author's note: Less than five months later, the children were departing Thanet for unknown destinations.)

* * *

The expected wide-spread bombing of cities and industrial areas of Britain during the first few months of the war never materialised. This period was known as the 'phoney war' and it was during this time that thousands of evacuees drifted back to their homes in evacuation areas. However, as 1939 gave way to 1940 enemy activity began to increase. By May 1940, those evacuees, brought into East Kent from London and the Medway Towns, were now being removed to safer areas. Most of these evacuees had left by the middle of May, but there were a few 'stragglers' left in the villages bordering the Isle of Thanet, as the following article from the Isle of Thanet Gazette *for 31st May 1940, shows:*

EVACUEES TO EVACUATE

The remainder of the Medway children who were evacuated to the villages of Eastry rural district are to be evacuated in the near future.

This decision was made by the Government on Tuesday, and will affect about 162 unaccompanied evacuees who have been billeted in Ash, Preston, Wingham, Minster, and other villages in the Eastry district since soon after the outbreak of war.

The Kent areas affected by the order are Eastry rural district, Bridge-Blean rural district, Dover rural district, East Ashford rural district, Elham rural district, Strood rural district and Swale rural district.

At last week's meeting of Eastry Rural District Council it was announced that the council had been ordered to make plans for the reception of another 400 children, but those at Minster were to be removed.

A fortnight ago a large number of evacuee children were removed from Sandwich to South Wales.

* * *

The following comments, from those who were eventually destined to be evacuated from the Isle of Thanet, give some good indications of life in that area during the first part of the war, and includes some vivid accounts of troops arriving in Thanet after being rescued from Dunkirk:

Irene Thornton: I was born in Margate, Kent in 1935 and started at a Margate infants' school at the age of four and a half. I had no brothers or sisters. My first memory of World War II was just after I had started school. I was playing outside the front of the house with my friends, when someone came rushing out of their house and said that war had been declared. All the adults went inside to hear the news, but the children carried on playing; 'war' at our age meant nothing to us. It was September 1939.

Janet Laker *(now Mrs Walmsley):* Before the war we used to go for afternoon walks, usually along the West Cliff from St Lawrence and then home for tea, followed by evensong at St Lawrence Church. I also remember listening to the band at the West Cliff bandstand. My parents, Charles and Edith Laker (now deceased) were very poor and worked hard to keep us well and happy. Mother did 'letting' in the summer to help pay the bills, and dad grew all his own vegetables. We had an air raid shelter in the garden and dad grew nasturtiums over it. Luckily we only had to use it for a few nights. We never went away for holidays, so when it came to the evacuation, it all seemed like a big adventure to us, without realising the seriousness of it all!

Roy Doherty: At the outbreak of the war my family was living in Stanley Road,

A royal certificate issued to householders who looked after evacuees

Ramsgate, near to the railway station. I lived there with my mother and two younger brothers, Alan and Brian. My father was serving in the Royal Air Force and was eventually posted overseas. I remember my mother telling us children that we may have to be sent away if the bombing got too bad. Although we had an Anderson shelter in our garden, mother thought we would be safer in the Ramsgate tunnels, the nearest entrance of which was in Ellington Park.

Peter Deacon: My brother and I were put into a children's home at Manston, Kent, sometime before the war began. The home consisted of about ten houses and each house had a house mother to look after us. These house mothers were not easy people to get on with! We each had chores to do like dusting, polishing, washing up etc. Sometime during 1939 workmen came into the homes and installed huge wooden beams into the houses, presumably to strengthen them against attack, but at the time we didn't know what they were for. It was about this time that we used to hear loud 'thumping' noises a good way off. We later found out that it was gunfire from across the English Channel. After a while we could see Wellington bombers flying out from RAF Manston, and these planes had huge rings fastened underneath from nose to tail. They looked huge and very frightening. Soon we were all taken by coaches to another children's home in the village of Eastry, near Sandwich. We were next door to what was then a lunatic asylum. We weren't at Eastry long before we were off again.

Magnetic mines, laid in the English Channel by the Germans, were exploded by aircraft with an electrified ring attached. It was very dangerous work!

Janet Small: I was 14 years old when war was declared in 1939. By the following April our schooling in Ramsgate began to be disrupted. Eventually we were told that our school, Clarendon House Grammar School, was being evacuated to Stafford (horrors! – the 'Black Country'!). and it was obviously important for my year to go as we were due to sit our General Schools Certificate that summer, and in those days it was a 'one chance exam'.

Antony Owen: Before the war we lived in Thanet, on the outer edge of Cliftonville, towards Broadstairs, and we had open views across the fields to St Peter's. I used to cycle to and from school every day, through St Peter's and past the old private aerodrome. I was a pupil at Chatham House Grammar School, Ramsgate, at the outbreak of the war and, consequently, when the school was evacuated to Stafford in

June 1940, I went with them.

Brian Sackett: The day war was declared I was walking along Church Road in Ramsgate, and I can remember the milkman coming along with his horse and cart. Suddenly the air-raid sirens started. I was close to home and my mother came running out and said, 'Come quickly, there is a war on.' Because the shelters in Ramsgate weren't finished, I remember we all had to go into the crypt of St George's Church, where there were hundreds of people. Anyway, things seemed to progress from that point until my school, Hereson Road School, was evacuated in June 1940.

M. A. Lawrence: On Sunday, 25th May, 1940, we were standing on Broadstairs seafront, looking directly out to sea. We could see the pall of smoke over Dunkirk and could hear the rumble of gunfire. At night we could see the glow of fires and flashes of explosions. Nothing could have prepared me for what we would find on Ramsgate railway station the following day. We arrived from Broadstairs on an early train, five of us, and we walked around the railings and stood in a line at the head of the subway steps. I suppose we thought the men lying solidly packed in the subway were dead bodies. Anyway, we hesitated for a long while before walking down, gingerly picking our way through. The booking hall was also packed with sleeping men, on the seats and on the floor. Outside a long queue stretched away down the road. I noticed the French fishing fleet in the Inner Harbour and there were several warships lying offshore waiting to dock. That weekend we were evacuated.

Beryl Price (*now Mrs Borne*): It was towards the end of May 1940 that bus loads of *poilus* (French soldiers) passed in front of our home in Ramsgate. Nobody knew what exactly was going on. My mother was so intrigued that she went to investigate. She saw a fleet of small boats unloading men on the beach, who were then being taken to

Thousands of British and Allied troops, saved from Dunkirk, arrived in Kent ports, some in small boats which crossed and re-crossed the Channel with their heavy loads

THE War Office has issued these diagram pictures of enemy troop-carrying 'planes. They are intended to guide Local Defence Volunteers and all members of the public.

Some of these pictures have been published elsewhere in the past few days, but this page contains many more details and also silhouettes of comparable British bombers. It is the only complete chart. Cut it out and hang it on your wall.

If you see an aeroplane that resembles an enemy, tell the police, an air raid warden, or the L.D.V., at once.

Here are some simple points to remember :
If the 'plane has more than two engines it is probably a German.

The 3-engined Junkers Ju 52 has one engine in the nose, looking like the head of a fly. These have been the 'planes most used for parachutists.

The Junkers Ju 90 has wings that sweep backwards like a swallow in flight.

Note the square-cut edges of the wings and tails of the Junkers 'planes.

If a bomber is flying low in daylight, note the colour. British bombers are mostly painted black on the underside. (There are some silver or light green.)

The badge painted on British 'planes is like a red, white, and blue target, with the red as the bull's-eye.

German bombers are painted light blue-grey under the fuselage and wings.

Their badge is a black cross, outlined with a white band. The white band itself is outlined in black.

A black swastika is usually carried on the tail of the 'plane.

THESE ARE THE TYPES OF GERMAN AIRCRAFT YOU ARE MOST LIKELY TO SEE

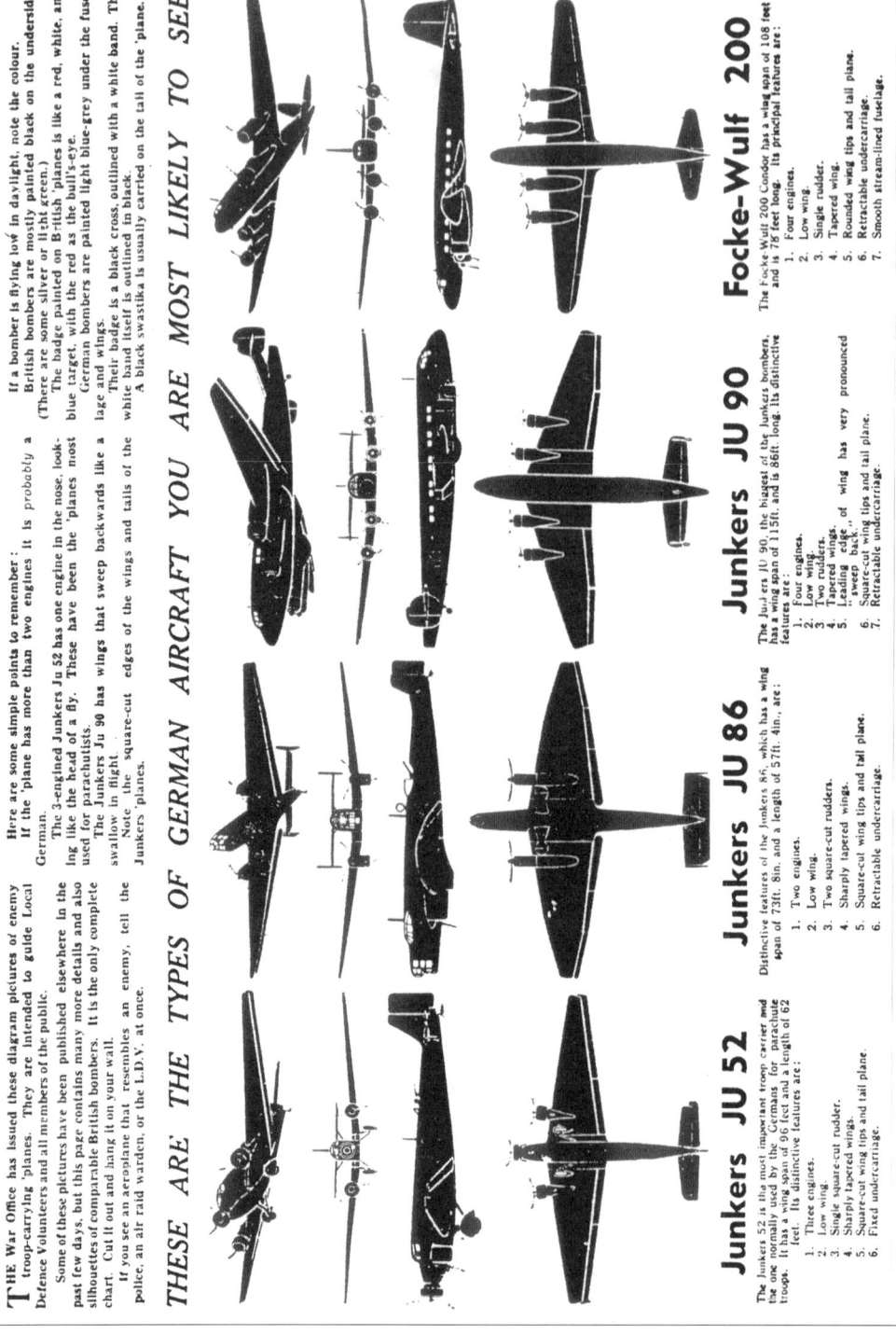

Junkers JU 52

The Junkers 52 is the most important troop-carrier and the one normally used by the Germans for parachute troops. It has a wing span of 96 feet and a length of 62 feet. Its distinctive features are :

1. Three engines.
2. Low wing.
3. Single square-cut rudder.
4. Sharply tapered wings.
5. Square-cut wing tips and tail plane.
6. Fixed undercarriage.

Junkers JU 86

Distinctive features of the Junkers 86, which has a wing span of 73ft. 8in. and a length of 57ft. 4in., are :

1. Two engines.
2. Low wing.
3. Two square-cut rudders.
4. Sharply tapered wings.
5. Square-cut wing tips and tail plane.
6. Retractable undercarriage.

Junkers JU 90

The Junkers JU 90, the biggest of the Junkers bombers, has a wing span of 115ft. and is 86ft long. Its distinctive features are :

1. Four engines.
2. Low wing.
3. Two rudders.
4. Tapered wings.
5. Leading edge of wing has very pronounced sweep back.
6. Square-cut wing tips and tail plane.
7. Retractable undercarriage.

Focke-Wulf 200

The Focke-Wulf 200 Condor has a wing span of 108 feet and is 78 feet long. Its principal features are :

1. Four engines.
2. Low wing.
3. Single rudder.
4. Tapered wing.
5. Rounded wing tips and tail plane.
6. Retractable undercarriage.
7. Smooth stream-lined fuselage.

'Merrie England', an amusement park on the East Cliff. These men wore very little clothing and all appeared to be totally exhausted and some were wounded. My mother found out that these were some of the soldiers being rescued from the beaches of Dunkirk and she immediately started to organise Ramsgate residents to collect clothing and blankets so that the soldiers had something to wear. My mother even helped to organise a team of writers who wrote on cards, 'Je suis en Angleterre', for the French soldiers so that they could post them home to France once they knew where they were going.

Then the British soldiers arrived. They were all in a state of shock and, after the processing, were taken to Ramsgate railway station and despatched to who knows where! I was a teenager at the time and my mother wanted me to see history in the making. We walked to the West Cliff and viewed the scene. The sea was as calm as a mill pond and there were hundreds of boats of all sorts arriving. Men were walking or being carried, or being lifted on stretchers from these boats and were taken into 'Merrie England'. Then we watched as the small boats put back to sea to return to Dunkirk. Visibility was good and we could see smoke rising from the French coast. Suddenly, from out of nowhere, came an aeroplane flying very low – almost on the water, and it strafed the ships close to Ramsgate Harbour. Mother was horrified and we hurried home. My mother and I couldn't believe what was happening. We were well aware that there were 22 miles of English Channel separating us from France, and that this silver sea had saved us from hostile attacks in the past; we were taught that at school.

As the long line of soldiers was leaving the area, the word went out that the Isle of Thanet school children were the next to go.

Cecily Matthews (now Mrs Poppy): I was eleven years old when war was declared in September 1939, and we were living in Margate, on the Isle of Thanet. It didn't seem long before the Luftwaffe began attacking the convoys as they passed down the English Channel, and most of our school days were spent in the air raid shelters. In May and early June 1940, things were beginning to look bad. The small ships were bringing thousands of rescued troops from the beaches of Dunkirk and we were expecting Hitler to invade at any moment. Posters were put up all over the town, advising people to leave as soon as possible. The authorities decided at that point to evacuate the school children to safer places away from the South East of England.

George Emptage: In 1939 my family was living in a small terraced house at 33 Byron Avenue, Margate. On Sunday 3rd of September 1939, I was playing in our small back garden with my friend, Lenny Wright, when we heard a load wailing noise. We had heard this noise before, but this time it seemed to go on for ever. We both ran indoors and found my parents and sisters listening to the wireless – an announcer was saying that England was now at war with Germany. Both Lenny and I were frightened, but my parents told us not to worry. Christmas came and went and life for us children went on

Opposite: These illustrations were issued by the War Office in 1940 and were published in national and local newspapers and other publications with the instructions to the reader to 'Cut it out and hang it on your wall'

as usual, but we did notice things going on that we didn't understand – like not being allowed to play on the beach and everywhere people were making frames out of wood and black material to fit over their windows to stop light shining out at night. Some people were even sticking paper on the windows in the shape of criss-crosses.

One day men came with horse and cart, loaded with steel air-raid shelters. They delivered one to each household and neighbours helped each other to dig holes in the gardens to put the shelters in. Then the shelters were covered with soil and sandbags, leaving just a small doorway to get in and out. Some nights when there was an air-raid we would go into the shelter, but it wasn't very nice, it was cold and damp. The school I attended at that time was Drapers Mills School in Margate and it wasn't long before shelters were built in the school grounds. After that, it was a regular part of school life to have air-raid practice. The bell would ring and we would walk in pairs with our teacher to the shelters and sit in a designated part of the shelter until the 'all-clear' went.

We were also issued with gas masks and taught how to use them. What with air-raid practice and gas mask drill, we seemed to have very little time for proper lessons! Anyway, the day came when Mr Bell, our teacher, told us that the Germans had invaded France and that we may have to leave Margate to go to a place of safety. A few weeks later Byron Avenue, Milton Avenue and Milton Square were packed with soldiers. They were lying or sitting on the roads and pavements with their kitbags and rifles by their sides. We were told that they had been rescued from Dunkirk.

Every house in the avenue opened their doors to the soldiers and served them with tea, coffee, cocoa, cigarettes and sandwiches. The soldiers were very grateful and there was a lot of hugging and kissing going on. Suddenly, a large man came marching up the street shouting orders and the soldiers got up and marched away. The air-raids were getting more frequent now and Mr Bell gave us evacuation forms to take home to our parents.

British servicemen saved from the beaches of Dunkirk during May/June 1940

Joycelin Ruth Holland: I remember, when I was 10 years old, the sound of marching feet that resounded through the air as hundreds of soldiers came into view, all looking dishevelled and weary. As they marched from Ramsgate Harbour, along Grange Road towards the railway station, a command rang out and the soldiers immediately lifted themselves up tall, and whistling, they marched on. Every conceivable type of seacraft had been used to assist in their rescue from the beaches of Dunkirk. It was the end of May 1940. The whole community pulled together to provide food and clothes, support and encouragement for these soldiers evacuated from France. The war was going terribly wrong and there was a very real danger of invasion by the Germans. It was only a few days later that all Thanet school children, including myself, were sent to a place of safety – another evacuation!

* * *

Although this book is primarily concerned with the evacuation experiences of the children from the Isle of Thanet, I feel it necessary to include some information about the Dunkirk Evacuation:

On 14th May 1940 the BBC Nine o'clock News requested that owners of all self-propelled pleasure craft of between thirty and a hundred feet in length send particulars to the Admiralty within fourteen days. It was not intended that the craft which registered with the Small Vessels Pool would cross the Channel, much less rescue an army.

Meanwhile, from his operations room in the tunnels deep beneath Dover Castle, Vice Admiral Bertram Ramsay and his staff were organising the operation, codenamed Dynamo, which was to rescue over 338,000 men (and women) from the beaches and port of Dunkirk in just ten days. The following information gives a day by day account of the Ten Days Of Dunkirk:

Sunday, 26th May, 1940 – Gravelines taken by German forces. 18.57 hours Operation Dynamo commenced with a view to lifting up to 45,000 of the British Expeditionary Force in two days. By 22.30 hours, 1,312 personnel had been landed at Dover from France.

Monday, 27th May, 1940 – Dunkirk was on fire and under heavy bombing. Evacuation only possible from the beaches. 5,718 troops rescued. The first of the Little Ships set sail for the rescue.

Tuesday, 28th May, 1940 – Belgium surrendered putting Nieupoort into enemy hands. Heavy casualties on the beaches near Dunkirk. Evacuation at night time only. Over 150 vessels were in operation. 18,527 soldiers saved.

Wednesday, 29th May, 1940 – Very heavy bombardment of Dunkirk and ships in the harbour. At least 14 ships lost and many damaged. Hundreds die but 50,331 were taken to safety.

Thursday, 30th May, 1940 – Mist and smoke clouds prevented German bombers from attacking ships. The East Mole pier at Dunkirk heavily used. 53,227 rescued.

Friday, 31st May, 1940 – French troops evacuated alongside British army. Dunkirk and La Panne beaches heavily bombed and machine gunned. Improvised piers and

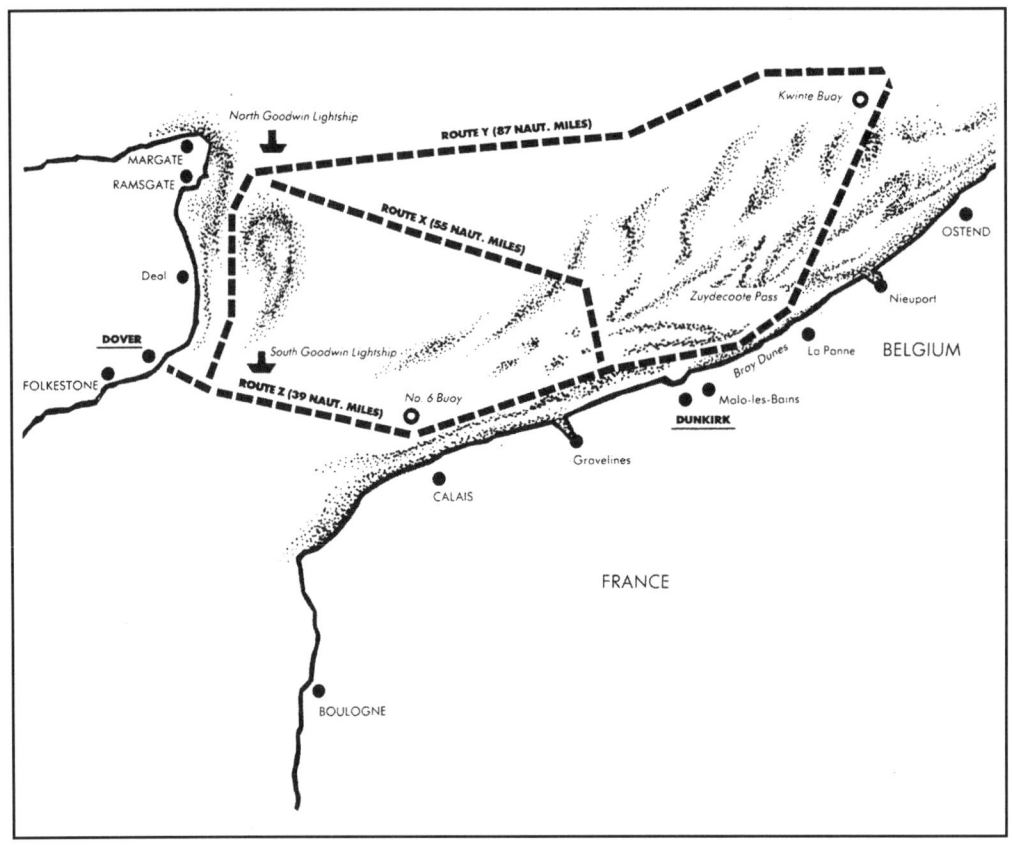

Routes X, Y and Z taken by the evacuating ships during the Dunkirk crisis, May/June 1940

pontoons speed up the evacuation. 64,141 troops rescued.

Saturday, 1st June, 1940 – Serious losses of British and French ships. 61,557 British, French and Belgian troops taken from the piers and beaches.

Sunday, 2nd June, 1940 – Daylight evacuation suspended. French and British troops are still defending the perimeter around Dunkirk, but most of the B.E.F. had by now been evacuated. 23,604 troops lifted. *(This was, of course, the day when the Isle of Thanet school children were evacuated to a safer place under the Government Evacuation Scheme.)*

Monday, 3rd June, 1940 – 29,641 French troops and some British stragglers evacuated from the East and West Piers at Dunkirk.

Tuesday, 4th June, 1940 – Operation 'Dynamo' terminated at 14.23 hours. 27,689 survivors taken. The brave and battered town of Dunkirk finally surrendered.

* * *

With the evacuees who arrived in the area in 1939 already removed to other locations by the end of May, 1940, it was now the turn of the Thanet children themselves to be removed to a safer place. The following report which appeared in the Isle of Thanet Gazette *for 31st May, 1940, highlights the preparation for their departure:*

EVACUATING SCHOOLS
6,500 CHILDREN LEAVING THANET
Parents Welcome Scheme

The parents of 6,588 children in Margate, Ramsgate, Broadstairs and Sandwich have welcomed the opportunity of sending their boys and girls to a safer part of the country under the coastal evacuation scheme announced by the Government on Sunday night. This represents about 70% of the school population last month, but since then a great many families have left the district, so the percentage may be higher than it seems.

The figures for each town are:

Margate	2,160
Ramsgate (including County Schools)	3,456
Broadstairs	506
Sandwich	466

About 120 of them are three and four years of age.

The children will leave by train on Sunday for a destination which was unknown to the local education authority yesterday (Thursday). Children from the newly-evacuated districts are to be distributed over the Midlands and Wales, and it is expected that they will go to the counties of Hereford, Nottingham, Shropshire, Stafford, Warwick, Worcester, Derby, Gloucester, Glamorgan and Monmouth.

The Government's broadcast announcement on Sunday night stated that as Holland and parts of Belgium and Northern France were in enemy occupation, the following towns were to be declared evacuation areas:

Yarmouth, Lowestoft, Felixstowe, Harwich, Clacton, Frinton and Walton, Southend, Margate, Broadstairs, Ramsgate, Sandwich, Deal, Dover and Folkestone.

Several of these towns, including Sandwich, Deal and Folkestone, were reception areas until recently.

The Government announcement also stated that the movement would start by special trains on Sunday, and that arrangements were being made for school children to be moved on the same day from Chatham, Rochester, Gillingham and Sheerness, which were already evacuation areas.

The Minister of Health, Mr Malcolm MacDonald, stated that the new evacuation areas had been chosen deliberately on the facts of the situation. The change was to be

THIS TABLET COMMEMORATES THE
LANDING ON MARGATE JETTY OF 46,772
TROOPS OF THE ALLIED FORCES ON THE
EVACUATION OF DUNKIRK IN MAY 1940

Plaque close to Margate Harbour

confined to the stretch of coast nearest the territory which was at present in the enemy's occupation, and certain urban areas on the coast, which was fairly closely populated.

With the departure of the children, all Margate's elementary schools will close, and the entire staff of 115 teachers will go with the evacuees. To make sure the youngsters are well cared for, additional women helpers are being engaged and there will be one teacher or helper for every fifteen children.

In a circular to the parents of children issued on Monday, Margate Education Committee stated:

'The responsibility for deciding whether or not your child should be evacuated is, of course, your own, for evacuation is entirely voluntary, but in view of the proximity of the enemy to this coast, you should lose no time in making your decision.

'It is likely that a limited number of billets will be allocated to Margate, and this number will be based on the number of replies received. If you delay beyond the time stated you will probably be too late. Only children who are registered will be allowed to participate in evacuation.'

The following instructions were given to parents:

If your child is not clean, he/she will not be happily received in a home where

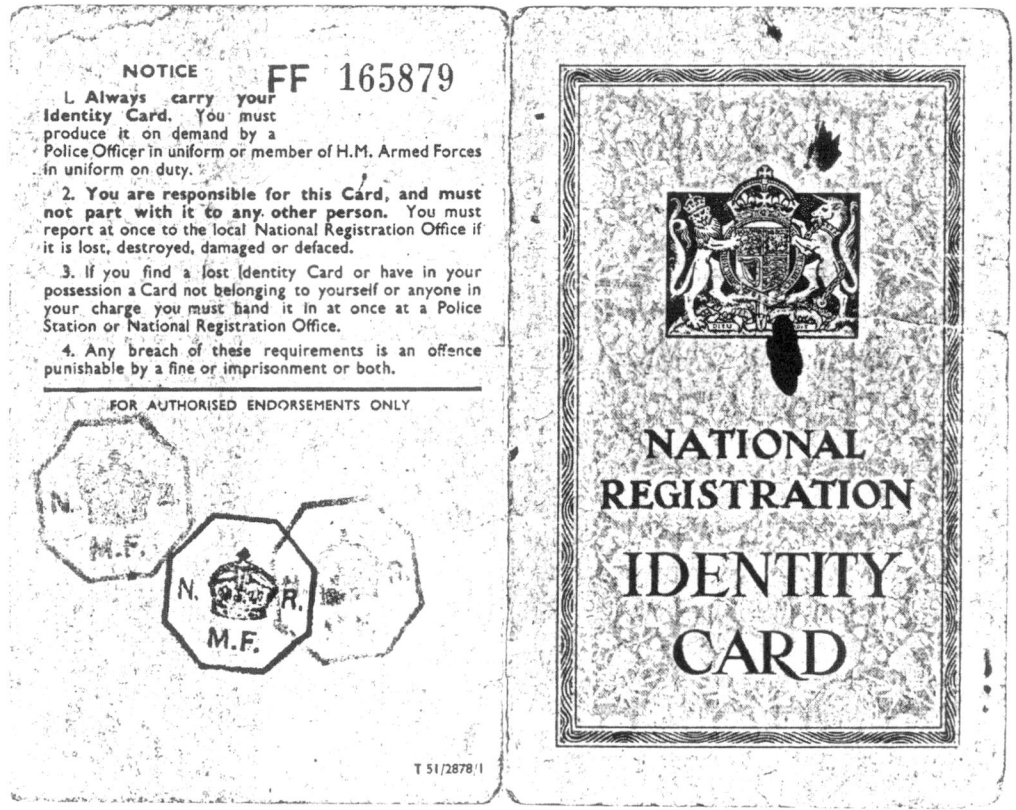

An example of identity card used during World War II

cleanliness is valued. Dirty children, even if evacuated, will be returned home at once, and the parents may be prosecuted. Before the child is evacuated, see that he/she is given a thorough bath. Keep your child's hair short and clean. You should also see that the child's clothing is clean and in good repair.

Parents will readily understand that no child suffering from an infectious disease or excluded from school because of contact with infectious disease, can be included in the evacuation party.

On the day when school parties are being evacuated, parents may help their children to carry their kit to the school playgrounds, but must not accompany them further. Parents will help by strictly observing this rule. Parents will not be allowed to enter the railway station. As soon as the child is settled in his/her billet, a postcard will be sent home, notifying his/her address in the reception area.

The following advice was given in regard to clothes and other requirements:

Clean serviceable clothing and strong footwear should be taken. Mark the child's name on all clothes and on the webbing of the gas mask.

The best carrier for the kit is an army pack or ruck-sack, i.e., a pack which is best carried by a strap around each shoulder so that both arms are free.

Suit cases should not be taken. Do not overload the child; additional articles can be sent afterwards by parcel post.

A luggage label with the child's name, address and school written on it, should be tied securely to the kit.

Every boy and girl will need:

Gas mask (in box)	Ration Card	Identity Card
Toothbrush	Face Cloth	Towels
Hairbrush	Comb	

Fork and Spoon (older pupils, knife as well)

A complete change of clothing, including two of socks, handkerchiefs, jersey or jumper or pullover or blazer.

One pair of sand shoes or slippers.

Night attire (two sets).

Boys: One vest, one pair of pants, one shirt and collars, one pair of trousers or shorts.

Girls: One vest or combinations, one pair of knickers, tunic and blouse or dress.

Blankets should not be taken; they will be provided.

Food: The child should carry food for one day: sandwiches, biscuits, oranges, apples are suggested. Bottles must not be taken.

The child should wear overcoat or mackintosh, strong boots or shoes.

COST TO PARENTS

The circular added: The law requires that parents should clothe their children properly, and the evacuation scheme does not relieve them of this duty. If clothing for neglected children has to be supplied in the reception area the parents must expect an officer of the Education Committee in Margate to collect from them the amount so expended.

No railway or bus fares will be charged. The people where the evacuees are billeted will be paid by the Government, not by the parents. After the child has been evacuated, parents will be asked to complete a form, and the amount they will be required to pay towards the maintenance of their children will be assessed according to the income of the parents and scale laid down by the Ministry of Health. Nothing is paid by parents in receipt of unemployment assistance or public assistance.

Forty-four million gas masks were issued during the war but were only ever used in practice

Chapter Two

TO A SAFER PLACE

THE EVACUATION OF SCHOOL CHILDREN from the towns of Thanet on Sunday, 2nd June, 1940, coincided with the evacuation of school children from Folkestone, Dover, Deal and Sandwich, and with the children from the Medway Towns. The only difference being that those evacuees from South East Kent and those from the Medway Towns were taken to the valleys of South Wales, whereas the Isle of Thanet children travelled to the rural areas of Staffordshire. So on that one day in June, 1940, more than 20,000 Kent school children and their teachers and helpers left their families and homes to travel to unknown destinations, and all this happening at the height of the Dunkirk crisis.

We start this chapter with the personal account of **Jeanne Bass** (now Mrs Dodson), who relates how evacuation was to change her life:

I was one of those children who was evacuated from Ramsgate in June 1940, immediately after the fall of Dunkirk. I was only

She looks after kiddies as well as coupons!

1. Since young Jim joined the R.A.F. Miss Roffey has busy days coping with the coupons at the village stores.

2. But, after hours, there's a bath waiting — and Lifebuoy Toilet Soap! That soon gets rid of stale perspiration and after-work fatigue.

3. So at seven she's off up the hill to "The Grange." There she mends for twenty little evacuees. A full life for Miss Roffey, but a happy one — she's doing her extra bit to help!

JUST as a measure of national economy, Lifebuoy Toilet Soap comes to you now without its familiar packet. But the soap itself still does the same grand job for Personal Freshness. No need to use it wastefully either! That deep-cleansing lather works quickly and thoroughly to free the pores of perspiration deposits. It gives you new vigour and freshness.

LIFEBUOY TOILET SOAP

Refreshes, Invigorates, Prevents "B.O."

THE NEW HANDY TABLET—PRICE 3D

LBT 548-836 ═══ A *LEVER* PRODUCT ═══

Many wartime advertisements made reference to the evacuees, as does this one for Lifebuoy toilet soap

East Kent children leave for unknown destinations in 1940

seven at the time but I can remember quite clearly certain events. As children we knew something was happening because our mums had been asked to help by going down to the harbour to hand out tea, sandwiches and blankets to the soldiers who were coming in on all sorts of boats from France.

The main road from the harbour to the railway station went past the bottom of our road and I would sit with my friends on the garden wall and wave at all the buses going to the railway station with all these poor soldiers. Some only had a blanket covering them and, although they looked so tired and weary, they still managed to smile and wave back to us.

Everyone thought that, after the fall of Dunkirk, invasion was inevitable and this started the rush to get the children away. I remember being taken to the railway station by my mum, and I had a big luggage label pinned to my coat, my gas mask and a packed lunch for the journey. I wasn't frightened or tearful. At seven years old it all seemed like a big adventure and, anyway, most of us had never been on a train before or away from home.

However, it was different for the parents. The decision to send their children away caused a lot of heart-searching. Mum told me afterwards that the scenes at the station were quite traumatic. On one platform stood the hospital trains with big red crosses painted on them, taking the wounded soldiers away and on the other platform were all the children being lined up to go away as well – and, of course, people were starting to believe that the enemy was on its way across the Channel.

To us small children the journey seemed endless and took all day. We finally arrived as it was getting dark, at a place called Denstone, a small village in north Staffordshire. On arrival we were herded into the village hall where we were handed over to the people who were going to look after us. I went with a farmer and his wife to their home, which seemed to be in the middle of nowhere. I was put to bed in a room of my own and it was only then that I started to cry. The couple were very kind and took me into their bed where I soon fell asleep.

The farmer had no children of his own and I was very lonely and a long way from the village school, so it was decided to move me nearer to things. For our first Christmas away the villagers gave us a wonderful evacuees' party and we soon started to feel at home and settled down to country life. We learnt about wild flowers and birds and other wildlife. One clear memory was being allowed to stay up late to help with the hay-making. The sun seemed to be shining at midnight because we were then on double summer time.

Ramsgate's Grammar School for Girls (Clarendon House) had been evacuated to the town of Stafford where they shared the local grammar school's buildings, but kept their separate identity. In 1943, at the age of eleven, I passed my scholarship and sadly left Denstone for Stafford and a grammar school education. I never really settled in Stafford and kept pestering my mum to bring me home. My mother, who was a widow, and my older sister, who was 18, had an invitation from relatives in Leicester to go and live with them as life in Thanet at that time was very uncertain. So mum locked up our house and travelled to Leicester where she got a job in a munitions factory, working 12-hour night shifts in the canteen. My sister worked in the food department of the local Co-op, where she met her future husband. They finally married and settled down to life in Leicester.

We managed to go back to Ramsgate several times during the war, just for short visits and to check on our house. Mum had to get a special permit proving that she was a genuine resident of Ramsgate. Every time our train got within a few miles of the coast, the train would stop and police would check all identity cards and special travel permits.

Our house was badly damaged by shelling during 1943. All our furniture was put into storage at one of the now empty schools, and the house was boarded up until after the war.

Everything was quietening down by 1944 and we decided to return home for good at Christmas 1944. Mum took a live-in job, looking after two elderly ladies until our house was repaired. My school had also returned to Ramsgate. I also remember standing on the West Cliff, watching all the activity out at sea as supplies and troops were being sent to France.

When victory came in 1945, everyone went wild with excitement. We had a lovely street party on VE Day in the form of a reunion for all of us kids who were finally together again. Our house was eventually repaired, with one or two modern improvements and we stayed there until June 1948 when it was decided to go back to Leicester. I have lived in Leicester ever since. I have only been back to Ramsgate a couple of times, but I always talk of Ramsgate as 'back home'.

Jeanne Bass's account refers to shelling of Thanet from the German guns mounted on the French coast near Calais. The following is a list of incidents relating to the shelling of the Isle of Thanet:

Ramsgate, 12.35 hours, Wednesday 12th February, 1941.
German long-range shells reach Thanet, after being fired from the French coast. A ranging shot fell in Ramsgate Harbour, but the next shell wrecked the bungalow called Shanghai Lodge in Whitehall Road. Another shell exploded close to No. 21 Wilfred Road. Although six buildings were reported damaged and a further seventeen slightly damaged, there were no casualties reported. A German news agency reported that '. . . important military objectives were shelled.'

Ramsgate, 22.43 hours, Tuesday 2nd March 1943.
Four large calibre shells were reported falling in Pegwell Bay.

Margate, 23.51 hours, Monday, 28th June 1943.
A shell exploded at Dowlings Chocolate Factory, Eaton Road, just before midnight and caused considerable damage to over one hundred dwellings. There were no reported casualties.

Ramsgate, 23.52 hours, Monday 28th June 1943.
Longe-range shells exploded near the gasworks and this was the beginning of intermittent shelling from the French Coast which was to last for nearly one year.

Ramsgate, 03.03 hours, Monday 5th July 1943.
At least seven shells fell in the Pegwell bay/Ramsgate area. Two people were killed.

Ramsgate, 22.43 hours, Sunday 3rd October 1943.
This was one of the worst shellings to affect the town and lasted for about four hours. Ten high-calibre missiles were plotted. Unlike bombs, shells arrived and exploded before anyone knew they were on their way. When dawn broke several houses had been demolished, and there were sixteen casualties.

Ramsgate, 22.39 hours, Wednesday 3rd November 1943.
A ranging shot fell in the sea before the next shell struck the town. It hit two houses in Grove Road. Another eighty houses were damaged by the blast. Two people were killed.

Ramsgate, 22.30 hours, Thursday 20th January 1944.
Nine long-range shells were logged. Seven of these fell harmlessly into the sea. but the next two shells exploded on dwellings in Finsbury Road and Denmark Road. Extensive damage was caused to eleven houses.

Ramsgate, 14.58 hours, Thursday 29th June 1944.
Two longe-range German shells exploded on the West Rocks.

Margate, 04.25 hours, Friday 1st September 1944.
In September the German long-range guns in the Pas de Calais were under siege. Nevertheless, they made every effort to discharge as many shells as possible. Determined to spread their shells as far east as they could before being overrun, the German gunners let fly at distant Margate. Ranging shots fell in the sea and then the next salvo struck Red House in Star Lane, causing considerable damage to surrounding property. No casualties were recorded.

Ramsgate, 04.25 hours, Friday 1st September 1944.
The rest of the shelling fell on Ramsgate and affected Station Approach Road, Lorne Road, Wildred Road, Royal Road, Sion Hill, Bradley Road and Coleman Crescent. There were at least eighteen casualties.
These were to be the last long-range shells to fall on the Isle of Thanet.

* * *

The following article appeared on the front page of the Isle of Thanet Gazette *for 7th June, 1940, and records in great detail, the exodus on the 2nd June, of children from Thanet and their reception at their various destinations in Staffordshire:*

THRILLED TO BE OFF
CHILDREN'S GREAT ADVENTURE.

No one in Thanet was happy to see trainloads of children steaming off for Staffordshire on Sunday; the streets seem empty and unnaturally quiet without them. But the great evacuation to a part of the country where war is more remote was a relief to thousands of parents anxious only for their safety.

The children went with a smile and a song, thrilled to be on the same railway stations as heroes of the British Expeditionary Force; thrilled to ride in carriages bearing the name of a famous train – the Flying Scotsman; thrilled again to start the biggest adventure of their lives in the company of friends.

Will they be homesick sometimes? Of course they will, but the kindly Midlanders have taken them to their hearts. While a *Gazette* reporter was with the Margate Director of Education (Mr J. C. Aspden) on Monday there was a telephone call from the billeting officer of Cannock Rural District. 'Your children are doing fine,' he chuckled. 'They are already getting together with the local youngsters, and everybody is happy.'

The Margate children – 2,097 under the care of 152 teachers and helpers – have gone to a district of which the centres are Lichfield, Cannock and Rugeley. The boys and girls of Broadstairs are in the Tamworth neighbourhood, and Ramsgate's are at Stafford, Gnosall, Uttoxeter and Madeley. The Sandwich children are in Wales at Gowerton, Glamorgan. Altogether, 6,500 children have left Thanet and Sandwich.

Kent road signs were removed during the war to 'confuse the enemy' in the event of an invasion

Proud to be the first authority in south-east England to complete plans for evacuation under the Government's announcement, Margate Education Committee should be prouder now, for those plans were carried out without a hitch.

First Again

The last of the three trains carrying Margate children away was due to leave at 12.35pm. It was one minute late. Within a quarter-of-an-hour the Ministry of Health were being told exactly how many Margate children, teachers and helpers were speeding across Kent, and the Ministry said, 'Well done Margate, first again.'

The staff of the education department remained on duty until nine o'clock that night, and did not leave until telegrams and telephone messages had established the safe arrival of every child. Notice boards gave the news to parents, who sighed a little wistfully and went back to uncomfortably tidy homes.

But we have reached the end of the story before the beginning. In many homes it began almost at dawn, for the first of the three Margate trains was due to leave at 9.45, and there was much to do before then.

Most parents took the sensible advice given by the Education Committee and packed a complete change of clothes for their youngsters in a haversack which could be slung from the shoulders without strain. There was so much to remember. The gas mask, ration card, identity card, brush and comb, toothbrush, fork and spoon, and a whole lot more.

But everyone was ready to time, and in most cases the 'goodbyes' were said at the schools, where buses waited to take the children to the railway station. Fathers and mothers were not allowed on to the station, which was a wise precaution.

If there was any tremor of early regret among the children they concealed it well. One little boy got as far as the barrier and could stand it no longer. He took to his heels and flew home. But the rest were safely shepherded aboard.

There was a great moment at one station when children lined up in the station approach saw 200 sailors, survivors of three ships lost in fetching the B.E.F. from Dunkirk, march by to their train. Bearded, ragged and cheerful, they smiled acknowledgement of the children's welcome. Tots shouted themselves hoarse and waved their little Union Jacks in frenzied excitement.

They cheered the sailors off and watched with wide-eyed sympathy while Steward M. T. Tinker, a pale-faced boy in borrowed clothing, was assisted to a seat on the platform to await an ambulance. He had spent five hours of the previous day swimming for his life, and could go no further.

The children of St John's School, Margate, had the school pet, a sheepdog, to see them off. He did his best to go with them. Several times he was pushed out of the train, and when his friends waved farewell he loped along the platform in hopeless pursuit.

Among the teachers and helpers were several men and women who looked after another generation of boys and girls through the last war. There was no evacuation then.

'Do you remember being told to lie under your desk while the German planes flew over?' one of them asked a *Gazette* reporter. He did remember. The teacher who jogged his memory used to shelter behind a blackboard!

Looked After Each Other.

On Sunday it was amusing to notice what good care the children took of each other. They were too well watched by helpers to go astray, but mites of three or four, below school age and only allowed to go because they had brothers and sisters in the party, looked to those elders for guidance in everything. Some of the 'grown-ups' were only six or seven.

The children were seen off by the Mayor and Mayoress (Alderman and Mrs G. B. Farrar), the Vicar of Margate (the Revd D. V. Beckingham), the Chairman (Alderman W. C. Redman, C.C.) and members of Margate Education Committee, and the Director.

The trains were made up as follows:

First train – Holy Trinity Junior School, 157 children and 12 helpers; Holy Trinity Infants, 55 children and 5 helpers; St John's, 205 children and 14 helpers; Drapers Mills Junior, 234 children and 16 helpers; Drapers Mills Infants, 64 children and 5 helpers. Totals, 715, 52.

Second train – St Gregory's, 149 children and 11 helpers; Pettman, 174 children and 12 helpers; Lausanne, 221 children and 16 helpers; Garlinge Junior, 128 children and 10 helpers; Garlinge Infants, 25 children and 3 helpers. Totals, 697, 52.

Third train – Westgate-on-Sea, 89 children and 6 helpers; King Ethelbert's, 245 children and 18 helpers; Birchington, 103 children and 8 helpers; Salmestone Junior, 207 children and 12 helpers; Salmestone Infants, 40 children and 4 helpers. Totals, 684, 48.)

The small numbers credited to infants' schools were due to the many registrations of infants at schools attended by older brothers and sisters.

Not more than half a dozen children from private schools were registered. Already the future education of the children has been closely considered by the Director of Education for Staffordshire (Mr F. A. Hughes) and the Director for Cannock (Mr S. C. A. Webb). This week arrangements were made for most of the children to be attached to existing schools, and some of them resumed their studies yesterday (Thursday).

Family Parties at Ramsgate.

Mayor of Ramsgate (Alderman A. B. C. Kempe) bade the Ramsgate children an official farewell. The reason for their leaving was obvious as the muffled rumblings of naval guns could be heard across the Channel.

Aircraft flew overhead as the children were shepherded into five trains. One of the features of the arrangements was that the children were allowed to travel in family parties. The eldest child of each family taking charge of his or her little group.

Parents waved goodbye to their children from behind barricades which were erected round the station.

The news, 'All safe and happy and are settling down well,' was received from Mr S. V. West, secretary of the Ramsgate Education Committee, who travelled with the party to their new homes. Later, parents were reassured when further messages revealed how very comfortable the evacuees were and how pleased their new 'parents' were with the Ramsgate children.

Prayers at Broadstairs.

Seven members of Broadstairs Council were at the railway station for the farewell scenes at Broadstairs. They were led by the Chairman (Councillor B. J. Pearson, JP, C.C.) and Vice-Chairman (Councillor H. Noble). The Rector (the Revd C. H. Hanley) and Bishop J. C. Magee, of Christ Church, were also there to see the children off.

A roll call was made by Mr E. Owen (clerk of the Council), who acted as evacuation officer, assisted by Mr F. H. Ward (deputy clerk), and the head teachers. When all the children were ready to depart, Bishop Magee led the gathering in a prayer for the children's safety. The children joined in the saying of the Lord's Prayer.

A few minutes later they were marshalled into the coaches and promptly at nine o'clock the train steamed on its journey to Staffordshire. Parents gathered at a few places along the line to get a last view of their children and to give a final wave.

On Sunday afternoon a message was received in Broadstairs from the chairman of a Midland Council stating that the children arrived safely at their destination at 2.30pm. Copies of the message were quickly obtained and posted about the town to give the anxious parents the good news.

Messages received in Broadstairs show that the children are settling down happily in their new homes and there are only one or two cases that are being adjusted of brothers and sisters who want to be together.

Parents have already received letters from their children saying how happy they are.

They are making friends with the local children, and the parents are showing the children around the district.

One youngster wrote home, 'There are two young ladies here, so I have my arms full!'

The Revd W. H. Bathurst, assistant priest of Holy Trinity Church, Broadstairs, has left the town to visit the children.

* * *

John Groombridge remembers in great detail, his departure with his school in 1940:

I was seven years old when I was evacuated with Dame Janet Junior School, Ramsgate, in 1940. My sister Marie, aged six, and brother Reg, aged four, were also evacuated. This still left a brother aged 18 months and a baby sister with Mum at home. We assembled at school on the day of the evacuation, and there was general chaos as we were sorted into groups in the school quadrangle. I don't think that I or the younger ones knew exactly what was happening.

We were generally 'parcelled up' with an identifying label pinned to our clothes and we each had a satchel or small case with a few belongings – and our gas masks over our shoulders. The next image of the day is of being on a train moving through the countryside. Excitement prevailed as we saw cows and sheep in the fields. Many of us had never seen sheep or cows before. The atmosphere of that early part of the journey was one of excitement akin to going on holiday.

The train journey became very long and tedious and there was a lot of curling up on seats and sleeping. Our teachers accompanied us on the journey. One of them was Miss Edmead who much later on was to marry a Staffordshire man, and became Mrs Handley.

We finally arrived at a station and then made the final stage of our journey by car. We were taken to a school room in a small village which I later learned was Rocester in Staffordshire. There were a lot of local people present and then the allocating of evacuees began. It was like a cattle market. Evacuees would be called up on to the stage and then an official would say, 'Who wants this boy aged . . .?' or, 'Who wants these two girls?' etc. When a selection had been made, both the new foster parents and the evacuee(s) left the hall, so that gradually the numbers went down.

Well, there were the three of us, myself, my brother and my sister, and I remember my mother insisting before we left, that we should not be split up. It wasn't until this point that I understood what she meant. Anyway, we were one of the last to be 'offered up' as a family. The three of us went up on to the stage and I remember vividly how the official tried to persuade those adults who were left, to take all three of us – but no such luck! Marie was taken by Mr Albert Bullock and was led away in great distress, crying, 'I want my Jacky, don't take me away from Jacky!' My sister's emotions went unheeded and she was bundled out of the room to her new home.

My four year old brother Reg and I were taken by Mr and Mrs H, and we were driven two miles up the hill leading out of the village to one of a pair of cottages which stood two fields back from the road. We were soon put to bed in a double bed in the small spare room. I looked around the room, put my head under the blankets and –

IMPORTANT NOTICE

EVACUATION

The public throughout the country generally are being told to "stay put" in the event of invasion. For military reasons, however, it will in the event of attack be necessary to remove from this town all except those persons who have been specially instructed to stay. An order for the compulsory evacuation of this town will be given when in the judgment of the Government it is necessary, and plans have been arranged to give effect to such an order when it is made.

You will wish to know how you can help NOW in these plans.

THOSE WHO ARE ENGAGED IN WORK OF ANY DESCRIPTION IN THE TOWN SHOULD STAY FOR THE PRESENT.

OTHER PERSONS SHOULD, SO FAR AS THEY ARE ABLE TO DO SO, MAKE ARRANGEMENTS TO LEAVE THE TOWN—PARTICULARLY
- MOTHERS WITH YOUNG CHILDREN
- SCHOOL CHILDREN
- AGED AND INFIRM PERSONS
- PERSONS WITHOUT OCCUPATION OR IN RETIREMENT.

All such persons who can arrange for their accommodation with relatives or friends in some other part of the country should do so. Assistance for railway fares and accommodation will be given to those who require it.

Advice and, where possible, assistance will be given to persons who desire to leave the town but are unable to make their own arrangements.

Information about these matters can be obtained from the local Council Offices.

(Signed) AUCKLAND GEDDES,
Regional Commissioner for Civil Defence.

2nd *July*, 1940.

(393/4177A) Wt. 19544-30 70M 7/40 H & S Ltd. Gp. 393

Shortly after the schoolchildren of Thanet had been evacuated, this public notice was issued to residents in the area, at a time when there was a real possibility of invasion

thought that this must all be a bad dream. I soon fell fast asleep, but when I awoke the following morning I gingerly peered over the blankets and looked around the room – it was no dream! I was now in strange territory and it was at that point that anxiety of my evacuation began.

Despite these initial anxieties I think we soon settled down. Being transported from a town to the heart of the country was real excitement. We climbed trees, roamed the fields, woods and valleys. We were surprised at rabbits starting up before us and seeing squirrels in the trees.

Our foster mother had a son, Kenny, who was about Reg's age and, during that summer of 1940, we spent a lot of time out of doors. Although Kenny could do no wrong in the eyes of his mother, and despite the fact that he had the knack of getting Reg and me into trouble, we all managed to enjoy ourselves.

Our cottage was one of a pair and in the adjoining cottage lived a very elderly couple, Mr and Mrs Collins, who we almost regarded as grandparents. They were exceptionally nice to us evacuees.

We went to the local school two miles down the hill in the village of Rocester and we would walk there and back daily. We had no trouble settling in at school. No doubt the presence of other evacuees helped a lot – and of course we had our own teachers.

Bathing arrangements at the cottage are one particular memory which has stayed with me. We would be given a bath at the weekends in a long tin bath in front of the fire. The water was heated in kettles and transferred to the bath, and we three boys took it in turn, using the same water. The following evening Mrs H's sister would visit and it would be the turn of the ladies to have a bath, one by one, in front of the fire. The fact that we three boys looked on seemed of no consequence to them – but we were very young at the time!

One day Mrs H was very tearful. She kept pulling out a letter reading bits of it and putting it back in her pinafore pocket. We found out that her husband Ken, who was by this time in the army, had lost one of his fingers and this was the cause of her distress. On another occasion several of us were playing near the 'big school' in the village when suddenly there were sounds of screaming and uncontrollable sobbing. Two evacuees, the Osborne brothers, had been told by the headmaster that their father had been killed in the war. It was their reaction that we could hear.

On Sundays we had to wear our best clothes and go to chapel. From time to time we would see other members of Mrs H's family, most of whom lived in another nearby village called Roston. I remember that we always had to wrap up well before going out in cold weather, and that there were all sorts of home-made remedies for various complaints and sicknesses. That for tummy ache seemed to be a vigorous rubbing of the belly!

The local people had their own morality and code of conduct – no lying, swearing, stealing or any other types of misbehaviour. The difference between right and wrong was always stressed.

Sometime in 1941 my mother and the two little ones remaining with her, were themselves evacuated to the town of Tamworth in Staffordshire. When she found out that Rocester was only some 30 miles away she decided to come and join us. After some temporary billeting she was put into a terraced house and some time later into a small cottage. This meant that for a few months we had our mother and our little brother and sister living in the village while we were still billeted with Mrs H. It was during this time that an incident occurred concerning my brother Reg. Up until that point, I can safely say that we were quite happy living with our foster mother

This particular incident happened on the way home from school one day, when Reg 'messed' himself. Mrs H was beside herself with anger. After cleaning him, she got a stick and thrashed his bare backside whilst holding him with her free arm. This beating resulted in the right side of his buttocks and his right thigh going black and blue which lasted for weeks.

When my mother saw him on her next visit, she was shocked and angry, and the whole incident resulted in mother taking Reg and me out of our billet, collecting our sister Marie from her billet, and taking us all to stay with her in her small cottage.

It was a pity it was to end like that because up to that point, Mrs H had been a fine foster parent. This was in contrast to Marie's foster mother. Marie was made to do a lot of housework and general 'skivvying' and I think that her life was generally made a misery.

Sometime later our father joined us in Rocester. We waited all day for him to arrive, but it was late at night before he finally came. I remember how glad I was to see him, and I jumped up and down with joy shouting, 'I knew you'd come, I knew you'd come!' Father was a builder by trade and was sent to work at an airfield nearby.

Our family was now altogether, but the problem was that there were now two adults and five children living in a one bedroomed cottage. About a mile out of the village stood a large three-bedroomed house in its own grounds. It was standing empty so my mother wrote to the authorities in charge of housing, stating the plight of her family and mentioning this empty house. The letter must have done its job because some time later we were all rehoused in this lovely detached house. My father was in his element.

He dug up the lawn to grow vegetables and used a yard at the back of the house to rear pigs, chickens and ducks.

Nearby was a derelict cheese factory and, in the grounds of this old building, the Home Guard trained and practised. These were mainly the older men who worked on nearby farms. I recall that they often drilled with pickaxe handles, and how comical they looked. It did not require the advent of the TV series *Dad's Army* to bring this point home to me.

War seemed remote. We used to listen to the comedy programme *ITMA*, the Saturday Night Theatre and the morning advice of the Radio Doctor. My father and mother listened to the news bulletins, but I never understood them.

On one occasion, while Reg, Marie and I were playing in a cornfield, dozens of aeroplanes came over and they were so low that we thought they would clip the tops of the trees. On another occasion we got up one morning and noticed that the field opposite the house was filled with army vehicles and soldiers. A convoy must have stopped there for the night. At about eight o'clock that morning, one of the soldiers knocked on the door and asked for a bucket of water and a chair to stand it on. He washed and shaved, dried himself with his towel, thanked Mother profusely, and left. This incident sticks in my mind because out of more than a hundred soldiers, only this one came to ask for help.

Another memory that sticks in my mind is of an evacuee lad who climbed a tree which overhung an exceptionally muddy pond. The branch on which this lad was sitting, broke, and down he fell. He emerged from the pond, a black silhouette of a figure, completely covered in mud from head to toe, with just the whites of his eyes showing through.

In March 1944, my mother gave birth to twins, a boy and a girl, so now there were seven children in our household!

While I was at Rocester Junior School I was aware of being well instructed. Despite the war and the absence of many teachers in the Forces, education went on apace, and was faithfully administered by both native and evacuated teachers. At the age of eleven I passed the scholarship to the Thomas Alleyne Grammar School in Uttoxeter, and started there in October 1944.

For some reason quite unknown to me, my mother decided, midway through 1945, to return to Ramsgate. Even stranger, my father did not return with her. To my utter chagrin and disappointment, neither did I. It was decided that my education at the grammar school was too important to disrupt. So mother took the rest of my sisters and brothers back to Coleman Crescent in Ramsgate. I remember as they left, how desperate I felt at being left alone with my father. Anyway, I recovered and I managed to do the shopping, the housework, help with the cooking and feed the animals. Father was something of a remote and stern man who never displayed much emotion unless it was anger, but looking back at this period, I think we got on all right together.

My mother's stay in Ramsgate was a short one. Our house had been bomb damaged with a gaping hole in the hallway. Anyway, mum and the kids were back in Rocester within six weeks. How glad I was to see them return!

My family never returned to live in Ramsgate. My father died in 1962 and my mother died in 1994. I was allowed to stay on at school until I was 18, did my National Service, then went to the University of St Andrews and, after my degree, I became a teacher. I finished my teaching career in Ramsgate, the place of my birth.

The Isle of Thanet Gazette *for 7th June, 1940, reports on the welcome given to Broadstairs evacuees:*

WELCOMED WITH WARM HEARTS
BROADSTAIRS CHILDREN AT TAMWORTH.
Headmaster's Letter

The 500 children of Broadstairs and St Peter's who were evacuated on Sunday, as reported on page one, have already endeared themselves to the people of Tamworth, and are settling down comfortably. This news is contained in a letter which the Editor received yesterday (Thursday) from Mr J. E. Bird, headmaster of Broadstairs Boys' School, who felt that the parents left behind would like to know how their children have been received.

Mr Bird's letter is as follows:

I feel sure that the parents of our St Peter's and Broadstairs children would appreciate an early report confirming the reception accorded to the evacuees in Tamworth. Many of our little ones are too young to convey very much to those at home, and for us to correspond with every family is impossible at this stage. Would you therefore, very kindly announce through your columns that our party of over 500 has been taken into the warm hearts of these Midland folk.

The utmost care has been taken in planning billets for the children and within a very short time of arrival everyone was safely installed. A fleet of private cars provided transport from the station to the medical examination post, the billeting centre, and thence to the billets. Subsequently a few – surprisingly few – changes have been made to get family parties together.

It is noteworthy that while making the initial survey for parties some difficulty had been met in securing offers – since the arrival of our party many offers have poured in. The exemplary behaviour of the Kent children has already endeared them to Tamworth.

On Monday, while staff conferences were held, the children made first acquaintance with the river, the castle, the swimming bath, and the spacious playing fields of Tamworth. Wednesday morning found them in the school to which they have been assigned – it has been decided that they shall receive full-time education in the school appropriate to their age, in nursery, infants, junior or senior departments. The schools are well equipped and there is, even after this invasion, no obvious overcrowding.

The great task which confronts the accompanying teaching staff is to make contact with the foster parents and to ensure the continued wellbeing of the boys and girls. Every endeavour will be made to keep in touch with those left behind in Thanet. Excitement and novelty are at present buoying up the children. All have received most generous kindness from their hosts, or, I should say, foster parents.

In the days to come they will miss you (their parents). We hope then to form a link between the home town and this town of refuge and, in due course, when danger is past, to return them to you fit and well, with much useful experience and a deeper appreciation of home, sweet home.

Mrs Bird is shortly going to Tamworth to join her husband and help in the work of looking after the children.

* * *

William Dorkings *was a pupil of Hereson Boys' School, Ramsgate, at the time of evacuation:*

The day we were to leave, my brother and I reported to our school, Hereson Boys' School. It was a bright, sunny Sunday morning and we all lined up in the playground with our teachers. Those I remember were Mr Lowman, Mr Young, Mr Harris, Mrs Harris and our headmaster, Mr Davis.

We each had our small case, a packed lunch and our gas mask and at about eight o'clock we marched from the school to Ramsgate Railway Station. I remember someone said that there were German soldiers at the station, so you can imagine the thoughts that went through our minds as we marched along. We all seemed to walk a little slower but when we arrived at the station, the 'Germans' turned out to be French soldiers who had just been rescued from Dunkirk.

The train left Ramsgate at about 9.30am. My brother John and I weren't all that bothered about leaving home. Two years previously we had both spent some time in a children's home, so being away from home was nothing new.

As our train passed through the large towns, it seemed that every house window had a Union Jack flying from it, and people waving to us. They were, of course, there to welcome back home the troops which had been saved from the fall of Dunkirk. The train finally arrived at its destination, Gnosall Railway Station, at 3pm. I remember it well because the local church clock was just striking three o'clock.

At the station were charabancs waiting to take us to various locations. John and I went with a large number of others to a place called High Offley to the village school where the local people were waiting for us. All the evacuees were then allocated to foster parents, but it seemed that my brother and I were left till last. Eventually we were taken to a Mr and Mrs Malpass. Mr Malpass worked on a farm at Adbaston and they had two children, Joan and Reg. They all made us very welcome, but Joan and Reg found us a little strange – as we did them at first!

We enjoyed life in the country, but we had to get used to an outside toilet which had to be emptied every day. All our water was drawn from a well and I remember it was so clean and sweet.

We attended church every Sunday and I had the job of pumping the organ twice a day – for which I was paid sixpence. During my evacuation I was confirmed at Market Drayton.

My brother and I attended High Offley School for about a year then I went to Ecceleshall School until I left at the age of 14. Shortly after I left school we had to change billets. I thought it was because we were too naughty, but I found out some time later that Mrs Malpass was having another baby. We were then billeted with Mr and Mrs Breeze and I stayed there until I got myself a job on a farm just outside

Stafford. Brother John stayed with Mrs Breeze and I went to stay with Mr Collier who ran the farm. I remember him quite well – he had a glass eye!

When I left to work on the farm I lost touch with my brother, and it wasn't until we met up again some years later that I found out that Mr Breeze had nearly killed brother John. Apparently, Mr Breeze was sent to prison for ill-treatment of an evacuee – my brother! John spent six weeks in hospital and was then put on a farm outside Stafford to recuperate. The irony of it is that John and I were just three miles apart and didn't know it.

I returned to Ramsgate in 1944. John went back some years later and visited Mrs Malpass. He found the whole family celebrating their golden wedding. Mr and Mrs Malpass and their son Reg have now passed away. Joan is living in Newport. I still have happy memories of my evacuation – harvest time, going fishing, bunking off from school, playing rounders with Joan and Reg – and many more.

Another Ramsgate pupil, **Jean Chamberlain**, *talks of her evacuation:*

I lived in Ramsgate and was attending Clarendon House Grammar School when war was declared in 1939. Early in 1940 my mother took me to Berkshire, but for some obscure reason I decided that I would rather live away from home than join a new school, so in the September my mother took me to rejoin Clarendon House, which by this time, had been evacuated to Stafford.

The school was still on holiday and all I can remember is playing rounders, supervised by the games teacher, on a public recreation ground.

I had three billets during my stay in Stafford. My first foster parents were an elderly couple with two married daughters. They also had an airman billeted on them. These foster parents were a kindly couple and, to my delight, they had a dog which I was allowed to take out. The man was a furniture remover and had relatives who kept a country pub, so sometimes on a Sunday evening we would go to the pub and be treated to platefuls of bacon and eggs, and other rationed foodstuffs! I had to leave this first billet after nine months because their elder daughter, who lived above her own hair dressing salon, became pregnant, decided to give up her business, and return to her parents' house – and what had been my bedroom.

My second billet was to be quite unsatisfactory. They resented having an evacuee and I was given a list of household tasks I was expected to do before school in the morning, and at lunch time. My evenings were spent alone in the kitchen doing my homework. I think I only sat in their lounge once the whole time I was there. We parted by mutual consent at the end of six months.

I was then moved to a vicarage where I spent three happy years. The vicar and his wife were childless and had had evacuees before with whom they had been very happy. I had a large bedroom with a wide window seat which overlooked the lawn and the church, and in the summer I sat up there to do my homework. There was a housemaid of about my own age who lived in, so in the winter I often shared her fireplace though I would have been welcome in the lounge. This was the time when I first realised that a church wasn't just a building, but a social centre.

Visitors were entertained every Sunday evening and I was encouraged to join them and also to join in church socials etc. There was a thriving youth club attached to the church and I became an enthusiastic committee member.

My hostess was in charge of the Saturday night shift at the YMCA canteen and, if she was short-staffed, I was invited to help. I was quite shy and preferred to spend the evening washing up rather than serving, but I enjoyed the company of the other helpers who were older than I was.

Clarendon House shared the local grammar school and a large country mansion named Baswich House, which had been a private boarding school. So that we could have full advantage of laboratory facilities at the grammar school building, we had to go to school on Saturdays – and have Mondays off.

Baswich House had extensive grounds which made marvellous playing fields. When we were in the top class we were allowed to 'fire-watch' in this building if our parents gave permission. There were two teachers and two pupils encamped in adjoining rooms.

As I could slip through a gap in the hedge at the vicarage, into the grammar school grounds, I was given the job of collecting our school's mail from the grammar school on the two days we were at Baswich House. I was also allowed to use the tennis court in the school grounds in the evenings and I became friendly with many of the grammar school girls through the Youth Club at church.

Although I missed my parents, I enjoyed evacuation. It made me much more independent, and at fourteen I was doing my own washing, ironing and mending, deciding myself when I needed to see a doctor, and managing my own finances to a limited extent. It also made me more adaptable – my three billets could not have been more different. Evacuation made me more sociable too. We had done very little entertaining at home because of my father's illness, so life at the vicarage was quite an experience.

It was during evacuation too, that we realised that teachers were human! In those days teachers were treated with great respect – almost in awe, something modern school children would find difficult to believe. However, they did become more human while we were away and took a more personal interest in us.

The only enemy action I can remember in Stafford was one Saturday when a German aeroplane machine-gunned the High Street.

As my mother was living in Berkshire, I went there for the school holidays until 1942 when my father had an accident. After that, mother returned to Ramsgate and, ironically, I was allowed home for the holidays!

I went to college immediately after leaving school, so I was away from home for a total of six years. I was very pleased to return home, especially as I was going into my first job, and the fact that both my parents had suffered physically through the war.

I visited Stafford three times after the war and I always kept in touch with my last hostess until she died.

The following 'rosy' report on the evacuees in Staffordshire appeared in the Isle of Thanet Gazette *for 14th June, 1940:*

NEWS FROM EVACUEES – PRAISE FOR MARGATE CHILDREN.
REPORTS FROM TEACHERS

'I like being here and I like the people and I like all my food, and I like going to school, and I like feeding the fowls, and Rex, the dog.' So wrote home a young Margate boy to his mother and father after a few days experience of his new surroundings in Walsall.

'I am proud to see that the children have won everybody's praise for their excellent behaviour, manners, cheerfulness and their excellent speech,' was the report of a Margate head teacher.

These two brief comments show how well Margate's evacuated children are settling down in their war-time homes. There has been practically no trouble in arranging satisfactory billets for all the children.

More To Go

As announced by the Government, a supplementary evacuation scheme is being devised to enable those who did not take advantage of the first scheme to join their friends in the Midlands. Registration took place on Wednesday and yesterday (Thursday), and as a result another ninety-nine are scheduled to leave Margate. There will be seventy from Ramsgate and fifteen from Broadstairs.

The date of the evacuation has not yet been announced.

Teachers' Reports

First reports from Margate head teachers reached the Director of Education (Mr J. C. Aspden) this week.

Mr A. T. Walker, of Salmestone School, stated that most of the billets were very good, and some children were exceptionally fortunate. He added, 'I have formed the helpers into a committee under the leadership of Mrs Roberts, a qualified nurse, and they are now visiting every child to make quite certain that the billet is suitable, and that the child is happy and well cared for and, if necessary, recommend a change of billet.' In case of sickness they will write to the parents in Margate giving full details of the progress of the child.

After paying tribute to the splendid work of the helpers, Mr Walker said during warm weather school work is to be carried on in the fields and under the trees. Two picnics were arranged for the children's first week-end away from home.

'All the people of Rugeley have been extremely kind to us and have done much to make us happy and comfortable,' adds Mr Walker. 'I have visited and thanked all those who have been very generous to us – those who supplied the children with refreshments and sweets on arrival, those who supplied transport and especially Mr Orton-Smith, an old Margate teacher, who has been most helpful in every way.'

Spiritual Welfare Assured

Miss Beresford, of Lausanne Girls' Central School, reported, 'Our first week-end has passed off very well. Most of the staff and myself, with about 100 girls, attended the parish church at Great Wyrley, where the vicar made us very welcome. The vicar also holds an afternoon bible class, to which he has invited the senior girls, so their spiritual welfare is assured.'

She added, 'Helpers are watching over our girls when they meet in the evenings in the local recreation room for games and take parties for walks.'

'Billeting officers are very kind and ensure comfort for the children,' reported Mr F. W. Shaw, of Holy Trinity Junior School. 'In each school our own children have been assembled for me to chat with them. I can assure you they are very comfortable and well fed.'

He stated that walks, games, visits to places of interest, and attendance at Sunday School and church are being arranged. 'It is hoped,' he added, 'that our choristers will make themselves useful in the village choirs.'

'Everyone seems out to make the Margate children happy. The welcome accorded us by the teachers and local inhabitants was more than cordial – it was most touching,' says Mr Shaw.

BEGGING FOR CHILDREN

Reporting on the activities of the Roman Catholic children who attended St Gregory's School, Margate, the headmaster, (Mr I. P. Ivory) stated, 'So pleased is everyone with our children that there is a long waiting list of householders who have begged the authorities to let them have any St Gregory children who may not be happy with their present billets. You can assure the committee and the parents that the children are having a wonderful time. I am proud to see that the children have won everybody's praise for their excellent behaviour, manners, cheerfulness and their excellent speech.'

St John's children have gone to Walsall and Mr W. H. Graham in his report wrote, 'On the whole the children have settled down quite well in their new surroundings, and the foster-parents are delighted with the appearance and conduct of the Margate children.'

Mr Graham added a word of thanks to Margate Education Committee for their kind thought in providing milk for the children on their journey.

LITTLE CRYING

From Hopwas, in the Lichfield Rural District, Miss Mongomery of Drapers Mills School wrote, 'The villagers have given us a very hearty welcome and think our children are heroes. There has been very little crying for mothers.'

She related how, during the journey from Margate, the children's train drew to a standstill by the side of a train carrying Canadian troops. 'They bombarded our infants with lovely Jaffa oranges, rhubarb tarts and jam tarts,' she said, 'and provided the children with cans of drinking water.'

Commenting on the uprooting of the children from their homes, Miss Montgomery said, 'It is surprising how easy these big changes can be overcome if everyone acts with common sense. There has been much common sense displayed by everyone, from the youngest to the oldest.'

FULL-TIME SCHOOL

Similar reports have been submitted to the director by other teachers. All tell happy stories of how well the children are settling down in their new homes. 'Very few cases have needed adjustment,' said the director to a *Gazette* reporter. 'Reports from the teachers lead one to believe that the billets are of the best. Any complaints, however, will be brought to the notice of the teachers and passed on to the billeting officers.

Most of the children are having full-time attendance at their new schools. In some cases they have mixed in with existing classes, but in others special classes of Margate children are being held and are taught by Margate teachers.

Letters From Boys

A series of letters from two Margate boys who are staying in Walsall, together with a letter from their foster-mother, was brought to the Director of Education this week by the boys' parents who are highly delighted with the reception the children have received.

The boys must have earned the envy of their school fellows for, in their first letter home, they said, 'We are staying at a sweet shop.'

Their foster-mother wrote, 'I know you will be glad to know that your boys have arrived here quite safe and in good spirits. They have settled down and made themselves at home and are quite happy. Everything possible will be done for them to keep them happy and well.' She added, 'We keep a good few fowls and Eric loves to go and fetch the eggs in.'

The boys themselves are quite emphatic that they like their new home. one of them wrote, 'I like being here and I like the people and I like all my food, and I like going to school, and I like feeding the fowls and Rex, the dog.' He adds, 'I am looking forward to Saturday as the people I am living with are expecting some baby chicks and I want to see a chicken come out of its egg.'

Behaviour Was Delightful

Reporting the reception of the evacuees in Lichfield Rural District, where the children are distributed in twenty villages, the *Lichfield Mercury* stated: 'The children presented a very pleasing appearance. They were well dressed, clean and healthy specimens of English childhood and their behaviour was delightful. Their appearance spoke well for the loving care of their mothers. They were of all ages from tiny tots to hefty youths.'

Lichfield had been told to prepare for 500 children, but 1,100 arrived. Fortunately, the assistant billeting officers had obtained sufficient billets to accommodate 2,000. Another 267 went to the Rugeley district.

Margate's 'Young Ladies'

Under the heading, 'Young ladies from Margate', the *Walsall Observer* published a happy picture of over fifty girls of the Lausanne Central School last weekend. It was taken in a field with the girls grouped round Miss Galloway, one of the teachers, who was playing an accordion. The girls are billeted at Great Wyrley, in the Cannock Rural District.

In describing the arrival of 538 of Margate's children at Great Wyrley station, the newspaper said, 'That cheerful, bustling Margate, with its sands and sailing boats winkles and piers, and all the other attributes that go to make up the cheerful air of a people's holiday resort, should be among the places from which the children have now to flee to safety is another count in Hitler's score. Yet so it is, and last week-end long trains brought young people from Margate, which is in the east coast danger zone, to Cannock Chase, where it is believed they will be able to carry on their education and daily lives in safety. They were almost uniformly glad to arrive, for the air raid siren's voice and the noise of guns from the sea have done much to break the serenity of life on the east coast.'

Members and officials of the local council met the children, and they were at once taken to a school for a medical inspection. Afterwards tea was provided for them by members of the Women's Volunteer Service before they were taken in cars to their billets in surrounding villages.

MEETING WITH WOUNDED

The *Walsall Observer* described a touching episode on the children's journey. 'Among the stories told of their trip to the Midlands,' the report stated, 'is one of a touching episode when at one station the train load of little evacuees met a train load of wounded soldiers. The soldiers made much of the children, and the children made much of the soldiers, and there were tears in the eyes of some of the men as they remembered the hideous hell to which they had seen German barbarity deliver the helpless and weak across the water. In their minds was an unspoken, but none the less real, prayer that these little ones might be spared. Wildly cheering, the youngsters sped the wounded soldiers on their way.'

SO HAPPY

Describing the reactions of the children and their activities, the paper said, 'They all appear to have settled down well in their new homes. Only a few have found it necessary to change their billets, and the majority have expressed themselves in terms of happiness. At least one has told her teacher who came with her, "We are so happy. We don't want to go back." '

'Everything possible is being done in homes and schools to see that they are happy. The schools are being opened in the evenings and at week-ends for various forms of social activity, such as concerts and dramatics – a choir has already come into being at Wyrley. Organised games, rambles and picnics are in the programme mapped out, and those who are connected with religious organisations are being put in touch with them.'

LOVINGLY CARED FOR

A splendid tribute to the behaviour and physical fitness of the Margate children is contained in a letter received by the Editor from Councillor C. Allen, of Sankey's Corner, Chase Terrace, near Walsall.

Councillor Allen writes: 'With a week's experience of the invasion of our village by the children of Margate, I felt you might like to know how very much the whole population of this parish (Burntwood Parish, 10,000 inhabitants) appreciate the splendid behaviour and general demeanour of the 500 children billeted among us. Everyone, too, remarks about their physical fitness and their very obvious good upbringing and education.

As a local councillor and voluntary worker I helped to welcome the first to step off the charabanc and by their frequent remarks soon found out they were glad to be away from the sounding of air raid sirens. Willing teachers and helpers and particularly the WVS very quickly gave them tea and then, with the aid of the Margate headmaster and staff, began to assign them to their various billets.

I personally took many in the car to their new homes and, mothers and fathers of Margate, if only you could have seen the ready and joyous reception that awaited your children, you would have felt very relieved.

I saw many very comfortably settled that night and have seen very many in their new homes and you may rest assured they are very happy indeed and are being very lovingly cared for. By the way, every morning the local postmen are waylaid for letters from Margate. It is 3.30pm Saturday, and many scores are in the local cinema at a penny matinee.

As a local trader who has naturally benefited by this invasion, my sympathies go out to the traders of your famous town and I do hope and trust that victory will soon be secured with a lasting peace, so that your children may return to you, and with them the many thousands you are so used to entertaining. Be assured, Margate, Burntwood Parish has welcomed and will continue to look after your children.'

MARGATE PARENT SATISFIED

Mrs M. Hassett, who went from Margate to Staffordshire a few days after the schools were evacuated, found her children very comfortable.

Writing to tell the Editor, she says: 'We have visited lots of the children and everywhere they are very happy and comfortable. It is a paradise for them, as they have such lovely playgrounds with swings and slides everywhere. The people here are very kind and fond of children and are doing their utmost to make them happy. I hope the mothers will be reassured by reading this letter. We came here on Tuesday and have found our children very comfortable.'

* * *

Irene Thornton *relates her evacuation experiences – and the problems she had when she returned home to Margate:*

War was declared in September 1939, but nothing much really happened until the following year. I was five years old and one day I heard my mother say to my grandmother, 'She may as well go, she will be safer there.' I did not understand what was going on, and I didn't know that the war had taken a turn for the worse with the threat of invasion looming closer. Anyway, on the 2nd June, 1940, my mum wrote my name on a card and pinned it to my coat. She gave me a bag which contained a change of clothes and some food, and took me to school. When we arrived at school we found lots of mums with their children dressed like me. All the children were given a small cardboard box which contained a gas mask.

Mums were crying and so were some of the children as we were put on to coaches and taken to the railway station. We were put on a train which stopped at other stations picking up lots of other children. After what seemed a very long time, the train stopped and coaches took us to a large building where we were given a meal and a toy. I was given a fluffy dog! Once again we were put on to coaches and taken to another station and continued our journey. By the time we reached Tamworth in Staffordshire, it was getting dark. I don't remember much about

Irene Thornton aged five, just after evacuation

Irene Thornton's mother with Uncle Jim and friend during the war

our arrival, but I remember a lady taking a boy and myself up a path to a house. Here a man and woman opened the door and took me in. The boy was taken to live down the road.

May and George Neal became my foster parents. They only had one child, a daughter in her early twenties who had joined the WAAFs. Once I was left alone with them I suddenly realised that I had been taken away from my mother. I was completely exhausted from the journey and, with the promise that I could go back to my mum the next day I cried myself to sleep. I would not let go of my fluffy dog, or some pennies that someone had given me.

My foster parents' house had three bedrooms, sitting room, kitchen and a small room downstairs which was used as a bathroom and wash room. Just outside the back door there was a porch; on one side was the toilet and on the other side the coal was stored for the fires. A black cast-iron range was used for cooking and for heating the water. At the front of the house was a flower garden. The houses, which were semi-detached, were built in a 'crescent' shape.

As the days passed I began to settle down. Auntie May and Uncle George as I called them were very kind to me and treated me as their own daughter. All the people in Hopwas village made me welcome and I soon made friends once I started at the local school. I soon started to feel at home although I missed my mum.

During the time I was evacuated my mother joined the ATS, but she managed to come to see me about twice a year. One of my uncles was in the army and was able to visit me until he was posted to Egypt. Another uncle who was in the Fire Service managed to come and see me a few times.

We always took our gas masks with us to school. Sometimes we would have 'Air Raid Practice', which meant that when the bell rang we would all make our

Wood Bridge, Hopwas, in the 1940s

way to the air raid shelter. This was on a piece of ground near the playground. The shelter was built under a small hill and consisted of a long room with benches on either side. During the day we would see the barrage balloons in the sky or see aeroplanes fly over. When the siren went we all either went inside or into the shelter. At nights my auntie only got me out of bed if the bombing was nearby, such as Birmingham or Coventry.

School supplied wool for knitting hats, scarves, gloves and pullovers for the army, navy and air force lads. Auntie used to knit them and taught me to knit as I got older. She also taught me to make rugs out of cloth, wool and sacking. I also learnt to embroider.

Food was scarce and rationed, so it was a sin to waste any. An apple starting to go bad with the bad bit taken out made a nice sandwich and stale cake was never wasted. Stale bread was made into either bread pudding, bread and butter pudding or broken up and put into a cup with hot water and a beef cube. The bread, milk, meat and coal were delivered by the Co-op horse and cart. Other things we needed were bought in Tamworth where there were queues for everything. One shop I hated going into was a hardware shop. Everything was scattered everywhere – on shelves, in boxes and all over the floor. It was quite dark in there with only a small pathway to walk in and out. My auntie always seemed to talk a lot in there and I had to stand perfectly still for ages. If I so much as moved a muscle I either knocked something down or broke something and ended up in trouble!

Fruit, like sweets, were also on ration, so they were a luxury. If, on my way home from school I saw bananas or oranges in the shop I would rush home to get my ration book. I was about nine years old when one day I saw some 'big yellow oranges' in the shop. I went in with my ration book but was only given one. I had never seen a grapefruit before!

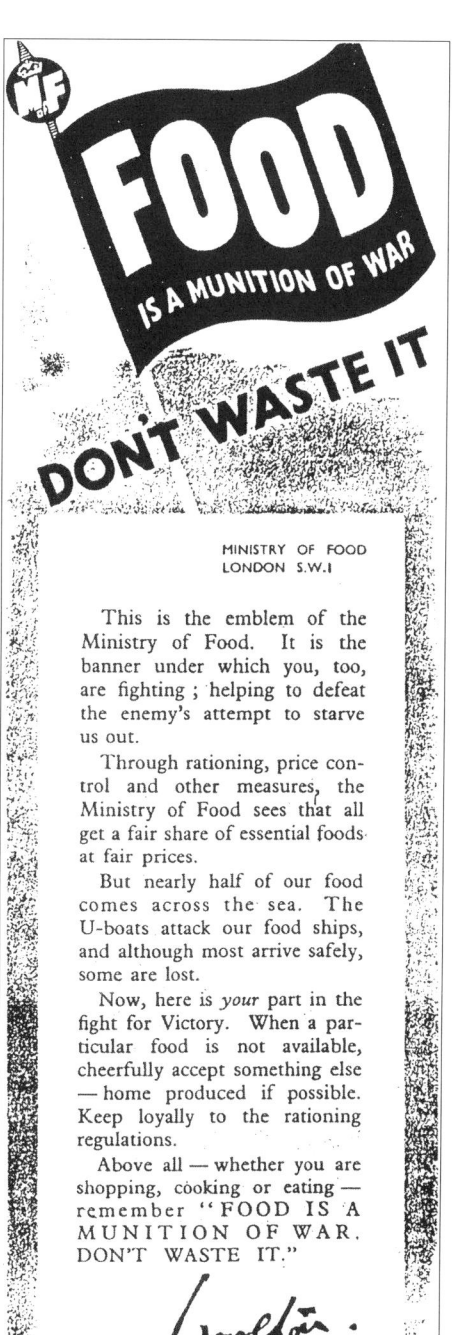

'Don't Waste Food' notice issued by the Ministry of Food, January 1941

The Church at Hopwas, 1940

On Sunday afternoons in the summer, auntie, uncle and I would go for a walk in the woods. We would collect blackberries and blueberries to make pies. Chestnuts and hazel nuts were kept for Christmas, and we collected wood for the fire. The children used to play hide and seek in the woods or just climb trees. It was safe enough in those days. We would swim in the canal or just watch the barges go by, some pulled by horses. Together we played Hopscotch or Five Stones. I had a whip and top and two tennis balls and also a piece of clothes line. The line was used to skip with or to tie on to the gatepost to make a swing. Sometimes I sat on the front step with a jar of soapy water, blowing bubbles with a white clay pipe.

On dark nights uncle would get the cards out and we would play rummy or patience. When we went to Tamworth auntie sometimes took me to the park to play on the swings. The rich people of Hopwas village used to put on fetes in their large gardens. I also went to Sunday School in the village hall. On Wednesdays we would go to the village hall to see pictures. The hall was also used by the local dentist for filling and extracting teeth!

During school holidays I went to stay on a farm. Uncle had relatives who lived and worked there. I loved it on the farm, but at first I was frightened of the cows. I soon got used to them and would help to bring them in to be milked by hand. I hated the turkeys running loose because they used to peck at me.

During my stay with auntie and uncle, I was allowed to 'adopt' a kitten which I used to play with for ages. When I was naughty my uncle used to tell me he would send 'Old Nick' after me. Old Nick was an old man with a long grey beard who lived locally. While I was staying on the farm, it was decided to go down to the village for a drink. While we were walking through the village, an old man with a long grey beard came walking towards us. He stopped to talk to my uncle and then bent down, took my hand, and introduced himself as 'Old Nick'. I was so frightened that I ran back to the farm and locked myself inside the cow shed. I was never threatened with him again.

Friday was Home Guard night at the Chequers

Our school sports day was always held on

May Day. I enjoyed this very much as I had become quite good at sports. Not quite good enough though because in the high jump and the running races I always came in second. After the sports were over we all danced around the maypole, singing and weaving the coloured ribbons around the pole. Afterwards we formed into a group and sang school songs.

At times the war seemed very distant from us in the village. Sometimes we would see the American army trucks go past the end of the road. We would always wave at them as they went past and they would give us sweets and chocolate. Friday night was Home Guard night and this was held in a room in 'The Chequers', the village pub. Friday was also my bath night. My hair was washed and rinsed in vinegar to make it shine. Then it was 'gone through' with the toothcomb. After this I was given the dreaded weekly dose of syrup of figs. I was then allowed to stay up until uncle came home with my weekly treat, a packet of crisps.

Irene Thornton's Uncle Jim and a friend with his army lorry named 'Miss Margate' during the war

At the end of the war some of the evacuees could not go home so other arrangements were made for them. My mother wanted me back so I believe I returned to Margate in March 1946. On returning home I found I had a stepfather who was not very nice to me. Because of this my mum would send me back to Hopwas on my school holidays. I also went back after I had left school. As I grew older I married a soldier and travelled around with him and we had three children. When my marriage broke up after thirty-five years, I brought my daughters back to Hopwas which I had always looked upon as my home.

As an evacuee I never really understood about the war. Life was so simple for us children. We had very little money, clothes or toys, yet we got on so well together and were happy with what we had. It was the happiest five years of my life!

Irene aged ten, just before she returned home to Margate

Beryl Price *(now Mrs Borne), writing from Florida, USA, after witnessing the terrible scenes of troops arriving from Dunkirk, remembers the heartbreak she felt as her family was torn apart during 1940:*

On the day of evacuation my father took me to join my school, Clarendon House County School for Girls. He asked the train driver where the children were going, but the train driver wouldn't tell him. My mother was at home busily packing and waiting for a lorry to arrive. My father's company had transferred him to some unknown destination, so my family was being split in two – and nobody knew where any of us were going! It was one of the most horrendous days of my life! I am still haunted by

*Clarendon House Grammar School for Girls in Ramsgate
(from a photo taken in 1998)*

the look on my father's face as he waved me goodbye.

We left Ramsgate and our school train passed through many stations before arriving at the town of Stafford where we were soon billeted with local families.

Separation leaves its scars and evacuation changed my life for ever. My own family names of Franklin, Price and Bundock had lived in Kent for generations. My parents and I vowed to return to Thanet after the war – but we never did!

Joan Heaton *was one of those, who, after being evacuated, never returned to her home town to live:*

At the outbreak of the war I was attending Dame Janet School in Ramsgate. By June 1940, Dad was in the army and the next thing I remember was being told that we were going to the country with the school for a holiday, and that our teachers were coming with us. I was 10 years old.

Mum and grandad saw me off and we all assembled at Ramsgate railway station. We wore our school clothes and I had a gaberdine raincoat with my label attached to it, my gas mask, and a small case with my Sunday best and a change of underclothes. I also had a plain post card to send home to let my mother know my new address.

Apart from the initial excitement of going away, the train journey was long, tiring and uneventful. We finally arrived at Uttoxeter in Staffordshire and were all taken to the town hall where we had some refreshments. Then we were all examined by a nurse before being sorted into groups for the buses which were waiting to take us to our final destination.

My bus took me and others to the village of Rocester where we assembled at the village school. By this time there were a lot of tears as the local people chose which evacuees they wanted. I was chosen by two lovely people whom I called Aunt Nell and Uncle Bert. My friend Vera and her sister were billeted two doors away, so I didn't feel too lonely or sad.

As soon as I got into the house I asked to go to the bathroom – and that's when I came down to earth. There was no bathroom, no water toilet and no tap water! I was taken to the end of the garden where a lamp was lit. There was a long wooden seat with two lids and the smell was disgusting. A man with his horse and cart used to come once in a while at night to empty the smelly pit. I hated it! Water for the house was drawn from a pump in the yard.

We shared the premises of the village school with the local children, but we had our own teachers for a while. Nobody told us about the cows that were driven down the village street twice a day for milking! One day we were walking home from school, and when we turned round, there was a herd of cows – with huge horns – right behind us. I had never seen a cow before and I ran screaming all the way home. The local children thought it was funny, but it took us a while to get used to the cows.

I was given the job of going to the farm, which was just across the road from where I lived, to collect cows' milk in a large jug. I also had a piece of muslin with beads all round the edge of it, to cover the milk jug when it was full. I wouldn't drink any of the milk and told Aunt Nell that our milk back home came in bottles. She solved the problem by getting some milk bottles from school!

Eventually, my grandad's house in Ramsgate was destroyed by bombing, so he went to live with relatives at Maidstone and, after two happy years with Aunt Nell and Uncle Bert, I also went to relatives in Maidstone, but never returned to my home town of Ramsgate. I kept in touch with Aunt Nell and Uncle Bert for many years. When I was sixteen I went back to Rocester for a holiday, then every chance I got after that, I returned there. I married my husband at Maidstone and in the course of time persuaded him that we should sell up and move to Rocester permanently. So I finally returned to the place of my evacuation to stay, but this time I was accompanied by my husband and my six children.

Peter Deacon *didn't have a very good start in life, but things improved from the time of his evacuation:*

On 2nd June 1940, buses took us to Ramsgate railway station where we joined hundreds of other children who were being evacuated. We had our gas masks with us and sandwiches to eat on the journey. To us small children it was a great adventure and the thought of not having to go back to those children's homes was great.

We travelled on that train all day and it was dark before it arrived at its destination. We were again put on to buses and my brother and I and many others were taken to the Institute in Abbots Bromley, which is near to Uttoxeter in Staffordshire. We were all put on to the Institute stage and the local people came and chose those whom they wanted to foster. The billeting officer asked my brother and me if we would like to stay together and I remember nodding at her. We then went by car to the outskirts of Abbots Bromley, to a place called Seedcroft and the house of a newly married couple, Mr and Mrs Tom Talbot. They were a nice couple, but my brother and I were only together for a few weeks because Mr and Mrs Talbot found they couldn't cope with two small boys. My brother was moved into the village and lived with the local blacksmith, Mr Bloor.

We went to school in Abbots Bromley and the headmistress was Miss Upton. After a few weeks we were surprised to see the arrival of Mr Pinder, our old headmaster from Manston Village School.

I remember some good times in Abbots Bromley. We used to walk to school from Seedcroft and, after being in a children's home, it was wonderful to be free in the countryside to do as I liked. However, being only eight years old and having lived through the trauma of children's homes and then being evacuated to a strange place, it took its toll and I started wetting the bed. The doctor in Abbots Bromley did his best to cure me, but to no avail. In the end I was taken from the Talbot's and put once again into a children's home, Kingstanding Hall, just outside Abbots Bromley. The strange thing was that once I was in the home with the other children, the bed wetting stopped!

After a few months I was found another billet with Mr and Mrs Moss, who lived on a farm called Sunset Rise in the village of Willslock. I had seen animals from a distance, but actually to be on a farm with them was something very different. There were cows, horses, pigs, sheep and chickens – and they all looked enormous!

Mr Moss worked very hard, but in the evenings he liked to go to the pub. What a life I led! It was down to the 'local' every evening, and I would sit in the back of the car with crisps and a bottle of Vimto. What a fantastic change from living in a children's home but, the only trouble was, I couldn't wake up the next morning to go to school. The local billeting officer happened to be Mr Moss's mother and, when she found out what was going on in the evenings, she was very angry – and I was on the move again. This time I found myself billeted with Mr and Mrs Swetnam who lived in the gardener's cottage at a place called Loxley Hall, not far from Willslock. They were good, kindly people with a son called Bill. The area was a great place for boys to play, with its woodland and old buildings, and we really had some wonderful times there, but in the end, because the cottage was so small and cramped, I was moved on once again! I finished up in Willslock again, with Mr and Mrs Plant, a farm working family. By this time I was about ten years old and used to go with Mr Plant to help on the farm; I think this was the start of a change in my life.

When I was nearly eleven, the headmistress at Kingstone School tried to persuade me to take the examination for high school, but I learned that, if I passed the exam, I would be sent down to Chatham. There was no way that I was going to go back down south – so I didn't take the exam! I left Kingstone School and went to the senior boys' school in Uttoxeter – and hated every minute of it. All I wanted to do was to go farming. It had got into my blood and that is what I intended to do when I left school.

I finally left school at fourteen and got the chance of a job on a farm and that is where my working life has been spent. I never returned to Kent and have lived in the Uttoxeter area ever since those dark days of World War II.

Joan Small *gives a very lucid account of her evacuation experiences:*

On 2nd June, 1940, we left Ramsgate railway station, complete with a small suitcase each, a packed lunch (that in itself was no mean achievement for our mothers, who had been turning out their cupboards for find something to help feed the hungry soldiers returning from Dunkirk), and some dried apricots to chew, as recommended by our form mistress.

Everyone carried a cardboard box containing a gas mask and all we children wore a large label which was crossed on the back. It was assumed by the children that the cross meant that you did not wet the bed! I can't remember feeling sad about leaving. To be going on a train journey with school friends was like an adventure. One thing that has surprised me is that the reason for our evacuation does not seem to have been understood. It was not the bombing that sent us away, it was the real threat of imminent invasion by the enemy and school children were being sent away from likely invasion points. All the adults who stayed behind had been given their instructions on where they were to go in the event of an enemy landing. It seems hard to take this seriously now, but at that time it seemed the expected thing – and even odd that it did not happen.

Stafford was not as we had expected it to be; instead, it was a lovely quiet, country town. When we arrived, we were taken to St Paul's church hall and given lemonade and buns. Then two by two we were taken by car with a billeting officer, to possible homes. My friend Sheila, who came from Westbrook, and I were just about the last to leave, and by now it was late afternoon.

I remember the billeting officer knocking on doors of two attached houses, and the ladies coming to the door together. They looked us up and down doubtfully – well, we were both grown girls. 'You see,' the ladies said, 'We've got sons!'

They said they would take us overnight anyway and we must have behaved ourselves because the next day they decided we could stay – and we both stayed until we left school at 17. For me it was a great experience. I was an only child and, being at a school that took its pupils from all over Thanet, my school friends lived in Margate and Birchington, not necessarily close at hand; here I was in Stafford with my friends all living in a fairly small area. My foster family had a car, which we didn't have at home, and we all went to church – which we didn't do at home. In fact, I was confirmed while I was in Stafford, something that might not have happened if I had stayed at home. Sundays back home were like any other day. My father, being a railway man, often had to work, and my mother worked too, so that her weekends were busy. I was old enough to appreciate this more ordered way of life in Stafford, and I am sure it was of benefit to me.

Once a week we were escorted by boys of our own age to the 'Green and Brown Club', named after the colours of the blazers we wore – brown for the Girls' Grammar School, and green for the boys'.

We found that the two households where my friend Sheila and I were billeted were almost like one. The ladies, although not sisters, had been brought up together and still did most things together. The houses had cellars and, later on when we had air raid alarms, we all went down to the cellars, which had been knocked into one, and quite enjoyed ourselves. When the all clear went we always had Horlicks – made with water

– before we went off to bed.

My hosts were extremely kind and, after a while, I called them Aunty Connie and Uncle Billy (Aunty Lou and Uncle Fred were next door). I eventually found out that they had agreed with my parents that if anything happened to my parents, Aunty Connie and Uncle Billy would adopt me!

The son in my billet was just starting his teaching career when I arrived and very shortly afterwards was called up for the Royal Air Force, which meant I was moved from my little bedroom into his room and I had all his books to read. I like to think that perhaps my being there helped Aunty Connie a bit, as she missed her son very much.

Aunty Connie was in charge of a shift at the YMCA near Stafford Station once a week, and Sheila and I were allowed to go down and help in the kitchen. We were never allowed the other side of the counter to clear tables – we would have been too close to all those soldiers!

One thing I remember about rationing was that there were always long queues at sweet shops when supplies arrived. We very rarely got a chance to spend our sweet coupons, so I sent mine home to Ramsgate and my mother sent me a monthly parcel, as there seemed to be plenty of supplies in Thanet. We also had our bikes sent up from home, which gave us more freedom to get around.

After a while the ban on people travelling to coastal towns was lifted and we actually went back to Thanet for holidays. Up till then we either stayed in Stafford or, as I had a grandmother in Welwyn Garden City, we went there, or to Sheila's family who had moved to Sidcup.

Some of my friends had several billets in Stafford. Obviously circumstances of the host families changed sometimes, which made having an evacuee inconvenient. I helped in the garden and did my own ironing and mending (we darned socks in those days!), but there were some cases of girls being expected to do too much in the house.

We had to share the local grammar school building by going there on Tuesdays, Thursdays and Saturdays. Wednesdays and Fridays were spent at Baswich House, a large rambling house in beautiful grounds on the edge of the town. When we first started using Baswich House there was no furniture, so we sat on the floor for our lessons. I remember a local farmer offering a prize of apples for a competition between our school houses, to see who could collect the largest amount of acorns, which were to be used for pig food. Besides our Green and Brown Club, a few of us belonged to a drama society held at St Chad's Hall, and which we called 'Stathane' – a name made up from Stafford and Thanet, as we had members who were local as well as evacuees. We never actually produced anything, but worked hard at play reading and rehearsing.

Eventually, in December 1944, my school returned to Ramsgate.

25th June, 1940, saw a second evacuation of children from Thanet. as the following Isle of Thanet Gazette *article for 28th June, 1940, shows:*

MORE CHILDREN GO
THANET'S SECOND EVACUATION

The second evacuation of children from Thanet took place on Tuesday, when nearly 200 left by special train to join the main body of Thanet's children who left for safer areas on June 2nd.

Most of Tuesday's party, who were given a second chance to leave the south-east coast by the introduction of this supplementary evacuation scheme, had been prevented from taking part in the first by illness.

Ninety-nine registered at Margate, fifteen at Broadstairs, and about eighty at Ramsgate.

When Margate children assembled outside the railway station at 7.30am there were only eighty-five. One had already notified the authorities that he would not be travelling with the party and thirteen others failed to put in an appearance.

They were seen off by Alderman W. C. Redman, C.C., chairman of Margate's education authority, and the Director of Education (Mr J. C. Aspden). Seven helpers went with the party. Councillor Mrs B. M. Giles was one of the escorts. While the children were preparing to enter the train she was to be seen quietening one or two small ones who became tearful as the time of departure drew near.

They went to Lichfield, Cannock rural area, Rugeley and Hednesford, in Cannock urban district.

*Also in the same issue of the **Gazette** appeared the following article:*

THEY WANT TO GO TO CANADA

The plan announced by the Government for the evacuation of 200,000 English children to Canada has created interest among Margate parents.

Between fifty and sixty mothers and fathers have made enquiries about the scheme at Margate education office and already some twenty definite applications to go to Canada have been made.

The children have to be medically examined and this is being carried out in Staffordshire where the children are at present evacuated.

Probably a greater number of Margate parents and children will have to be disappointed for, unless the Government's scheme is increased in scope, only a limited number of the children of England can be accommodated on the first trip across the Atlantic.

Evacuees were sent to various overseas locations such as Australia, Canada, New Zealand, South Africa and the U.S.A. during the last war. Most of these were evacuated under the C.O.R.B. scheme (Children's Overseas Reception Board). Not all evacuees reached their destination safely. The ship City of Benares *was carrying children from Britain to Canada. The voyage across the Atlantic from Liverpool was passing reasonably smoothly when, on the 17th September, 1940, disaster struck as the ship was torpedoed by an enemy submarine. 77 young evacuees and many members of the crew lost their lives on that terrible day. 46 of the surviving children spent eight days in an open lifeboat before being rescued. The whole of the free world was shocked to hear of the tragedy and Winston Churchill was so distressed he urged the cessation of the overseas evacuation and no further sailings took place under the C.O.R.B. scheme. Official figures show that only just over 70,000 young evacuees were sent abroad before the cessation of the C.O.R.B. scheme.*

During the research for this book no evacuee could be found who actually went to Canada from the Isle of Thanet. However, the following account is of an evacuee from the south-east who went to the U.S.A. and gives some indication of the experiences encountered by those evacuees who were sent abroad. Here, **Betty Kentish** *(now Mrs Betty Booker) recounts the events of those days:*

My parents decided to send my sister aged seven, my brother aged 11 and me aged 15 to the United States, thinking that the war would only last a year. We duly went for medical checks, had passports arranged and were told to report to Grosvenor House Hotel in London.

Our parents were up on a balcony watching, while we children were all assembled below, complete with hand baggage, sandwiches for the trip to Liverpool, and our names and addresses pinned to our coats. We were ushered to buses as we waved goodbye to our parents, singing of all things, 'Wish Me Luck As You Wave Me Goodbye'. It was a heart-breaking moment when the buses moved off and my mother ran after the bus waving her arms.

The journey to Liverpool via Euston was a nightmare, with hold ups for air raids – and children fighting each other! It was to be two more days before we actually reached the ship, R.M.S. *Samaria*, and sailed. The voyage wasn't too bad. We were divided into groups of six under an escort who had the responsibility of looking after us.

Lots of entertainment was provided for us - films, 'Silly Symphonies', P.E. lessons and, towards the end of the trip, there was a concert performed by talented young people. Seasickness was common among the children and one girl managed to swallow a sixpence with no dire results.

I have often wondered if those cheerful sailors survived the war. They all gave us their autographs with messages of good luck. The captain even signed my book – E. M. Fall.

The Seamen's Institute was our temporary home once we landed in New York, then from there we were billeted out to families in the area. We were fortunate to be placed with families nearby so we children kept in touch. My brother was placed with a family who had one son and my sister and I were a couple of blocks away where they had two older children attending Mount Holyoke College.

Homesickness affected us all of course, but all in all, our three and a half years in the U.S.A. were filled with warmth and kindness from all who came in contact with us. The High School I attended had 2,000 pupils – a bit different to my previous school. I had come from a boarding school with only 70 girls. But I was made to feel welcome in my new school and I enjoyed my years there.

News from home was always worrying, with my father working in the city where the air raids were so bad but we could never imagine the horror of the bombing. I used to feel guilty being in such a comfortable home away from all the danger.

There were times when I felt we would never get home as the years went by, but in 1944 I was allowed back to England to attend Goldsmith's College – which had been evacuated to Nottingham – to continue my teacher training. My brother came back in 1945 as did my sister, though she didn't return until later in the year.

So many children had dreadful experiences when they were evacuated. We were the lucky ones! Our guardians eventually came to England to visit us and our parents went to America for a visit to meet the kindly folk who opened their homes to us. I still write to several old school friends in the U.S.A.; it was a fantastic experience – but I could never have sent *my* children!

* * *

Audrey Collison (now Mrs Jones) was evacuated from Margate with her sister in 1940:

On the day of evacuation my sister and I assembled with the rest of the children at Holy Trinity School, Margate. I was just eight at the time and my sister Shirley was just six. My most vivid memory of that day is the noise at Margate railway station where hundreds of school children were waiting to board trains. Some were crying because they didn't want to go and some mothers were crying because they didn't want to let their children go. I can remember my mother and my grandmother having a terrible argument about my sister and me and whether we should go or not.

Parents were not allowed on to the platforms with the children and one of the last things my mother said to me before we left was, 'Look after your sister, don't let her out of your sight.' Eventually our train left the station and we were on our way, though we didn't know where we were going.

Apart from the fact that the journey seemed to last all day, the only other thing I can remember about the journey is that, as we went through some stations, there were lots

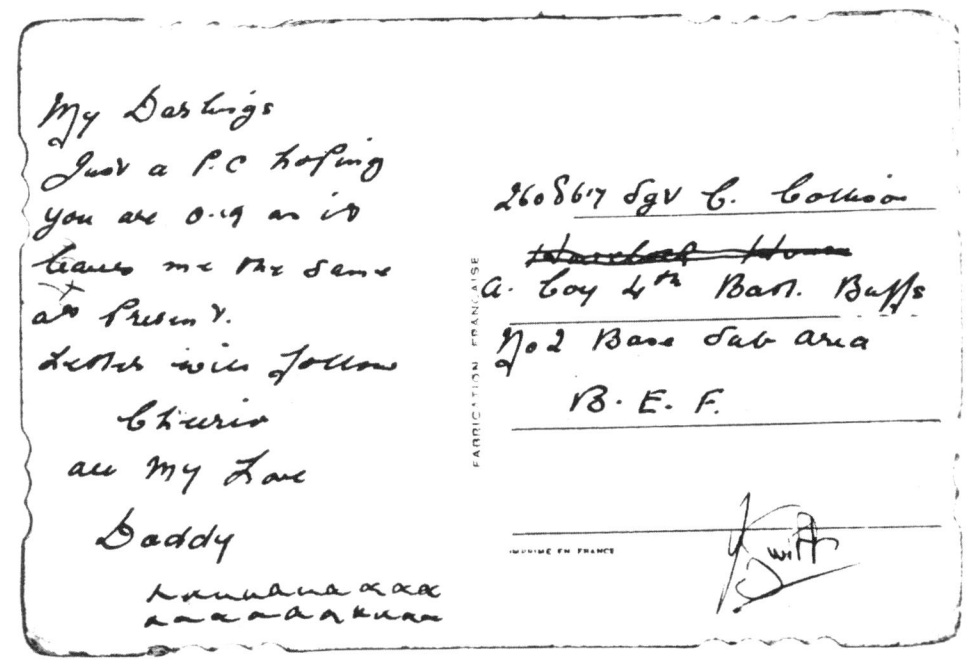

A wartime postcard sent to Audrey and Shirley Collison in Staffordshire by their father who was then a sergeant in the British Expeditionary Force

of soldiers waving to us. Our final destination turned out to be the village of Wall, near Lichfield in Staffordshire. We were all taken to the village hall where we waited to be allocated to foster parents. Most of the children had left when I suddenly had this dreadful feeling come over me that nobody wanted us. Suddenly a lady burst into the room and said, 'The two little girls in blue coats and red berets are mine!' That was our first encounter with Mrs Emily Threadgold, who became our Auntie Em. She had been held up for some reason and was late in arriving at the hall.

Em was a widow. Her husband had died in the influenza epidemic of 1919 and she lived all alone in a house at Pipe Hill. Her brother and three sisters and a brother-in-law all lived at the family farm called Fossway Farm, just down the road from Pipe Hill.

My sister and I were very happy living with Aunt Em. The local school was very small – we only had one teacher, Miss Dowling. The first winter we were in Wall, the pond in the field next to the school froze over, and the teacher told us not to slide on it. Not many of the children took any notice of this order, including myself, so I got caned – along with a few others! Needless to say I never did it again.

Our free time was spent on the farm, and a week or two after we had arrived from Kent, 'Uncle' George Oliver white-washed the barn and all the evacuees in the area were invited to a party to welcome us into the district. A few months later near to Christmas, we gave a concert in the same barn. My sister and I took part and we dressed up from a large trunk of clothes which they kept on the farm. I can remember my sister singing 'Little Old Lady Passing By', dressed in a black, beaded cloak and bonnet, and me reciting;

'Auntie' Gertie Oliver and Audrey Jones (nee Collison) on Auntie's 96th birthday in 1997

> Podge the puppy found a box
>   And thought perhaps there'd be
> A nice big juicy bone inside,
>   Said he, 'I'll look and see!'

Can you imagine it! We also sang 'Two Little Girls In Blue', 'One Finger One Thumb Keep Moving' and a song called 'God Bless Our Soldier Daddy'.

At the time of the first heavy snow, men from the farm had to come and dig us out before Aunt Em could open the door, but this did not stop us from going to school. We used to walk the two miles there and two miles back every day. Also during the winter we used to collect the red holly berries and thread them on to cotton with a needle, until we had a long string of them, and make Christmas decorations. We would also make Christmas presents by knitting scarves and socks, embroidering tray cloths and handkerchiefs. I have a cloth that Shirley and I embroidered during our evacuation. It was made as a present for my 'Auntie' Gertie Oliver, who lived on the farm, but she never used it, and on her 90th birthday in 1991, she gave it to me. It is a very treasured possession of mine.

It was peaceful and pleasant in Wall and one was not always aware of the war, although once we saw the flames of Coventry as a red glow in the distance.

When the war came to an end, I joined my mother, who was by now living in Wolverhampton. I was with her on VE Day. People cried and laughed a lot. Somebody took a fish from a market stall and threw it up on to the tram wires – and brought all the trams to a halt! My sister Shirley stayed on with Auntie Em in Lichfield.

I left school in 1946 and returned to Margate to live with my grandmother – who had refused to leave her home during the war. In 1948 I joined the Women's Royal Army Corps, met my future husband, and eventually settled in Wales. My father joined my mother in Wolverhampton after the war, where they both stayed until they died.

I have been back to where I was evacuated. The farm has gone, but other things have changed surprisingly little.

Anthony Owen *was a pupil at Chatham House Grammar School in Ramsgate and was evacuated with his school to Stafford. He was another evacuee who never returned to his home town to live after the war:*

My sister Hilary, who was with Clarendon House Grammar School, Ramsgate, also went to Stafford. My father was a teacher at the time and he went with his school to Chasetown.

My first billet in Stafford was in the last house of Brunswick Terrace, but very quickly moved from there to Cresswell! After a few months I made my final move to Cannock Road where I spent the remainder of my schooldays.

I lived with an elderly couple called Hollison who were kindness themselves, although always very strict. In 1943 I left school to go to University and then into the army. For most of my working life I lived near Derby, eventually returning to Stafford in 1981.

By the end of the war my parents were living near Tunbridge Wells in Kent and, except for one brief visit, I never returned to Thanet.

Chatham House Grammar School for Boys, Ramsgate, founded in 1797. Photo taken in 1998

Chapter Three

MEMORIES OF STAFFORDSHIRE

This chapter continues with more personal accounts and newspaper reports of those children evacuated from the Isle of Thanet.

Brian Sackett *was just six years old when the experience of evacuation was thrust upon him. Although being very young and only being evacuated for a short while, he still has some happy memories of his time in Staffordshire:*

I was just six years old and I remember we said our goodbyes to our parents then marched from the school to the railway station, carrying our little cases and gas masks. I can't remember much about the actual journey, except we were shunted into sidings from time to time.

When we finally reached our destination, it was the village of Gnosall near Stafford. When we got off the train we all marched up to the local village school, where we were herded into the playground, then the local populace arrived and started picking out the evacuees they wanted. I waited and waited and I think I was one of the last to be chosen.

Shortly after I arrived in Gnosall I contracted pneumonia and was taken to Stafford Infirmary and, during my stay there, I was given M and B tablets. I must have been quite poorly because they sent for my mother and she came up to see me. My father also came up, but he could only stay for a day because he had to return to his work at Chislet Colliery.

When I recovered from the illness I moved to another address in Gnosall where my hosts ran a small hardware business and I remember they had a van which they used to go to the surrounding villages selling paraffin and brushes, etc. On Saturday mornings they would take me with them as they drove round the countryside. One thing that really sticks in my mind was the complete contrast from our home in Ramsgate to living in a country village with wide-open spaces – and hills, which to me at the age of six, looked like mountains!

I don't know why, but I moved again, this time to a farm labourer's cottage where I slept on a straw mattress. They had the usual bucket toilet down the garden. I remember one day when my mother was there, I went to the toilet and I stood on the wooden seat to look out of the window – and took a step backwards! I fell down the hole in the seat and I was suddenly up to my waist in the 'proverbial'! It took my mother ages to wash me down with endless pans of hot water from the hob.

There were occasions when I used to peer out of my bedroom at night-time and look at the orange glow in the sky, and I would be told that Wolverhampton was being bombed again.

I used to like going to the farm because it was like a new world to me, with all the animals and tractors. I remember in particular one of the horses whose name was Captain, which was the biggest and strongest of the four horses they had there. I also remember the old threshing machine and the hay making.

There were a few cattle in the field next to the farm and they were sometimes fed with swedes which were taken around the field by horse and cart. They used to sit me up on the front of the cart holding the reins and I would drive this cart around the field whilst the farm labourer scattered the swedes behind us. On reflection, I suspect that the horse would have walked around the field without any help from me, but at the time it really felt good.

I went to the local primary school in the village and I remember at one time there was some local flooding when we were told not to go near the water. The next morning on the way to school there was flooding across the road. I had my wellingtons on so I went through the water, but it was deep and the water went over the top of my boots. As I walked across the playground with my wellingtons squelching, the other children shouted, 'Teacher, Brian Sackett's been in the flood!' I had to take all my wet things off and stand in the corner of the classroom as a punishment.

Sunday afternoons we used to go for walks and sometimes we would walk down to the Shropshire Union Canal. I used to sit on the bridge and watch the horse-drawn coal barges pass by. I think it was seeing that canal that fostered my interest in canals later in life.

I had only been in Gnosall a few months when our house in Church Road, Ramsgate, was damaged by enemy action. My father found alternative accommodation in the village of Upstreet and, as this was considered to be much safer than Ramsgate, I returned home in time for Christmas, 1940.

In the 1980s I had a boating holiday on the Shropshire Union Canal when we stopped at a place called Brude and walked up to the village of Gnosall, but I didn't recognise much at all. After all, I was only there for a short while, but my memories of my evacuation there are happy ones.

Peggy Horn *(now Mrs Campany) was barely school age when she was evacuated to Staffordshire:*

Prior to going to Staffordshire I lived at 12 Milton Avenue in Margate, with my parents and younger brother. (My sisters had already left!) I was five and a half years old when I was evacuated. I didn't go when the schools went on 2nd June 1940, but followed some time later.

I remember being on a train with lots of other children. When we left the train we went on to a couple of charabancs as coaches were then called. My next memory is of arriving at the cottage of Mr and Mrs Bradbury, seeing a large open fire with a big black pot of water bubbling away on it – the only way to get hot water there!

Peggy's foster father, Mr Bradbury

Peggy Horn with Mary Bradbury in Kings Bromley, Summer 1942

There were three children in the foster family, but they were much older than me. One daughter was married and a son was in the armed forces, but there was still a girl, Mary, at home with her parents. The strange thing I remember about the cottage is that it had an outside, bucket-type toilet and a water pump in the yard, although we did have a cold water tap inside the cottage. Mr and Mrs Bradbury were kind to me and treated me as one of their own children. I was well fed and clothed and was often taken on outings to nearby towns and villages. Buses were few and far between so we didn't travel too far from home.

The school in Kings Bromley was two rooms in a large house, which is where I first started school. One room was for the infants, and the other for the juniors. The older children went to schools in Lichfield or Rugeley. I was introduced to the Peter Rabbit stories and soon learnt to read.

I don't recall having any trouble with the local children. I did have a special friend, Lucy, but as I was only eight years old when I returned to Margate, we soon lost touch with each other.

I have been back to Kings Bromley twice since the end of the war. The first time when I was fourteen years old. I went for a week with my sister Joyce, and stayed with her foster parents, Mr and Mrs Jackson. The second time I went back was with my husband and our two children in 1970. We met some of the family that my husband had stayed with, but we didn't meet anyone that I knew.

My own foster mother, Mrs Bradbury, came to see me in Westgate soon after I was married, and it was nice meeting her again.

The only thing I recall that was in anyway related to the war, whilst I was evacuated, was when a convoy of army lorries drove through the village. Mostly I remember my time in Kings Bromley as a peaceful time; a happy childhood paddling in the streams, walking through the fields, and picking blackberries and wild flowers.

I returned home to Margate in late August

Salmestone County Primary School, Margate, in 1998

1943. I went to Salmestone School – and spent most of the time in the shelters, having spelling-bees while the air raids were on. We were not allowed on the beach because it was covered in barbed wire. Apart from that, life went on as usual.

Joan Horn (*now Mrs Jevons*) *was evacuated with Drapers Mills School, Margate, and relives below her memories of Kings Bromley:*

I can well recall the day we left Margate, with my gas mask in a tall tin, tied with string and slung over my shoulder, and a small attache case with my meagre belongings in. It was Sunday 2nd June 1940 and it was the first time I had travelled such a long distance. I can well remember that on the way our train stopped and there opposite was another train crowded with troops, who passed meat pies and oranges over to us.

When we arrived at Lichfield we were put on to coaches and sent to the out-lying villages and towns. Our own destination was to be Kings Bromley and in the village hall we were all offered a glass of milk from a churn, which to me was the best drink I had ever had, ice-cold and very refreshing!

My sister Joyce and I were collected by Mrs Bailey who lived in the 'new council houses'. It was all beautifully clean and bright. Mr Bailey worked on a local farm. We stayed with Mr and Mrs Bailey for two years, then Mr Bailey secured another job in Alrewas and we were unable to go with them.

Next door was a family named Evans, and I became very friendly with Margaret their daughter, whom I still visit to this day.

We spent some lovely times in Kings Bromley, taking packed lunches down to the fields, catching minnows in the streams. It was especially exciting at hay-making times, as we used to get a ride back and forth on top of the wagons. We also went mushrooming – nothing tastes quite so nice as when you have collected them yourself.

The road we lived in stretched from one end of the village to the other and, in holiday times, we would use the banks and grass verge opposite to lay out our 'houses' with bricks and stones and play 'happy families'. On reflection, this was truly an idyllic time.

Margaret, my friend, once wrote in a composition, 'Joan Horn and I played mud pies in the holidays, this was making cakes out of mud, and opening a shop!' This must have amused the teacher, because Margaret had to read the composition to the class!

After leaving the Baileys', my sister and I were split up. She went to Mr and Mrs Jackson, and I went to Mr and Mrs Wood who were retired farmers. They had a daughter, Mrs Harris, who helped to look after me. She is now in her late eighties and I go to see her most years. They were all very kind to me. Mr Wood loved teasing me, and when he found out that I wasn't particularly fond of my second name Maud, I was for ever after called 'Maudie'!

Mr and Mrs Wood had a son and daughter with farms; I would go and stay with them in school holidays and when it was potato picking times. All in all, I was a very lucky evacuee. I think I found it hard to integrate into my own large family when I first came home, because I had been the only child for quite a long time during my evacuation.

The village of Kings Bromley is now very built up, and the lovely cottages are mostly occupied by people who travel daily to Birmingham and other places. Mrs Harris was, until 1997, treasurer at the local church, and she is truly a wonderful lady.

When my husband and I go to stay, she still does all the cooking.

Incidentally, my husband was evacuated to Chase Town, but I didn't know of him at the time.

The following article appeared in the local press in Lichfield on 7th June, 1940, documenting the arrival of evacuees from Margate:

HAPPY EVACUEES
Hospitable Reception in Lichfield Villages.
Homes Found For 1,180

For years Margate has been accustomed to being invaded by thousands of children bent on pleasure, but last Sunday saw Lichfield and its surrounding districts invaded by the children of Margate seeking safety from the threatened bombing of their homes.

It had been arranged that 300 children should be sent last Sunday to Lichfield from Margate, and the city billeting officer (Mr. Fineron) had arranged compulsory billets in the city accordingly. Early in the day the town clerk received word that they were not coming to the city, as Lichfield was being reserved for secondary school children. Notices were accordingly sent to the expectant householders on Sunday afternoon to inform them of the change of plans. Whilst some of the householders may have been pleased, most were disappointed, as they had been busily engaged in making preparation for the reception of their young expected guests and would have preferred to have received them then than at a later date.

Councillor Jonah Deakin (the vice-chairman of the Rural District Council) and the billeting officer for the Lichfield Rural District (Mr. B. L. Illingworth) had had a busy time. In each parish there was an assistant billeting officer and a willing band of workers to find billets for the expected children. They were told to get ready to receive children, the number of whom would be notified on Thursday after the parents at Margate had registered their children on Wednesday. The figures came through as 500, but when the children arrived they amounted to 1,180. Fortunately the assistant billeting officers had obtained sufficient billets to accommodate 2,000 children.

The children assembled at their respective schools in Margate at 8.30 and were medically examined and entrained shortly after 10am and commenced their long train journey to Lichfield.

The first train steamed into Trent Valley station at 3.45pm. The children quietly and orderly, under the care of their teachers, formed up on the platform in their classes and schools. They were then taken in coaches to the Central School in Frog Lane, where they were medically inspected by the school medical officers of the county council. The local teachers were there to help with the children.

Distributed in Twenty Villages

The children then went in coaches to their billets at Chasetown, Chase Terrace, Colton, Drayton Bassett, Elford, Elmhurst, Fazeley, Gentleshaw, Chorley, Hamstall Ridware, Mavesyn Ridware, Hammerwich, Hints, Kings Bromley, Stonnall, Shenstone, Wall, Weeford, Hopwas and Wigginton. The assistant billeting officers, with the ready and sympathetic help of the women of the parish (and also the men) gave refreshments to the children and did their best to give them a hearty welcome and to make them feel at home in their new and strange surroundings. The teachers also greatly helped. The newspapers say the children left Margate with all the hilarity of a Sunday School treat, but when they arrived at Trent Valley Station they were a very quiet, orderly, and somewhat tired contingent.

The children presented a very pleasing appearance. They were well dressed, clean and healthy specimens of English childhood, and their behaviour was delightful. Their appearance spoke well for the loving care of their mothers. They were of all ages, from tiny tots to hefty youths. There were several coloured children and Jewish refugees.

The day was hot and sunny, but all wore their overcoats. Some carried attache cases, others had knapsacks, kit-bags and brown paper parcels. Some girls hugged their dolls and some boys carried cricket bats.

It speaks well for the inhabitants of the rural district that in their country's hour of need they were all willing to do their bit, and that all the children were accommodated voluntarily without the need of compulsory billeting.

Secondary School Children for Lichfield

It has now been ascertained that Lichfield itself has been reserved for secondary school children from the Camp Hill Grammar School and it is anticipated that the number of children to be received will be in the region of four hundred. The chief billeting officer (Mr J. Fineron) informed a *Mercury* representative on Tuesday, that at the moment it is not possible to state when these children will arrive in the city, but when the council receive such notice they will notify householders as early as practicable.

Warm Welcome at Rugeley

On Sunday, Rugeley welcomed 267 young evacuees from Margate. With them were sixteen teachers and helpers. The children were met at the Trent Valley Station shortly before 6.30pm by coaches, which conveyed them to the Talbot Street Church of England School. There they were medically examined and given light refreshments, later being taken to their billets by local teachers and officials. By 10pm all the evacuees were safely in their new homes. Everywhere they were met with that kindness and sympathetic understanding which characterises the people of Rugeley. The billeting arrangements were very efficiently carried out by Mr W. H. Beresford (billeting officer), with the assistance of local school teachers and helpers. Interviewed by the *Mercury* Mr Beresford said that not once, in the whole of the urban district, was he compelled to exercise compulsory billeting powers. In all cases, people were ready and willing to do their little bit to help others less fortunate than themselves.

In addition to the evacuees brought to the town on Sunday, there are about thirty others who were evacuated from West Bromwich to Rugeley a few days after the outbreak of war.

Lord Dudley's Thanks

Following the reception in Midland areas of 16,000 evacuees from the East and South-East towns, Lord Dudley, Regional Commissioner of Civil Defence, has sent this message to the heads of Midland local authorities, including the chairman of the Lichfield Rural District Council:

'Please convey my sincere appreciation and gratitude to the officers of the Council, teachers, voluntary helpers, householders, and all concerned in the splendid work done on Sunday last in connection with the reception of children from the East Coast.'

(Signed) Dudley,
Regional Commissioner.

* * *

Marjorie Horn (now Mrs Kelsey) gives her view of the evacuation, even though she was only away for about two months. She was thirteen years old at the time:

There were six children in our family and four of us were at various schools in Margate. My sisters Joyce and Joan were at Drapers Mills School. My brother Jack was at Pettman Central School and I was at Lausanne Central School.

On the day of evacuation in June 1940 we all reported to our different schools. Because Joan and Joyce were the youngest, it was only right that my mother should see them off from their school, so Jack and I had to say our goodbyes at home before we left. Because we went to different schools, we were destined for different areas of Staffordshire!

The train journey was very long and it was late in the afternoon when we arrived at a place called Great Wysley. After leaving the train I remember we had to line up in front of people sitting at a long desk and then we were allocated to our new foster parents. One lady asked for me but I had promised to stay with my friend Patricia Whitehead and eventually we were both chosen by a couple who already had a son and daughter. Our home was to be at Laney Green, some distance from Great Wysley. It was a small house with no running water. We had to collect water from a well several hundred yards down the road by another house. A bit further on was the 'local', a little thatched inn called 'The Wheatsheaf', where we used to call for our sweet ration.

We had three fields to cross to get to school, so we were away all day. For the first few days we were there they didn't know

Drapers Mills County Primary School, Margate, in 1998

what to do with us, so they sent us to a hall where they were staining the floor boards – we had to go over the floor boards with a rag and polish them! We also used to go on the fields across the road from where we lived, to thin out sugar beet and earned our pocket money that way.

Eventually we went to Brownhills High School. I made friends with a girl, but she went off to Canada. Pat and I really didn't have a lot to do with the local school girls and of course there was nobody when we got back to the billet. The neighbours only had boys and I don't think they thought much of us 'vacees'!

I heard from my mother that my brother Jack had gone to Hednesford and that Joan and Joyce were living in Kings Bromley. I managed to save enough money to go and see Jack, who was the nearest. He lived with a very nice couple at Hill Street. They made me very welcome, but Jack was very homesick. I made other visits to see him.

Even the 'Bisto' kids were evacuated

Cannock was near and I remember we went to the cinema there to see Charles Laughton in *The Hunchback of Notre Dame*. That was the only time I went to the cinema whilst I was in Staffordshire. My time there was really short. I was fourteen on 3rd August 1940, so when we broke up for the summer holidays I was put on the register to start work at Courtaulds in Walsall. In the meantime my mother came up from Margate with the two younger children, but she couldn't settle and wanted to go back home. My father's job took him all over the country delivering all sorts of things, and he had to come close to where we were living to collect some mattresses. When he arrived he said he would take us back home. The problem was that only father had a permit to allow him to enter Thanet which by this time had become a restricted area.

Anyway, we travelled back as far as Canterbury and then mother, the two youngsters and I all hid under the mattresses for the rest of the journey to Margate. We had to stop at a checkpoint at St Nicholas-at-Wade, but we all kept quiet and managed to get through without any trouble. There were only four families left in our road when we got home. I spent the rest of the war in Margate. I shall always remember watching the 'dog fights' in the sky over Kent, being machine-gunned on my way home from work and watching from my office window as the bombs were falling. The 'doodlebugs' were scary at first, but like the bombing we soon got used to it – and survived!

I managed to save enough money after about a year, to go and see Joan and Joyce who were still at Kings Bromley.

Finally, when we were all back together as a family towards the end of the war, it was noticeable how the characters of each one of us had developed, having lived with different people. One sister was very domesticated, another was very spoilt, and my other sister had become a real country person.

Arthur Campany remembers the day he was evacuated with his school, Holy Trinity School, Margate:

At the outbreak of the war I was ten years old and living at Fort Mount, Margate. On the 2nd June, 1940, I, with many other children, was evacuated from Margate. It was a lovely day and we all had to assemble at Holy Trinity School by 8.30am. There were lots of people there, mothers, fathers and teachers. Some mothers were crying, but to most of us children, it was like starting out on a big adventure.

Mr Gilbert, a retired school teacher, was in charge of all the children. We were each given a blue card with our name and the name of the school on it. There was also a party number, my number was 14, and we had to pin these cards to our coats.

At 9 o'clock 'East Kent' double decker buses arrived ready to take us to Margate railway station. We all said our goodbyes and set off. When we got to the railway station we found that many other Margate schools were already assembled there. The station was also packed out with hundreds of troops recently evacuated from Dunkirk. We all walked on to the platform and then on to a train which was to take us to Staffordshire.

The train standing next to ours was full of soldiers and they threw fruit to us. Some of the boys asked them for their steel helmets and other things that they had brought from France, but the soldiers wouldn't part with anything.

The journey to Staffordshire was long and we finally arrived at Lichfield at about 4pm. After alighting from the train we were put on to coaches and dispersed to our various

To The Women of Britain
GIVE US YOUR ALUMINIUM

Out of the frying pan . . . into the Spitfire.

WE want aluminium, and we want it now. New and old of every type and description, and all of it.

We will turn your pots and pans into Spitfires and Hurricanes, Blenheims and Wellingtons.

I ask, therefore, that everyone who has pots and pans, kettles, vacuum cleaners, hat pegs, coat hangers, shoe trees, bathroom fittings and household ornaments, cigarette boxes, or any other articles made wholly or in part of aluminium, should hand them over at once to the local headquarters of the Women's Voluntary Services.

There are branches of this organisation in every town and village in the country.

But if you are in any doubt, if you have difficulty in finding the local office of the Women's Voluntary Services, please inquire at the nearest police station or town hall, where you will be supplied with the necessary information.

The need is instant. The call is urgent. Our expectations are high.

Beaverbrook

An appeal for aluminium by Lord Beaverbrook, the wartime Minister for Aircraft Production

villages. My party went to Stonall, which was between Lichfield and Walsall.

When we reached Stonall, we assembled in the village school and met a lot of the village ladies who then picked out the children that they wanted. I sat there with a school mate named Bertie Clayton. One lady came and asked if there were any girls left, and someone said, 'No, only boys!' The lady then said, 'Alright, I will take these two boys.' We were then introduced to her. She was Mrs Ball and she took us both to a lovely farm cottage where we met her husband. Mr Ball was a blacksmith and his forge was next to the cottage. They were very nice people and we lived with them for two years. Being a blacksmith, Mr Ball was called to do war work at a big factory at Darlaston. When he came from work, he would shoe the farmers' work horses. Both Bertie and I would pump the bellows for the forge fire. Mr and Mrs Ball had a son, Alan. He was very well educated and had attended Walsall High School. While we were living there, Alan went into the Royal Air Force and trained as a pilot.

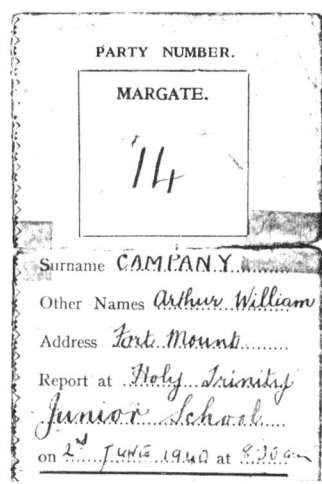

The rail ticket issued to Arthur Campany for 2nd June 1940

Mrs Ball's father, Mr Oakley, was the village builder and lived with his unmarried daughters in a nice house in the village. They had two evacuee boys staying with them, the Stone brothers.

Bertie and I used to play down at Mr Bower's farm at Lower Stonall. He had two sons and two daughters. Sometimes we would go to Mrs Smith's poultry farm to play. They had a large family – and I still get Christmas cards from one of the daughters.

The thing I missed most while being away was the sea! My father was a local boatman back home in Margate and I often used to be with him in the boat. It was quite different being in the country, playing in the fields and on the farms. Bertie and I used to spend quite a lot of time at night just watching the Germans bombing the Midlands.

One night, five bombs fell in a field just down the lane from our cottage and we went down to see the craters they had made. I think the only casualties were several sheep killed.

My mother came to see me while I was away in Staffordshire and she stayed for a week. Both mother and father came to visit just before I returned home, though my father couldn't stay long because he was one of the Margate lifeboat crew and had to sign to stay with the boat during the war.

I attended school in Walsall Wood until I returned home to Margate in September 1942. It was nice being home again, but I enjoyed being away. I left school the following year and started work as a carpenter/joiner apprentice.

Arthur Campany and Bertie Clayton shortly after their arrival in Staffordshire in 1940

STAFFORDSHIRE EDUCATION COMMITTEE.

WALSALL WOOD SENIOR COUNCIL SCHOOL.

Report for Term ending April 9th 1941.

Name Arthur Campany   Age 11 ½ yrs   Form IB
Position in Form 31st   Number in Form 46   Mark 507.
Attendance: Absent 3
Late 1   Conduct Very good.

Subject		Marks		Report
		Term	Exam.	
ENGLISH	Composition	—	52	Has begun to improve. ERB.
	Literature	100	75	Good. ERB.
	Poetry / Grammar, etc.	30	26	Good. ERB.
MATHEMATICS	Arithmetic	150	54	Very weak, but is trying hard with this subject. ERB.
	Algebra			
	Geometry			
HISTORY		100	83	Has done good work. ERB.
GEOGRAPHY		100	71	Very good. Keen worker.
~~SCIENCE~~ Writing / MECHANICAL ~~DRAWING~~		30	20	Fairly good. ERB.
HANDICRAFT	Wood	100	66	Fairly Good.
	~~Metal~~			
ART ~~AND CRAFTS~~		100	60	Fairly Good CH.
MUSIC				
NEEDLEWORK				
DOMESTIC SCIENCE				

Form Mistress E. R. Belasco.

Remarks Arthur has tried his best to give satisfaction and is making steady but slow progress.   B. O. Smith. Headmaster.

Arthur Campany's school report for Easter Term 1941

Another evacuee, who was 12 years old at the time of evacuation, recalls details of her departure and of her time spent in Stafford:

That first weekend in June, 1940, we were evacuated and our school assembled outside Ramsgate station on the opposite side of the road to the men evacuated from Dunkirk, who were by now, mainly French and French Colonial troops. I remember buying sweets from a nearby shop and giving them to the men. They responded by giving us badges and rosaries. We waited there for a very long time before we started on our journey, each with a small suitcase, gas mask, a name and school label attached to us, and a packed lunch.

There isn't much to tell about the journey itself, and I don't recall knowing exactly where we were going – Stafford would have meant nothing to me anyway! As we got to London, the houses backing on to the line were decorated with flags to welcome the men home from Dunkirk.

We arrived at Stafford at about teatime and were taken to a school hall where we were given something to eat and were then distributed to our billets. I was put with a wealthy family who lived in a big house in its own grounds. This was something of a culture shock. The chief difficulty for me was that the wife of the house treated me in exactly the same way as her little boy. For those who offered to house evacuees, the responsibility of looking after someone else's teenage child and keep them out of danger and trouble, in wartime at that, must have been considerable; as an adult I can appreciate that now, but at the time it all added to the misery.

All too soon our welcome grew a little thin; the restrictions placed upon us became irksome. We were only allowed out in groups or accompanied by an adult – and there was nothing much to do! On top of that, we were worried about the war and about what was happening at home.

The teachers did their best. Miss Palmer, our form teacher, invited us out to a meal and a trip to the cinema to see either *The Wizard of Oz* or *Hitler, the Beast of Berlin*. We voted for the escapism of 'Oz'. The teachers of course had problems of their own. They too had been uprooted, but were still responsible for the houses they had left behind.

There was uncertainty about future exam arrangements and lack of books and equipment, especially lab equipment. Only Miss Hancock, the chemistry teacher, fell on her feet. Her sister was head of a nearby school. One moment of recorded pleasure was when all our familiar text and exercise books arrived from Ramsgate.

News from home was eagerly seized upon and passed round. Most people had left the street where I lived, and most shops and places of entertainment were closed or boarded up. We heard that our school was being used as a police canteen.

It was a long hot summer in 1940. The fields near the riverbank were filled with frogs and snakes, something new to us and unpleasant. There was no beach and no swimming. However, there was a nearby heathland called Cannock Chase which was nice for outings.

I went to Sussex for the school holiday. Many children must have returned to Thanet. Often their parents made fresh arrangements and they did not return. The school dwindled in numbers and this made change possible. Instead of dividing our school week between two schools in Stafford, we now had our own building – a large house in its own grounds called Baswich House – some way out of town.

I moved to a new billet, to a family who had a gorgeous white bull terrier, but I was only there a few weeks as they found me too quiet! I then moved to an elderly woman and her son. They treated me more like an adult. My host had another guest, a friend who had been bombed out in Liverpool and she described to us how people had been buried in mass graves. We had no air raids in Stafford, except an attempt by the enemy on the Siemens factory in October – but we often heard the German planes overhead on their way to bomb the big cities.

An example of a poster issued by the government during the war

There were six of us left in the 6th Form and we were preparing to sit the Higher Certificate. We were all a lot happier now; some were planning to go on to college, two to the WAAF, and we knew that our days as evacuees were numbered.

Baswich House was full of nooks and crannies. One classroom had an alcove above the door into which someone could climb and play a practical joke. On one occasion a bag of flour was dropped on my head! I stood in the middle of the room covered in flour and laughing at how funny I must have looked. All around me was total silence; I think they were dumbstruck by their success. My landlady was not amused. Neither was the next girl they tried it on – she went straight to the head!

Another thing I remember was our Sunday evening ritual at the billet. Before the nine o'clock news on the wireless they played all the national anthems of the Allies. We sat in complete silence throughout this and then solemnly stood for *God Save The King*.

That spring people began to drift back to the Isle of Thanet now that the threat of invasion had receded.

I went home briefly at Easter and I remember the excitement when, on Good Friday, a fish and chip shop opened in Broadstairs High Street.

From now on most of my letters dealt with future plans and the final journey we would all make home. Afterwards, although I kept in touch with school mates and was involved with an independent Old Girls' Association for a while, I have no idea when the school returned to Ramsgate, and I have had no contact with Stafford or with the school itself from that day to this.

Eileen Norris, *although quite young at the time, remembers her evacuation with detail:*

I was a pupil at Drapers Mills School, Margate, at the outbreak of the war and, in June 1940, just before my seventh birthday, I was evacuated with my school. We travelled by rail from Margate Station and I remember there were soldiers also entraining. Our escort gave them the usual greeting of the time, 'Are we downhearted?', and received the reply, 'No!'

We travelled to Tamworth in Staffordshire and from there we were taken to the village of Hopwas, where we were billeted with the local residents. During my time there, I stayed in several different places; as a toddler I had had a bout of whooping cough which left me with an annual cough which lasted most of the winter. This tended to disturb the man of the house. My final 'resting place' was with a family with a girl a little younger than me, called Joan, and a boy of four, called Peter.

Their grandparents owned quite a lot of property. There was a farm, run by the elder son, and his younger brother, Edward, my host, ran a sand and gravel pit on part of the farm. The old folk owned and ran a small shop on the canal bridge approach and there was also a daughter and her husband who had a shop in Tamworth.

We children had a wonderful time playing in the sand pit. We were occasionally allowed to ride on the back of the lorry when a delivery of sand was being made. Once 'Uncle' Edward lifted his son, Peter, down from the lorry, but left Joan and me to hang on for dear life while he tipped out the load! He made us a kind of sledge out of a panel of corrugated iron, which we used on the great piles of sand, but once we came to grief when we attempted a much steeper slope of stones.

We attended the village school and we were lucky enough to have two of our own teachers from Kent: Miss Montgomery, our headmistress and a younger woman whose name I can't recall. The village school teacher was a Miss Jackson. She generally wore a navy suit and white blouse and always looked neat, with not a hair our of place. Miss Montgomery was quite different. I remember she had grey hair cut in a fringe which followed the rest of her hairline right round her head, like a cap. In my memory she was not unlike Margaret Rutherford as Madame Arcati in *Blithe Spirit*.

That summer the school ran a competition for the best collection of wild flowers, pressed in a book. When the winners were announced, two prizes were given. One, for the best collection, was won by Joan; the second, for the best collection by an evacuee, was awarded to me. They must have decided that we evacuees from the towns didn't really stand much chance in competition with the village kids.

There was a cane at the back of the stationery cupboard. I never saw it used, but she found a useful substitute in a ruler – or even two! I cannot speak from experience, but I understand two rulers together pack a real sting.

There is one incident which I remember and still resent. It was the night before my birthday and we children had gone to bed. Joan's mother came and called her downstairs, where it later transpired she had been shown my presents. Next day, of course, when I tried to show them my presents, I was completely deflated.

In January 1943 my mother decided to take me back home. I had been taken to Coventry the day after the city had been blitzed, because my hosts had relatives there, but my mother was furious when she found out. She said she had evacuated me to get me away from the bombs, not to go sightseeing in a blitzed city. During my time away I had had jaundice, measles, and cold after cold. Back home the air raids continued, but I think by that time the worst was over.

I went back to Drapers Mills School and in 1944 I passed for Clarendon House Grammar School in Ramsgate – which had been evacuated to Stafford! So back I went to the Midlands, but only for one term. After the end of the autumn term our school returned to Ramsgate and I only had one further term at Clarendon House before my family moved to Dartford.

I didn't analyse my feelings at the time of my evacuation but, looking back, I realise now that I was clinging to my mother long after most children are trying to break free. Still, it was an experience!

Although not a Thanet girl, **Olive Degg** *(now Mrs Harris) remembers her time with Clarendon House Girls' School from Ramsgate, in Stafford:*

I had been evacuated to Stafford from Essex and the local education authorities sent me to join the evacuated Ramsgate school of Clarendon House and I can truly say they were the happiest years of my school life. I can remember most of the teachers: Miss Koller, Miss Masson, Miss Uffendell, Miss Gosling, Miss Honey, Miss Wisendon, Miss Palmer, Miss Lacy, Miss Ormiston, Miss Curran, Miss Sorrell, Miss Segal, Miss Raynor, Miss Harris, Miss Jones and Miss Helm.

I used to adore the days we spent at Baswich house and still have a great affinity with the place. In later years it has been developed into a police training establishment and my son has since completed his initial police training there. It seems strange to think of his working in those same rooms where I sat so long ago.

The most tragic memory of my time in Stafford was when it became known that one of our classmates was dying of sleeping sickness. Her name was Barbara Walkling and she died on 30th May, 1942, at the age of twelve. It remains so clear in my mind because she sat next to me in class and we were of an age when death seemed very awesome. I can recall so vividly, even now, the sadness that hung over us all when she died. As the day of the funeral arrived, my friend, Pauline Bray, and I picked a big bunch of hawthorn blossom and tied our hair ribbons together to make a bow, and I copied out a verse from my own mother's memoriam card. When we got to school, Miss Helm allowed Pauline and me to take our 'bouquet' to Baswich Church.

Years later, when in my sixties, I returned to find the grave of Barbara Walkling and asked the vicar to search the records. We found the grave. It was waist high in weeds, nettles and brambles, but fortunately close to the path. I went back the following morning suitably equipped to restore the grave. By evening I had only managed half the job. As I was packing up for the day an old gentleman came up to me and asked if he could help. I explained what I was trying to do and he said that he remembered the 'little lasses from Kent'. He then said that if I came back in a day or so I would have a nice surprise. When I returned a few days later, true to his word, Barbara's grave was like a little oasis in the wilderness. Not a weed to be seen and the gravestone cleaned with all the lettering clearly visible. I laid a posy of summer flowers on behalf of all the girls of Clarendon House, and said a little prayer.

Life in Stafford wasn't all gloom. We had great fun too. There are so many things I can remember, such as the days we 'went' to Art School. Most times 'our gang' used to skive off and go round Woolworths instead – no one ever seemed to find out! Then there were the times we would make toys and do other things for the 'Ministering Children's League', whatever that was!

I remember the upstairs corridor in Baswich House was out of bounds and everyone thought that it was haunted. We all took part in the 'Dig for Victory' campaign with our little plots of land. School dinners remain a firm memory. The least favourite of which were called 'bullet pudding' and 'concrete pie'.

I still have pangs of guilt about how we used to tease poor Miss Payne. It couldn't have been much fun trying to impart the finer points of the English language to the unwilling – especially in those troubled times, when goodness knows what personal problems she might have had.

When it was time for me to leave Clarendon House School I recall being interviewed by Miss Helm. She sighed when it was my turn, as well she might. I had no certificates or anything to commend me. It wasn't through lack of intelligence. Because of family circumstances I had only attended intermittently during my last five years at school. Miss Helm said to me, 'My dear, I don't know what to suggest you do. I think the best thing would be for you to marry and have a large family.' I finish with the words of our old school song:

> Forty years on, when afar and asunder,
>   Parted are those who are singing today,
> When we look back and forgetfully wonder
>   What we were like in our work and our play.
> Then maybe there will often come o'er you,
>   Glimpses of notes like the catch of a song,
> Visions of girlhood will float then before you
>   Twenty and thirty and forty years on.
>
> Forty years on, growing older and older,
>   Shorter in wind than in memory long,
> Feeble of foot and rheumatic of shoulder,
>   What will it help you that once you were strong.
> God give us bases to guard or beleaguer,
>   Games to play at whether earnest or fun,
> Fights for the fearless and goals for the eager,
>   Twenty and thirty and forty years on!

*   *   *

Eileen Walker (now Mrs Eileen Tobin) was living in Percy Avenue, Kingsgate and attending St Mildred's School, Broadstairs at the time of the evacuation:

My sister Sheila, my little brother Tony and I were all evacuated on Sunday the 2nd June, 1940, and I remember us and the rest of the school being lined up in twos at the station approach in Broadstairs. We all had our gas masks over our shoulders – and huge name tags pinned to our coats. I don't think any of us was frightened at what was going on, in fact we were all quite excited about going on

Eileen and Tony Walker with their foster parents, Frank and Milly Jackson, at their home in Rene Road, Bolehall in 1940

St Mildred's County Infant School, Broadstairs, photographed by the author in 1998

a train, although nobody knew where we were going.

I don't remember much about the train journey except that we were shunted into sidings several times to let the troop trains go through, which were carrying those rescued from Dunkirk. But we finally arrived at Tamworth in Staffordshire. We were then taken to a public house where the locals just came and picked out who they wanted. That was quite upsetting and distressing be-cause no one seemed to want to take the three of us. Mum had given me very firm instruc-tions about looking after my little brother who was only five years old, and not to let anyone split us up. Sheila went to one family, but moved several times; she was never really happy and never settled.

Anyway, on the day of our arrival Tony and I were walked out into the street, and what luck it was for us. A lovely couple named Milly and Frank Jackson said they

Sisters Eileen and Sheila (foreground) with wartime mum Mrs Milly Jackson (third from left) and Rene Road childhood friends Brenda Morris, Lilian Rowley, Jean Leedham and Brenda Cooper, photographed in 1990

would take us until a permanent billet for the both of us could be found, so off we went with them to their home at 22 Rene Road, Bolehall, Tamworth. This couple had no children of their own and they both worked full time, which was the reason why they said they couldn't take us permanently. But after a short while we became part of a very happy family. Our new foster parents were very kind to us and treated us as their own – and we stayed with them for the duration of our stay in Staffordshire. One abiding memory I have of Tamworth is that of being sent to the local public house every Sunday at 12 noon, with a miner's water-can to fetch a pint of beer for my foster father Frank. All the local children would be doing the same thing – apparently it was the usual custom up there. My foster father was so pleased to have a 'little girl' of his own to fetch his beer.

Because of our ages, it was unfortunate that we three children had to go to different schools. Sheila went to Marmion Juniors, Tony went to Kettlebrook Infants and I went to Croft Street Seniors. Perhaps if we had all managed to go to the same school, things wouldn't have been so bad for my sister Sheila. She never settled, perhaps because she was on her own and wanted to come home. In the end, in 1942, our mother came to Tamworth to collect us all and to take us home. We hadn't seen anything of the war in Tamworth, but as we arrived back in Margate, the sirens sounded and guns started firing at German aircraft that were flying in low over the town. I really upset my mum by crying and saying that I wanted to go back – where the war wasn't on!

Tony and I stayed in contact with Milly and Frank Jackson, our Staffordshire foster parents and, in fact, they came many times to Kingsgate for their holidays. Mr Jackson has now passed away, but I have been back to Tamworth several times to see Milly Jackson, who is now in her nineties, and I continue to keep in touch.

Mrs Milly Jackson, *the foster mother of Eileen Walker, remembers the moment when the children arrived in Tamworth:*

My husband told me that there were two kids at the top of the street with nowhere to go. And there they were with their gas masks and labels on. So we said we'd have them. The children were never any trouble and they were some of the happiest days of my life.

Janet Laker *(now Mrs Walmsley) remembers the experience of her evacuation to Staffordshire in 1940:*

It was the 2nd of June, 1940, and I shall always remember the scenes at Ramsgate railway station. There were hundreds of children with their labels, gas masks and small hand luggage gathering in a large 'crocodile' as parents were waving their goodbyes. We all went down the far steps at the station, and coming from the opposite direction were hundreds of injured soldiers and sailors who had been rescued from Dunkirk. We were all agog watching these poor men arriving.

The journey to Staffordshire is a bit of a blur, but I remember getting off the train and being taken to a large hall were we were medically examined. From there we were taken by coach to Newborough, near Burton on Trent.

Our group of children from St Lawrence School waited with our headmistress, Miss

Children from St Lawrence C of E School, Ramsgate, pictured outside Newborough Church, Staffordshire, 1940

Huggard, in the local school hall, waiting to be picked by local families. I had been told by my mother that I must look after my brother Norman and we were not to be separated. Because of this we seemed to be the last ones to be picked, but at least we were still together!

Our foster parents had a four year old son and while we were there, another baby was born. I was so thrilled when I was allowed to help look after the new baby. We stayed in Newborough for two and a half years and finally left when I passed the scholarship to go to Clarendon House School which had been evacuated to Stafford.

I returned home to Ramsgate that summer, for a holiday with my parents before joining my new school in Stafford. Norman also went home. He stayed with mum and attended St George's School which had reopened for the evacuees that had returned home.

After the summer holiday I met a friend from my infant days and we travelled to Stafford together, to be 'delivered' to our foster parents – an elderly couple who greeted us with 'We don't really want you, but we need the money!', which did nothing to put us at our ease. However, they gave us a bed and fed us, but apart from that there were no real home comforts. We were not allowed to stay indoors once we were up; we had to go out no matter what the weather! On Sundays we would walk the two miles to church to attend two separate services, even in the winter.

Luckily, during our stay in Stafford we were allowed home for school holidays. We didn't tell our parents or teachers about our awful billet in case our foster parents made life worse for us! But I have to say that some of our friends had wonderful foster parents.

We shared the local grammar school and had the use of Baswich House on certain days of the week. It was a lovely old building set in grounds with beautiful beech trees.

I cannot remember the exact date when Clarendon House School returned to Ramsgate, but we were in Stafford for more than two years. At some time during our evacuation my father, who was in the local Home Guard, was later sent for a while to Staffordshire, to supervise the making of charcoal by Italian prisoners of war. My mother went to friends in London for a year or so, working in the Lucas battery factory, before returning to Ramsgate where she kept the vegetable garden going. She also used to make clothes to send to us.

After the war the family was all back together and life in Ramsgate gradually returned to normal. We resumed our Sunday afternoon walks along West Cliff to the bandstand, but it was a long time before the barbed wire was removed from the beaches.

Roy Doherty *remembers the experience of being evacuated with his younger brother in 1940:*

In June 1940 came the worst moment we had all been dreading – the evacuation of school children from Ramsgate! I was at St Lawrence School and my brother Alan was attending Ellington School. My mother decided to allow myself and Alan to be evacuated and so on 2nd June 1940 we walked to Ramsgate railway station. Alan and I weren't very keen on leaving our mother and youngest brother behind in Ramsgate.

It was a lovely sunny day and when we got there we found hundreds of children lining the platforms, although the scene I shall always remember was that of many, many wounded soldiers, rescued from Dunkirk, laid out on stretchers on the platform

Actually we boarded the train, not knowing where we were bound for. The journey was long and wearisome and seemed to go on for ever. We finally arrived at the small village of Draycott-in-the-Clay, about six miles from Uttoxeter in Staffordshire. The reception centre was the old village school where we were given lemonade made from the yellow powder which was so popular in those days. We were also given buns to eat. By this time we were all

Ray Doherty's first billet at Acton's Farm, Draycott-in-the-Clay Staffordshire

very tired and bewildered, and my brother was very upset. The reception centre was packed with local people waiting to choose the children they were to foster. I was chosen by a farmer and his wife, Mr and Mrs Acton, and was whisked away to a small farm about half a mile outside the village.

I was now separated from my brother Alan, who was taken to a house in the village itself. It all seemed a very traumatic time for both of us and the only time I could see Alan was at the school each day. I couldn't settle with my new foster parents. They were very different to what I was used to. One abiding memory of my stay there was that my packed lunch for school each day consisted of beetroot sandwiches, which never varied! I was never really happy at the farm.

Meanwhile, my brother was having a rough time at his billet. He had to sleep on a camp bed on the landing of the house. I complained to the billeting officer on his behalf and she promised to get in touch with my mother. After a short while I was moved from the farm and my brother also moved to a better billet.

My new foster parents, Mr and Mrs Sanders, ran a smallholding with chickens and ducks, etc., and their home was situated at the other end of Draycott. They had two

The village water supply pipe, known as 'The Fountain'. This was the only water supply to Drayton-in-the-Clay during Roy Draycott's evacuation there in the early 1940s

daughters, Marjory and Joan. I was much happier with this new family.

In about October 1940, I received a letter from my mother to say that she had arranged to send my youngest brother Brian to join me at my new billet. A week later, Brian arrived accompanied by a care nurse, but he never really settled. This prompted my mother to come up to Draycott-in-the-Clay, to see if she could find accommodation so that we could all live together as a family again. She eventually succeeded in finding four furnished rooms in a large house in Draycott. The owner was a dear old lady by the name of Miss Thompson and, although she had two cats and a dog, she was happy for us to stay and to keep her company.

Once we moved in together, life became less stressful and it was lovely to be living as a family again, but of course mother then had to adjust to a different kind of lifestyle. Draycott-in-the-Clay was quite primitive in those days. There was no mains electricity, no gas, and no running water! The only water supply was from a spring at the top of the hill. Water from the spring was piped down to what was known as The Fountain, where villagers collected their water in buckets. Sometimes we had to queue for water and occasionally in the winter The Fountain would be frozen solid!

Lighting was by oil lamps and there were no flush toilets, but we all got used to it in the end. We all had our own jobs to do. One of mine was to go to the woods and fetch back wood for the fires. To make this job easier I made myself a four-wheeled cart to carry the wood.

I had my twelfth birthday at Draycott, which meant that I had to change schools. I had to travel daily to my new school at Tutbury, near Burton-on-Trent, and I quite enjoyed it there.

Though we were evacuated to a supposedly 'safe' area, we did experience some bombs that dropped nearby and, on occasions, we could hear the bombing of Derby and Stoke-on-Trent. It was 1942 when my mother decided that we would all return to Kent – and take our chances through the rest of the war – we were quite happy with that decision. We eventually packed our bags, said our goodbyes and returned to the village of Minster, near Ramsgate, just in time to celebrate Christmas. Meanwhile our house that we had left in Stanley Road, Ramsgate, in 1940, was too badly damaged by enemy action to return to.

Hazel Knight *(now Mrs Hazel Kelly) was only four years old when she was evacuated with her sister and two brothers:*

Douglas and Patrick Knight, his mother, Florence, with Grandma Hawkinge in Staffordshire

When we were evacuated I was just four years old. My sister Joan was six, my brother Douglas was eight and Patrick was almost ten. My first memory was of us all at Ramsgate railway station, with labels tied to our clothing and gas masks around our necks. We each had a box containing a few clothes.

I can't remember much of the journey, but my brother has since told me that the train never stopped and that we didn't have a drink until we reached Stafford, by which time we were all very tired. When we arrived in Stafford we were taken to a hall where there were lots of people. My brothers were chosen by a farmer and were taken to a farm somewhere between Weston and Uttoxeter. Joan and I were very frightened but we eventually left with an elderly couple.

When we arrived at our billet the couple took our few possessions and put them on top of a wardrobe and then said we had to have a bath. That really did upset us. We told them that we had had a bath before we left home. By this time we were both crying and my sister was sick. The elderly couple tried to pacify us with sweets, but nothing helped. We managed to get our things down off the wardrobe and by then I think these poor people had had enough and a car came back for us. We were taken to the farm where my two brothers were enjoying dishes of fruit and cream. After some discussion it was decided that my sister would stay at the farm with my eldest brother Patrick. My brother Douglas and I were then taken into the village of Weston, to a large house with its own lake, swans and boathouse. The house was called Pond House and the canal ran close by.

Our hosts made it quite clear from the outset that we were not welcome, but because they had spare rooms they had to take us in. They had one very spoilt son named Robin. Douglas and I were very unhappy there. If I cried I was put into the boathouse with a bucket to cry into until I stopped – I was very scared of the water. When my brother got home from school each day he was made to sit and knit. He was forced to sit so long he ended up with boils on his bottom.

Luckily all four of us went to the same village school so we saw Patrick and Joan on school days. Patrick used to suffer from terrible nose bleeds and more than once he was turned off the school bus and had to walk the rest of the way to school. I can't remember how long Douglas and I stayed at

Joan and Hazel Knight with their father, Flight Sergeant Arthur Knight on one of his visits to Staffordshire to see the family

grandmother came to Staffordshire, my mother was so upset by the way we were being treated that she found two rooms in a farmhouse in Weston and we four children joined her there. Patrick, Douglas, Joan and I slept in one room and my gran and mother had the other room which doubled as a sitting room.

Laurie Johnson, wartime friend of Hazel Knight, in May 1995

While we were at this farm, the farmer's wife, Mrs Pattison, took me into the barn where they were slaughtering a pig. I had to hold a bucket to catch the blood for her to make black pudding. I had nightmares for weeks after that – and I can still see that poor pig now!

We stayed in Staffordshire for about four and a half years, then mum brought us home to Thanet. As our house had been destroyed by a direct hit we had to live with gran until we found another house to rent. We spent the rest of the war in Ramsgate.

In May 1995 an evacuee reunion was organised as part of Thanet's VE and VJ Days' anniversary commemorations and a group of us travelled back to Staffordshire for a nostalgic visit. The little school I attended in Weston is now a private home, but the village post office opposite has hardly changed.

I met Laurie Johnson, who was working on Taverner's Farm, opposite where we lived at Pattison's Farm, and before I even spoke he said to me, 'You are one of the four Knight children!' He was four years old when we first met and was apparently my little boyfriend all the time we were in Weston. He took me up the road to where all the villagers were waiting for us to arrive. It was a very moving experience.

Ramsgate evacuees who made a return journey to Staffordshire in May 1995

Chapter Four

MORE MEMORIES FROM THE MIDLANDS

Joyce Horn *(now Mrs Morrell) together with her two sisters, Peggy and Joan, was evacuated with Drapers Mills School, Margate, to Kings Bromley in Staffordshire:*

We were evacuated on 2nd June 1940, when the evacuation of Dunkirk was taking place and the threat of invasion seemed imminent. At school we were given a list of things we were to take with us: a clean change of clothing; toothbrush and toothpaste; flannel; hairbrush, etc., plus the issued gas mask!

On the day of departure we assembled at school and were given labels to attach to our coats, then we were taken to the buses waiting outside. Many parents were there to see us all off and most of them in tears as we said our goodbyes.

When we arrived at Margate station there were lots of troops; some of them wearing funny shaped tin helmets! They were survivors from Dunkirk.

Once aboard the train we set off for Lichfield in Staffordshire and the journey took most of the day. When we arrived at our destination we were put on to buses and taken to a hall and given orange squash and biscuits. Then a nurse came to check us over. We were then sorted into groups and put on more buses to go to our final destinations.

My sister Joan and I stayed together – because my mum had told me to look after her! We arrived at the local school in Kings Bromley and were given a large glass of milk straight out of a big milk churn. Then a group of people who were to be our foster parents came forward to take us to their homes. Joan and I were lucky. We were taken in an open top car and when we got to our new home, there was a picnic set out with sandwiches, cakes and strawberries and cream.

We settled down really well, made many friends and we were invited into many of the houses for parties. Many of the local children laughed at the way we spoke.

Schooling was arranged so that one week the evacuees used the school and the local children used the institute, and the following week we would change around, alternating between the two locations. We spent a lot of time outdoors. The summer of 1940 was wonderful. We would play in the meadows, paddle in the streams and walk along the country lanes.

When our time came to leave the junior school, we went to Rugeley Secondary School. A bus collected us and brought us back each day. During harvest time we were allowed two weeks off school to help the farmers potato picking. We also picked sprouts which was very cold to our hands. I think most of the children in Kings Bromley were happy and had decent foster homes.

The nearest we ever got to the war in Kings Bromley was one night while I was lying in bed, I heard lots of aircraft flying over. I jumped out of bed and looked out of the window and could see that the searchlights from the air base at Fradley, about a mile away, were lighting up the skies. Suddenly there was a terrific bang. One of the German planes had released a bomb on its way back from bombing Coventry. Luckily it had exploded in the River Trent. Another exciting memory is when a Spitfire crashed in a field just up the lane from our school. We were all very curious and went to see the wreckage. We managed to get some perspex from the aircraft and my friend Margaret's brother, who was home on leave from the RAF, made us a pendant each out of it, and a little figurine for his mum.

One very sad incident that happened at Kings Bromley was when one of the young evacuees was drowned. Her name was Eileen Hills. She was with her sister and a friend walking over a little wooden bridge over a weir. The water was very high and Eileen slipped on the wet surface, lost her balance and fell into the water which was flowing very fast. She was wearing wellington boots and a 'teddy bear' coat when she fell. She was pulled under the water and was later found a mile away downstream.

Joan and I were separated when our foster father left his job as head cowman to take up a job with the Forestry Commission near Birmingham, but we were both very lucky once again to go to very nice families. Joan still visits her foster family once a year. I have been back four or five times since the end of the war and I still keep in touch with one of the girls.

I think it was a great experience; my sisters and I often talk over different things that happened in our young lives. After four and a half years away from home I was probably the last evacuee to leave Kings Bromley; I returned on a train full of troops. My brother Jack and sister Marjorie met me in London.

When I had been home a month, I got my first job. It seemed very strange being back with my own family – and two new brothers! But I eventually settled down. When I was sixteen, I was asked to join the WVS, along with my sister Marjorie and her friend Barbara Stockbridge. We would either work in the canteen in Margate High Street, or the NAAFI along the seafront. We made friends with the services and watched them go off to Arnhem in the gliders and planes.

I was ten and a half years old when I left Margate in June 1940; little did I realise the day we left home, that it would be such a long 'holiday'!

There were many evacuees from her school, but the following list of names are those that Joyce personally remembers as being evacuated from Drapers Mills School, Margate, to Kings Bromley:

MRS WALTERS (TEACHER IN CHARGE)

Joyce Horn	Joan Horn	Peggy Horn	Pat Saxby
Derek Saxby	Esme Woodward	Joyce Heggs	Doris Heggs
Eileen Morley	Phyllis Allen	Pat Garratt	Arthur Verrall
Albert Laver	Joyce Pilcher	Margaret Pearce	David Walters
Geoffrey Harding	Eric Saddington	June Edwards	Pat Hinds
Margaret Edmonds	Betty Whitehead	Eileen Hills	Violet Hills
Joyce Jezzard	Dennis Jezzard	Frances Terry	

June Edwards *(now Mrs June Cawood), and one of those mentioned in the above list, now gives her impressions of her own evacuation experiences:*

We all met outside Drapers Mills School, Margate, on Sunday 2nd June 1940, with our gas masks and rucksacks. I was just two months short of my tenth birthday. Coaches took us to Margate station where we boarded a train which was to take us direct to Lichfield in Staffordshire. The journey took ages and there were many stops on the way to let troop trains pass.

When we got to Lichfield, coaches took us to Kings Bromley village school where we were all given a glass of milk and then we were allocated to our foster parents. My friend Eileen Morley and I had been told to stay together. The two of us and a third girl, Phyllis Allen, were allocated to Mrs Allen the local vicar's wife. Phyllis was crying as we walked up through the village, dropping evacuees off at different houses. It was a very rural village and we had to tread carefully on the path to avoid 'cow pats'. On reaching the vicarage a flock of geese came hissing and honking at us and the three of us were terrified.

The vicarage was like a mansion with a huge tiled hallway and at the top of the staircase was a balcony with rooms leading off. Outside there was a dairy, stables, orchards – and many chicken, geese and cats etc.

We went to the village school where at ten years old we made our first dresses by hand and they were very nice. We were not allowed out to play with the local children. Shortly after our arrival at the vicarage, two nephews and a niece of Mrs Allen arrived from London. They were one, two and three years old and Eileen, Phyllis and I had one each to look after. Being an only child I suppose I 'played up' a bit and soon I was found another billet, this time with Mr and Mrs Rock. They had two grown up children and one of them lived next door where a school friend, Margaret Edmunds, was billeted. Mr Rock was the village blacksmith.

The vicar's wife found out that I hadn't been christened, so in April 1941 arrangements were made for me to be confirmed. My mother travelled up from Margate for my confirmation. She had never left Margate before so she found the journey daunting. I was very shy at meeting her again.

I was very happy living with Mr and Mrs Rock. I had a lot more freedom and their daughter taught me a lot about sewing which I still enjoy doing. I still have particular memories of my time in Kings Bromley: like the milkman, 'Old Groves', who had a wonky eye and drove a high stepping pony and trap. He brought the milk round in a large churn and we would leave a jug on the wall for him to fill up. Then I remember when the Hills girl was drowned and the time the army convoys passed through the village. During harvest time we were given time off from school to help with the potato picking, probably because most of the village men were away at the war.

When I reached eleven years old I went by bus each day to Rugeley senior school. It was a ten miles journey by 'double decker', with all the boys upstairs and girls downstairs. We were always mucking about on the bus and one day Margaret Pearce fell out!

June Edwards at Kings Bromley, 1942

The war came quite close to us on a couple of occasions. I remember the milk factory on the outskirts of the village being bombed, and once a plane crashed in the village, leaving the pilot dead in a tree!

Over a period of time many of the evacuees had drifted back home. Of the 52 evacuees I started with, by the time I left to return to Margate there were just 3. One of the girls from Margate was abandoned in Kings Bromley by her family and was eventually taken into care. When I finally returned home I had such a strong accent that mum and dad couldn't understand me at first. I have very fond memories of my stay in Kings Bromley. We had a lot of freedom and I think we grew up and matured quite fast.

Don Wright *from Ramsgate remembers his time in Uttoxeter:*

I was attending Chatham House School, Ramsgate, at the outbreak of war, and in June 1940 the whole school was evacuated to the Midlands. I was in the first year group and went with about 40 other juniors to a little market town on the borders of Staffordshire and Derbyshire called Uttoxeter, whilst the majority of other pupils went to Stafford.

The day of the evacuation was most poignant. We were gathered at Ramsgate railway station together with many soldiers who had just been rescued from the beaches of Dunkirk. The whole of the railway station seemed to be in a state of chaos. I had just had my twelfth birthday and had never been away from home before. As I kissed my parents goodbye I was old enough to realise that I might not ever see them again. I found the parting very traumatic.

The journey to Uttoxeter seemed to last for ever but eventually, in the early evening, we arrived and lined up in the station yard, waiting to be allocated to our foster homes. Some went off in twos and others, such as myself, went alone. I was billeted with what seemed to me at the time to be an elderly couple, who must have felt just as strange and ill at ease in accepting an 'unknown' into their home, as I was to be there. I remember to this day my first supper in my new billet which consisted of a thick slice of bread covered in dripping and red pickled cabbage. Surprisingly, after what had been to me an horrendous journey, it was most welcome.

The emblem of Chatham House Grammar School, Ramsgate

We did not, of course, have a school building of our own; but we had the use of two rooms in the local Methodist Primary School. For science subjects (chemistry and physics) however we joined forces with and went to the local Alleyne Grammar School. Our physical education was attended to by the gym mistress of the local girls grammar school where we went once a week and where we were prohibited from fraternising or speaking to the girls whilst on their premises. On summer days when a classroom was, for some reason or another, unavailable we were taken to 'Oldfields' – the local cricket and sports ground where we did lessons sitting on the grass. As we had the use of this ground for our sporting activities it was not unknown for lessons to be given a miss on some occasions so that 'volunteers' could be enlisted to cut and roll the cricket square.

Some of my most pleasant memories which remain with me to this day are cycle rides with friends to Dovedale, some 16 miles away, where the day was spent climbing Thorpe Cloud, one of the highest peaks; playing about on the stepping stones across the River Dove; eating our picnics of jam sandwiches and visiting the little sweetshop in Ashbourne on the way home for a drink of 'fruit-cup'. It seems unbelievable now that we would arrive at Dovedale, leave our bikes by the stile and return several hours later never dreaming that they wouldn't be there. Goodness knows what we would have done if the bicycles had ever been stolen.

In September 1943, those of us at Uttoxeter were moved to Stafford to join the main school and to make room for an intake of juniors in our place. I and several others preferred to remain with our landladies in Uttoxeter rather than move to Stafford, so we were permitted to travel daily by bus. The conductor, known only as Jim, was quite a character who delivered parcels, newspapers and anything else from the bus along its route from Uttoxeter to Stafford. Halfway along this route stood the ruins of Chartley Castle. On one occasion I recall Jim became quite excited and spoke quickly to the driver who by this time had passed the ruins. After a short discussion the bus was 'backed up' whereupon both Jim and the driver hopped over the fence into the castle grounds. After many minutes had passed, both eventually returned laden with freshly picked mushrooms!

My general impression as an evacuee is one of long, hot, carefree summer days and an almost complete unawareness that there was a war on – the only reminder being a number of American troops who were stationed nearby. All in all I had three billets during my stay from June 1940 until September 1944 when the school returned to Ramsgate.

The first meeting with my parents was almost like strangers meeting for the first time, but it wasn't long before the closeness of family life returned to normal.

I still have a great affinity for Uttoxeter and I return periodically to meet old friends and acquaintances.

Barbara Tilbrook's (now Mrs Wood) evacuation experiences cover several locations and two schools:

Towards the end of May 1940, I was told that I was going on holiday to the countryside and that I would be going on a train. This was thrilling news because I had never been on holiday and I had never been on a train!

On 2nd June 1940 I was taken to school where everyone assembled in the hall. The registers were marked then we all filed out to the buses which were to take us to the railway station. We all had our gas masks over our shoulders and a small suitcase, plus a carrier bag containing a packed lunch for the journey. Our mothers waved us off with very few tears!

Once we had started on our journey, we were all wondering where we were going and for how long. Memories of that first day are now very hazy, but I remember arriving at some unknown place and being examined by doctors and a 'nit nurse'. My next clear memory is of arriving at Ellastone School where we were divided into groups and taken by cars and vans to meet the people who had agreed to take us.

I ended up in the village of Wootton on the borders of Staffordshire and Derbyshire. I was fortunate in that my two cousins were at the bottom of the hill in the village, my best friend was at the top and my billet was about 50 yards along the road from her.

It was about 10pm before I was introduced to my foster parents, Mr and Mrs Bott and their daughters Sheila and Hilda. They were a nice friendly family and we all got on well together. Sheila was 14 and due to start work as a housemaid when the summer term finished. Hilda was six weeks younger than me and we became great friends. Mrs Bott was a small, motherly, kind woman who always wore a long white pinafore. Mr Bott was tall and thin and also very kind. He was a road mender and, I learned later, a water diviner.

When we went to school, which was in the next village, Ellastone, all the evacuees and the local children met at the bottom of the hill to walk together. Sometimes we would be passed by milk lorries full of churns clanking away. One day on the way home, we all stood aside to let a lorry pass and I happened to look up at the cab and saw a soldier who looked like my dad. When the lorry drew up and the soldier jumped out, it was my dad! I jumped into his arms, so did my cousins and my best friend, Joyce, and the poor man walked the rest of the way to my billet with four little girls weighing him down. Dad had just got back from Dunkirk and, although he couldn't stay long, it was wonderful to see him even for just an hour

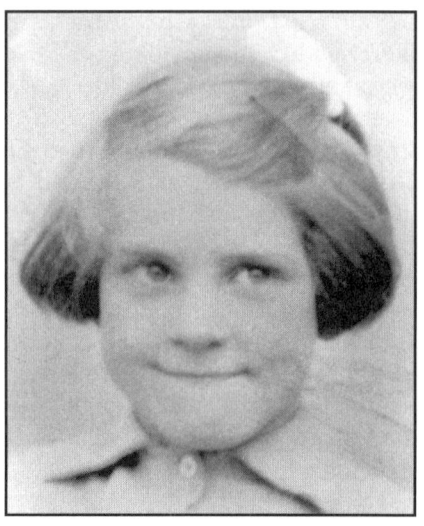

Barbara Tilbrook, aged six years. Photo taken at Dame Janet School, Ramsgate for Christmas 1937

We all seemed to get on well with each other at school. The school's headmaster was Mr Walker and the building consisted of a large hall, in which we had assembly and the top class was taught, and two smaller classrooms; one for the infants who were taught by Miss Prince, and the other for 7-11 year old pupils taught by Miss Richards who had travelled with us from Ramsgate.

After I had been at Mr and Mrs Bott's for about six weeks I was disappointed to hear that they were moving to Uttoxeter – too far away for me to go with them, so I had to find another billet. Fortunately one of my school friends was billeted with a couple who agreed to take me, so I moved to Ellastone to stay with Mr and Mrs Cope on their small farm. They were both in their 60s and they were very kind. Sylvia, the other evacuee from Ramsgate, and I helped with collecting the hens eggs, feeding the pigs and even learned to milk the cows! We also drove the cows to a field at the other end of the village and brought them back in the evening. We helped with haymaking, went blackberrying, collected watercress and mushrooms, and picked rose hips which we took to school to be collected for making rose hip syrup.

Eventually I sat and passed the entrance exam for grammar school. Little did I realise that it would mean leaving my billet. I was very sad to be leaving Ellastone. Mr and Mrs Cope had been really good to me and they took mGrammar Schoole to Uttoxeter to catch the bus to Stafford where my new school, Clarendon House Grammar School from Ramsgate, was situated.

My new foster parents were in their mid-thirties and had a daughter, Sheila, who was eight years old.

I was introduced to an older pupil of my new school. She was a prefect in the 5th Form and she took me to school and showed me my classroom. Our form mistress was a lovely lady called Miss Koller. We spent two days a week at Stafford Girls' High School and the other three days at Baswich House out at Weeping Cross. I didn't like the high school. It was large and impersonal to me, having just come from a tiny village school where all the pupils knew each other. Baswich House was a delight, rambling but not too large, with narrow passages and spiral staircases – and a panelled dining room. At the back was a large playing field and we all had a small allotment for growing vegetables and flowers.

Barbara Tilbrook in the uniform of Clarendon House Grammar School, Ramsgate, photographed in Stafford in August 1942

I became very unhappy in my billet. It seemed that my foster mother and I 'struck sparks off each other'. With hindsight, it could have been that I was growing up. It was hard getting used to doing homework each evening and weekend, especially with

Evacuees from Ramsgate at Ellastone on the borders of Staffordshire and Derbyshire, 1940

Sheila wanting me to play all the time and her mother insisting that I did.

After being on holiday with my parents during the summer of 1942, my dad saw me off on the train and I burst into tears which was something I'd never done before on returning to a billet. I told him that I didn't like it in Stafford and didn't want to go back. It must have upset him because I soon received a letter from him in which he promised that after the next holiday I wouldn't have to go back.

During the next few months my mum had my younger sister and mum and dad opened up our bungalow in Ramsgate. Mum and we children moved back there – but dad was posted to Italy for the next three years!

Some years ago I went back and visited Wootton and Ellastone. The cottage in Wootton where I used to be billeted is now a lovely holiday home. I returned again, this time to Stafford, and was allowed to look around Baswich House, which is now a police training centre. Stafford itself has obviously changed in fifty odd years. It is no longer a dirty, dingy place as I remembered it. I had steadfastly refused to go back to Stafford before, but I am glad I went. It gave me the opportunity to 'lay a few ghosts'.

Violet Cox *(now Mrs Warren) remembers when her school, Dame Janet School, Ramsgate, was evacuated to the village of Rocester in Staffordshire, and how, after the war, family life was never to be the same again:*

Before the war my family lived at 40 Allenby Road, Ramsgate, and I and my three sisters, Pat, Dorothy and Betty, attended Dame Janet School in Ramsgate. I remember the day of evacuation in June 1940 as being very emotional, tearful and fearful. We all had to meet at the school with our gas masks and case. Coaches then took us on our journey to Rocester, a small village in Staffordshire.

After we had arrived, the long drawn-out procedure of sorting us all out for billets seemed to take hours. Eventually, my three sisters and I were told to get into the back of a van and to go with these people with whom we would be temporarily staying. At this stage I was really frightened and wondered where we were being taken. I honestly thought that something awful was going to happen to us, but we soon reached a really big house on top of a hill and discovered that there were two school teachers staying there. The house was called Red Hall and the people we stayed with were Mrs Simister and her daughter Betty. Once we had settled in I can remember being very happy there. However, it was only to be for a short time then we got split up. My sister Dorothy and I went to live with a lady named Miss Bennett in Station Road. She seemed quite old and had grey hair – and didn't seem to know too much about young children! We had to be in bed by six o'clock every night and any money that was sent to us was taken away and put towards anything we needed.

The four Cox sisters at the time of evacuation: left to right Violet, Dorothy, Betty and Pat

Dorothy used to throw tantrums over this, but I was much too timid and shy.

Sisters Pat and Betty were billeted next door to us with Mr and Mrs Chritchlow. They were nice people who had a much better understanding of children and my sisters were happy there.

I became friends with a girl named Vilma Johnson who lived in a big house in the village and I used to think that her family were very posh. I lost touch with Vilma when, after two or three years, I went to live with my mother in Uttoxeter when she moved up from Kent because my father was away in the army. Family life was never to be the same again because my father and mother eventually separated.

The government printed 1.5 million of these notices in May 1944, down from 3 million two years earlier. Payment rates went up by only one shilling a week for each age group in that period

I have no really bad memories of my evacuation. The food was alright and I don't ever remember feeling hungry. We were not expected to do jobs – just to behave ourselves and do as we were told. Overall I don't think evacuation affected us in any great way.

I went back to Rocester in 1998, the first time since my evacuation. I found the house where we were billeted; it is still there but now stands derelict!

The sister of Violet Cox, **Betty Cox** *(now Mrs King), adds her comments of their time in Rocester, Staffordshire:*

I was little more than six years old when I and my three sisters were evacuated with our school, Dame Janet School, in Ramsgate on 2nd June 1940. I know I was quite upset at leaving my home and my family. Being so young, I can remember nothing of the journey to Rocester, Staffs, but I do remember our first billet where we all stayed for a while. It was a lovely big, old house and our host was Mrs Simister. She also had some of our teachers from Ramsgate billeted there.

After a while we moved to other billets. I went with my sister Pat, and my sisters Violet and Dorothy lived next door. Pat and I were very happy with our hosts Mr and Mrs Critchlow, but Violet and Dorothy were not so lucky. They lived with an older person who didn't have children of her own and probably found that looking after two girls was too much for her.

My strongest memories of our stay in Rocester are of the long, hot summers, and playing on the farm at the top of the road – and just being happy!

We stayed in Rocester for about three years, but we didn't return to Ramsgate. My parents' marriage had broken up and my mother moved to Uttoxeter where we were reunited with her.

Douglas Philpott *recalls his short stay in Draycott-in-the-Clay:*

I was born in Ramsgate in 1929 and at the time of our evacuation I was attending St Laurence Church of England School, Newington Road, Ramsgate. Dunkirk was in full swing when we were marched to Ramsgate railway station, and we had no idea where we were going.

On two platforms at the station there were wounded soldiers being loaded on to hospital trains – while we were being loaded on to another train. Once we set off into the unknown, the journey went on and on and it seemed like the middle of the night when we arrived at a place called Draycott-in-the-Clay. We found out afterwards that it was near Uttoxeter.

My younger brother and I, and the deputy head of the school, were billeted with the people who lived in the village school house. There was no running water and no water closet, just a dry toilet at the bottom of the garden. What a place after Ramsgate!

The next morning we all assembled in the school with the local

---

*A Message from the Minister of Health
to Parents who have Evacuated their Children*

*Ministry of Health
Whitehall S.W.1*

You are among the many fathers and mothers who wisely took advantage of the Government's scheme to send their children to the country. I am sorry to learn that some parents are now bringing their children back.

I am writing to ask you not to do this. This is not easy, for family life has always been the strength and pride of Britain. But I feel it my duty to remind you that to bring children back to its congested towns is to put them in danger of death or what is perhaps worse, maiming for life. You will have noticed that the Enemy is changing his tactics.

He is now concentrating heavier air raids on one or two towns at a time, leaving others alone for the moment.

Nobody knows which town he will attack next. So don't be lulled into a false sense of security if your home district has been having a quieter time lately.

Remember that in April over 600 children under sixteen were seriously injured in air raids. So keep you children where they are in the reception areas.

Don't bring them back even for a little while. This is your duty to the children themselves, to the A.R.P. Services in your home town, to those who are working so hard for them in the country, and to the Nation.

Please read this message as the sincere words of a friend both to you and the little ones.

*Yours Sincerely,
Ernst Brown, June 1941*

The serious problem of evacuees drifting back home made the Ministry of Health issue this letter to parents – despite the misprints – including the minister's first name!

pupils – all twelve of them! The people of Draycott thought that as we evacuees were from Ramsgate, we were rich and that we were all little 'Lord Fauntleroys' – a myth we quickly dispelled!

My brother and I stayed in the school house and, although the couple who lived there did their best for us, they were really too old to look after young children, but we all made the best of it.

I still remember what we did every Saturday morning. The old man would get his horse and cart, then my brother and I would help him to empty all the dry toilets and take them to a farmer's field. I didn't go to the village school for long as I was of an age to go to a higher school, which was at Tutbury, about fifteen miles away.

I think the times we liked best while we were evacuated were on market days in Uttoxeter. We would catch the bus, which would be full of people, geese, dogs, chickens and anything that was going to be sold. We were only evacuated for about a year then our parents took us back home to Ramsgate. It was more fun being back in Ramsgate, playing on the big guns and watching the aeroplanes coming and going at RAF Manston.

Joan Parker *(now Mrs Foad) recalls her evacuation to various areas of Staffordshire:*

I was an avid reader at the age of ten and had read so much about the Spanish Civil War. I was convinced that once war with Germany started, bombs would rain down on us and there would be fighting in the streets. I couldn't wait to get away to a safe haven.

I had been born in the heart of Buckinghamshire, but spent most of my school years in Kent and therefore considered myself a 'townie'. Anyway, in June 1940, I was evacuated with all of my friends from Ramsgate, and we were scattered into the villages of rural Staffordshire.

My friend Shirley and I were sent to Doddlespool Hall at Betley. The grounds of this lovely old house straddled two counties. A small stream running through the grounds divided Staffordshire from Cheshire. The lady of the house was a member of the famous pottery family of Wedgwood. This new world was fascinating to us. We ate in the servants hall and the staff included a cook, a parlour maid, a kitchen maid and a chap who must have been the butler – well there was a butler's pantry!

Cook was fat and jolly and would slip us the odd titbit. Dorothy, the kitchen maid, was a local girl from the village and saw to our needs (baths, etc.). Mary the parlour maid was older and a little austere and we didn't have much to do with the butler. The food at Doddlespool Hall was very good. On rare occasions we took afternoon tea in the drawing room with Mrs Wedgwood.

I remember a magnificent dolls house that we were allowed to play with – if we were careful! Every cup and saucer, vase – and little potty under each bed had the Wedgwood mark.

Our room was off the great hall and it was huge. We more or less camped in the middle of it. Every evening Mrs Wedgwood dressed for dinner, came to say goodnight to us and to draw the interior shutters over the huge windows. Sometimes there were cocktail parties or other gatherings. We had a wonderful view through the door which we opened just a crack.

There seemed to be lots of visitors to stay, mostly in uniform. Those I remember by name were Miss Felicity, a nurse, and son-in-law, John Cunningham, who was a pilot in the Royal Air Force, and his wife who was expecting a baby. We caused a right old scare when we evacuees both went down with German measles.

The walk to school was about a mile and a half and we always encountered the same farmer with the same herd of cows. Shirley would boldly go forth where this timid person hung back until all was clear! I was always late and in trouble with the village school master. The school was one big room divided into three classes. Thanks to this small seat of learning I can remember to this day every word, note and pause of 'Nymphs and Shepherds'. I must surely take it to my desert island!

This rural idyll was shattered when Shirley and I learned we had passed our scholarship exam for high school. We went to the county town of Stafford to join Clarendon House School for Girls from Ramsgate. We shared the high school in Stafford with local pupils for three days of the week, and the other two days were spent out of town at Baswich House.

Our billet this time was very different. Our hosts were a childless and, looking back, a loveless couple who lived in a semi-detached house on the outskirts of Stafford. The husband worked at Siemens, a vast engineering works where everyone seemed to work. Our hosts were good to us in their way but the house lacked warmth (of the soul)!

We still had a long walk to school but now it was past houses and into the town. The days we spent at Baswich House were the best. It was a big rambling place a few miles out of town. I remember the winters mostly, playing hockey and one poor girl losing her front teeth from an ill-placed ball. I remember the frosty walks – and we learnt the carol *In the Bleak Midwinter* there. It never fails to bring it all back. Another memory of Baswich House is that the cook always managed to burn the milk when she made the mid-morning cocoa!

I didn't stay in Stafford for the duration, but plagued my mother to have me home. My family moved to Northolt in Middlesex and after two years in Stafford I eventually joined them there – to survive the 'doodlebugs' and the V2 rockets.

Jean Fuller, *although quite young at the time, remembers her evacuation to Staffordshire:*

I was evacuated to Staffordshire on June 2nd 1940, at the age of six, with my brother who was eight. Prior to my evacuation I can remember my mother collecting up sheets and towels, which had been requested for the soldiers arriving from the Dunkirk evacuation. When we arrived at Ramsgate railway station on the day of our departure, I can remember the soldiers sitting along the walls, many of them bandaged around their heads and limbs, and they waved to us as we went by.

We left with one small bag each and our gas mask in its cardboard box. I can't remember much about the journey except it took a very long time, and we were given green apples and tea by soldiers en route. We finally arrived at Norbury, near Stafford, where we were taken to the village school, where I presume we were chosen to go to our allotted billets.

Three children from the same family, and my brother and I, went with a rather glamorous woman to the local vicarage, where we were to stay for about six weeks. It was then that my mother was able to visit us and discover that we were not at all well cared for. We already had 'nits' in our hair and were generally unkempt and neglected. My late mother had often related this to me in later years, so I am sure it must have been true. The five of us slept in the attic bedrooms and the vicar, who was a surly old man, hardly ever acknowledged us. We had porridge with black treacle every morning and we had to go to church three times on Sundays. In retrospect I can only presume that the vicar's wife had to be seen to be doing her duty for the war effort, and we children were basically left to look after ourselves.

My mother was able to visit the billeting officer in Stafford, and my brother and I were promptly moved to stay with Mrs Winnie Oulton at Gayton – another village on the other side of Stafford. The other three evacuees were left at the vicarage and I often wondered what happened to them.

Winnie Oulton proved to be a kind, caring lady who had a nine-month old baby – and a husband who had just been taken prisoner of war, and remained so throughout the war. My brother and I were very happy with Winnie. We settled in well and were treated as if we were her own. My brother, having just had his ninth birthday and a new bike, cycled each day to school in the next village of Weston, where he presumably received a better education than the tiny school at Gayton which I went to.

Being in a small village in those days, there were no modern conveniences. There was a smelly outside toilet – and a chamber pot to use at night. There was no electricity, so oil lamps were used and a Primus stove when the fire wasn't alight. A big copper was heated on a Monday to do the weekly washing and water came from a pump in the yard. This pump was shared with the next cottage where 'Aunty' Alice lived. She had two boys whom we used to play with.

There were three farms, the church and the school in Church Lane where we lived. The farm almost opposite kept cows and we had to take the milk can to fetch milk fresh from the cow. Another larger farm, Moat Farm was where my brother used to help at harvest time; I can remember riding home on top of the hay in a horse-drawn cart. At the end of the lane was Bill Upton's farm. His farm ran alongside a brook which had stepping stones over it and we would often go across and up a little lane where violets and primroses grew and where we could hear frogs croaking.

Winnie kept a pig which we used to feed. She also had chickens so there was always a plentiful supply of eggs. Winnie also cultivated a very large garden with the help of her father who lived with her. I can remember with horror when the pig was taken to be killed.

The Red Bus came to Gayton twice a week on market days, Tuesdays and Saturdays. I usually went in on a Saturday, when Winnie helped in her sister-in-law's shop, and I stayed with the grandma. We always took the accumulator for the radio with us to be recharged; it was very heavy to carry. We would also collect the weekly rations from the Co-op. Winnie's sister and her boyfriend visited every week and they were also very kind to us, buying us presents at Christmas and on our birthdays.

We were evacuated for about two years, but my mother did visit us once or twice during that time and I think we must have come home at least once for a holiday, because I can remember my grandfather meeting us at the station and having delicious rabbit pie that my granny had made. I still keep in touch with Winnie and she came down to visit us in 1995.

After we had come home for good, we had to move because our house was damaged by shelling and flying bombs also disrupted our lives. On passing my 11+ in 1944, I was re-evacuated for one term, from September to December, because Clarendon House Grammar School for Girls was still in Stafford, but again I was well looked after. My friend and I stayed with an elderly Canadian couple.

In retrospect I suppose we were fortunate in that during our evacuation our parents were able to keep in touch and showed concern for our well being. Others I fear were not so lucky.

Vera Booth *(now Mrs Clayton) remembers, with detail, the day of her evacuation:*

I was evacuated with my elder sister and brother on 2nd June, 1940, the day before my 11th birthday. I was attending Dame Janet School in Ramsgate but, as my elder sister was a pupil at St George's School, Ramsgate, my brother and I were evacuated with her and her school in the hope of all of us staying together.

I remember feeling excited as we stood in a great long line in Station Approach Road, shuffling slowly to the railway station, with parents lining the pavements waving us goodbye. We had labels tied to our coats and carried our gas masks over our shoulders. The evacuation, or retreat, from Dunkirk was also in progress and busloads of soldiers, having just landed at the harbour, were now coming to the station.

Our train journey was long and hot. I remember the train stopping at some station and a soldier giving me an orange. We did not know our destination until we arrived. It was a town I had not heard of – Stafford! We were then taken to a hall and, from there, volunteers with cars were driving the children to their new billets. My brother, sister and I wanted to stay together, but nobody wanted three children.

We were driven slowly along Lovatt Street and a woman, Mrs Bailey at number 45, called out that she would take the two girls, though she had asked for boys! So my sister and I went with her and my brother was driven away. We all met the next day at a local school, which we attended until the summer holidays. I then heard that I had passed the scholarship to attend Clarendon House Grammar School, and joined them in the September.

We shared the premises of Stafford High School for Girls for three days of the week, and spent two days at Baswich House on the outskirts of Stafford. We remained a separate school and did not integrate with the Stafford school at all

Our foster mother was a kind lady and, on reflection, we must have been a 'handful'. She did not have a bathroom. Instead, a tin bath was carried in from the garden on Friday nights and filled with kettles of hot water from the fire.

When my sister left school the following year, 1941, I was moved to another billet nearer my school. After a few months my new hostess, as we were taught to call them, decided to go out to work instead of having an evacuee. It was compulsory by this time to do one or the other. I moved again to Windsor Road in Stafford and remained there until Clarendon House Grammar School returned to Ramsgate in 1944.

I believe our hostesses received a government allowance of 7/6d a week for each evacuee, which was recovered from the parents. Looking back I realise how kindly I was treated in my billets, not always appreciated by me at the time!

Of Stafford I recall the park by the station, the swimming baths and castle. There was very little socialising and my life revolved around school, church and Girl Guides. We followed the war news, but felt detached from it – until we spent holidays at home from 1942 onwards! I never doubted we would win the war, a tribute to the optimism of our elders.

There were no other children in my billets and, except for a few at Guides, my friends were, like myself, evacuees from Thanet. I corresponded with my host and hostess for a few years after the war and, although they invited me to visit, I never returned to Stafford.

Joycelin Ruth Holland (now Mrs Bromley) from Ramsgate recalls the day she was evacuated:

On Sunday, 2nd June, 1940, with labels attached to our coats, gas masks over our shoulders, clothes and food for the journey, we assembled in the huge playground at Ellington Girls' School in Ramsgate. My sister Jean, my two brothers, Kerry and Gethin, and I, were told to stay together, to look after each other and to make sure that we behaved ourselves. So after hugs, kisses and a few tears, we marched off to Ramsgate railway station. The road was filled with hundreds of children making their way to the station on that day.

Parents were not allowed to accompany their children on to the platform. My parents' last words to me were to make sure we all stayed together. There was a train waiting for us and we climbed aboard, chatting excitedly. There was another train standing in the station which was filled with more soldiers who had been rescued from Dunkirk. They asked us where we were going to, but none of us knew our destination. Suddenly our train started to move. As it did so, a young soldier shouted, 'Hey kid,' as he grabbed my hand and placed in it a shamrock medal which he had taken from around his neck. He said, 'This will keep you safe, it has brought me safely through that Hell Hole!', meaning Dunkirk, and then he was gone.

Two of our teachers, Miss McKenzie and Miss Jones escorted us on the journey. We did not reach our destination of Stafford until after dark and

Kerry, Gethin, Jean and Joycelin Holland on Ramsgate seafront just before they were evacuated

we waited in a church hall to be billeted with local families. Because I tried to keep our family together, we were the last to leave. In the end they split us up with the promise that we would all be together the following day. Jean and I went with Mr and Mrs Dix to Rose Cottage at Sandon Bank, about seven miles from Stafford. Kerry and Gethin went with a farmer and his wife, Mr and Mrs Plant. I don't remember seeing much of them after that!

It was very different from back home in Kent where we had shops near to where we lived. We were now in the country and the only 'shop' came once a week, but we got eggs, butter and cheese from the farm, and watercress grew in the stream.

I missed my mum and dad a great deal and I don't think any of us realised, in our wildest dreams, that we would not return home to Ramsgate for several years. Some evacuees never returned. Two of my friends from the Brownies lost both their parents when a land mine exploded. They were twins. The war had a terrible effect on many families. One day our foster parents, who were very kind to us, said that if my mum and dad were killed, they would adopt us. This sent Jean and me into hysterics. Jean cried all night long and in the end I said, 'I'm going home!, I'm going to follow the railway lines back to Ramsgate!' Because of this, Jean and I were put into separate rooms. It must have been very hard for Mr and Mrs Dix. Jean and I were very close and I suspect we were quite a handful!

When my baby sister Barbara was about three years old, she came to Sandon Bank and was billeted next door to us with Mr and Mrs Farmer. They had two small children of their own – Babs and Brian. Eventually, we had a lovely surprise when my father managed to get a job in a munitions factory in Stafford, and rented a cottage, Skeath Cottage, in Sandon Bank. It was wonderful. No more crying oneself to sleep, even though we had to cope with oil lamps and a lavatory at the bottom of the garden! We returned home to Ramsgate when my father thought it was safe to do so, but we hadn't been home long before the shelling started, so we were packed off to an auntie in South Wales – but that's another story!

My brothers will not talk about their evacuation. They will only say that it split families up, never to be the same again.

I have thought many times of that young soldier who gave me that shamrock medal so many years ago. Did he survive the war I wonder. The medal, which I treasured for a long time, was given to my mother to keep her and dad safe back in Ramsgate – and it did! Both parents lived to over 80 years but, after my mother died, the medal was never found.

Ivy Sutton (now Mrs Wilson) was evacuated from Margate at the tender age of five and a half years old. Her account highlights the problem many evacuees went through in 'fitting back into family life' when they finally returned home:

I can recall the excitement of waiting for the big red double-decker buses which transported us from Holy Trinity School in Margate to the railway station in June 1940. We all had our labels on our coats, our gas masks and packed lunch. I can't remember anything about the journey except our arrival at a station which I was told later, was Rugeley in Staffordshire. I was then taken on another journey with two or three other evacuees, to a small village near Tamworth called Hints.

Another girl and I were taken to a lovely lady who at the time seemed very old to me. I never discovered her age but, thinking back, I suppose she must have been in her fifties because she had a grown up son in the Royal Air Force. The evacuee who was with me didn't stay very long. She was too homesick and soon returned to her parents.

After coming from a poor home and a large family – which obviously meant shortages and cramped conditions, I couldn't get over this beautiful 'posh' house. I had my own bedroom, was taught to keep myself clean and, each evening before bedtime, I had a chapter of a book read to me. I then had a square of chocolate before I cleaned my teeth. This became a routine before bedtime and prayers.

The other which always makes me smile when I think of it was that I had to wear a Liberty Bodice with rubber buttons. How I hated that wretched garment and couldn't wait each year for the May Blossom to appear and I could leave it off!

My foster aunt never once smacked me. Her discipline was maintained by talking and explaining things to me and, if I was really naughty, I was sent to my room and my books taken from me for however long it was decreed – that was punishment indeed to me. My weekly chore (which was my choice) was to black-lead and polish the kitchen range, in which I took a great pride, and I was always rewarded with affection.

We had exercises as to what to do in the event of an air raid. A man used to walk around the few houses, ringing a hand-bell. I don't think there were any air raid shelters because we were told that if an enemy plane came over, we must throw ourselves flat on the ground until we were told it was safe.

Our school was tiny, with just a few pupils. One of our war efforts was to gather the sheep's fleeces as they were sheared, then we had the job of picking out all the horrible lumps of dirt and grease. Then we washed the fleeces and watched them being spun and dyed into khaki wool. Both girls and boys were then taught to knit socks and balaclavas for the troops.

I was with my foster aunt for five years and came back to Margate sometime between VE Day and VJ Day. I can remember the trauma of leaving my foster aunt, and it must have been dreadful for her too. To this day, I can see me hiding under the kitchen table with the over-hanging chenille cloth, holding on to the table leg with all my might and screaming wildly.

After the long journey home my first impressions of Margate was of rolls of barbed wire along the beach and, the next morning, on waking up in a strange bedroom to look out of the window and see no fields or trees. I was very unhappy and to make matters worse I had to share everything with my family who I didn't know. My accent was different and my manners were such that I earned the nickname of 'The Duchess'. The lasting impression evacuation has had on my life has been thankfulness for my lovely upbringing and sorrow for the hard times I must have given my own mother for bringing me back.

I did go back to Hints when I was 20 years old, but my foster aunt had died. I felt so sorry that I hadn't managed to keep in touch. The village itself hadn't changed, and I felt as though time had stood still.

Chapter Five

UNHAPPY BILLETS AND TRAGIC MEMORIES

In contrast to the rosy picture presented by the newspapers of the day, there were those whose evacuation experiences were unpleasant, to say the least. All children of school age evacuated under the Government Evacuation Scheme had already gone through the trauma of leaving their parents behind. Many evacuees then had to cope with being separated from brothers and sisters once they reached their destinations. But there were other problems as well for some of the unfortunate ones.

Edna Tipping *(now Mrs Weaver) was living in Norman Road, St Peters, Broadstairs at the start of the Second World War. Here she recalls her evacuation to Staffordshire in 1940:*

In June 1940 we were told by our teachers that we were being evacuated, because there was a threat of invasion by the German army, now in France and just across the English Channel.

Our school, St Mildred's Girls' School, was being sent to Tamworth in Staffordshire. My sisters, Sheila, Audrey and Peggy, and I were all going together. My older sister, Doris, who went to St George's School in Ramsgate was going to the town of Stafford, leaving our younger brother, Raymond (Buster), aged three, at home with my mother. At the time our father was in the Royal Air Force somewhere in France.

We had to assemble on the slope of Broadstairs railway station at 9am on Sunday, 2nd June, with a small suitcase each, and our gas mask. We all climbed on to one long train and set off on our journey, which to most of us seemed like a big adventure. It wasn't until we arrived that the real upset began. I don't know how it was done, but the train went straight through to Tamworth and we never had to change trains at all.

Edna and Peggy Tipping at Tamworth in 1940

We did stop on the way and I can remember there was a train full of soldiers alongside ours and they were throwing apples and oranges into the carriages. We all had sandwiches on the way and we arrived at our destination in the early afternoon.

When we left the train we were taken to Tamworth Girls' School and assembled in the quadrangle, where our foster mothers were waiting to collect us. It was very much a game of chance who you went with. My mum had told me that if we couldn't all be together, I was to go with my younger sister, leaving Peggy and Audrey to stay together.

Sheila and I duly went with one mum and I hadn't a clue where my two other sisters had gone! I was anxious to know where they were and so our foster mum said that we would walk round the castle after tea where we might meet them – and we did!

My sister Peggy was sobbing her heart out. The two foster parents decided to swap us over and so I went off with Peggy. When we got to where she was staying I could see why she was so upset. The foster family was very poor. We had a bedroom with a double bed and nothing on the floor apart from a piece of sacking; all we had for our clothes was a single drawer placed on the floor. The following morning we were given a boiled egg, but no egg cups! We had to hold the hot eggs in a piece of cloth.

We were all instructed to meet at the local cinema that morning and when I saw my teacher, Miss Rouse, I told her she had to find me somewhere near to Audrey and Sheila or I would write to my mother to fetch us home! This went on until the Thursday when Miss Rouse said, 'I have found somewhere nearer your sisters.' And that was the excuse she made for moving us.

We didn't see much of the war in Tamworth, but I was there when the Germans raided the city of Coventry.

After one more move, my mother decided to join us in Tamworth. By this time, my dad was back in England having been evacuated from Dunkirk where over 300,000 British and Allied troops had been safely taken off the beaches of France, and ferried across the English Channel.

My mum rented two rooms at the top of a three storey house, where she had to go down two flights of stairs to fetch water. She had just one gas ring to cook on. Eventually, the local council gave her a little cottage to rent – which had been condemned! But it was home to us. There was one living room and two bedrooms, with a scullery across the passage and a toilet across the yard – which we shared with another cottage nearby. Later, my mother took a job at the Nuffield aircraft factory at Lichfield, where aircraft flown from America were taken apart, crated up and sent to Russia.

It was after mum had had an accident and hurt her back that we decided to return to Thanet. This was just before the doodlebugs started coming over from France. They mostly passed over us on their way to London. We used to listen for the engines of these rockets to stop – when they didn't we knew we were alright!

I think evacuation made us more independent than we would otherwise have been. We had to stand on our own two feet. I have been back to Tamworth a couple of times, but it has all changed so much, I have a job to find my way around! When I asked my daughter-in-law if she could have sent her three girls away as we had to go, she replied, 'No way!' How our mums didn't all have nervous breakdowns being parted from their children I will never know!

Ron Toole *has few pleasant memories of his evacuation to Rugeley in Staffordshire:*

After spending several days with my mother, by the harbour at Margate watching the troops coming back from Dunkirk to see if my father was among them, we were told that my school, Salmestone Junior School, Margate, was to be evacuated. We were assembled at the school with our gas mask in its cardboard box, a 'luggage' label and a small suitcase of belongings, put on to buses and taken to Margate railway station. The worst emotion I had was of leaving my dog behind, a large Airedale terrier. As I recall, there were no parents at the station to see us off.

After a long journey we ended up at Rugeley, a mining town in Staffordshire and, after being registered at a school, we were taken round estates in a coach and taken out to billets. I was put with a mining family who lived in a council house. To me they seemed to be a tribe of savage and strange people who spoke an odd language, and whose food was totally different from anything I had seen before. Lunch could be a slice of bread with H.P. sauce, children ate raw potatoes and bad language was rife. My clothes were stolen and at the age of eight I began bedwetting! This was the most embarrassing part, getting out of bed, which was often shared, and not daring to admit your guilt!

My mother, who was looking after my grandmother, later arrived in the Birmingham area and took on war work in a factory, but I only visited very infrequently. I subsequently went to another mining family – tin bath in front of the fire, *et al*, where a cracked mug was passed around the family for the nightly cocoa.

After 18 months I went to bed one night fully clothed and, after the family was asleep, I climbed out of a first floor window and dropped, very heavily, to the ground. I made my way to my mother in Birmingham, but how I can't remember. My mother took me to a doctor who advised returning to Margate. We returned home and, after many examinations and the removal of my tonsils, I was found to have a TB infection of the neck glands and was sent to a hospital in Chatham where I spent two months after an operation for their removal.

I have visited Rugeley twice since the war. When I went back in 1993, the last billet I stayed at had been knocked down, but the other side of the street is still there, and it is still, to me, an awful, grubby place.

Being such a young age in 1940 it is difficult to record impressions but I think I felt the crudeness of the people, the poor living conditions and the absence of books – although somehow I managed to keep reading!

Mothers, I learnt later, were discouraged from visiting their children, in order to assist in the war effort – and bed-wetting among evacuees was a national problem. One word to describe evacuation is 'bewilderment'. We were carted around, and dumped off with totally unsuitable people who didn't really want you.

My memories of that time are not happy ones – and it was even worse on returning home. My one thought, as soon as we reached home, was to fetch my dog from an aunt who had undertaken (so I thought) to look after him. On rushing into the house to see where my dog was, my aunt informed me that he 'had to be put to sleep'. One can see in old newsreels, the queues of dog owners outside the local offices waiting to have their dogs put down but that day, for me, was probably the worst memory of all.

I am sure that evacuation changed me from a trusting little boy, to someone who never really trusted anyone again and my attitude to authority has always been one of mistrust – perhaps rightly so!

The following advice was given to foster parents in a wartime leaflet entitled Information for Householders Taking Evacuees *and issued by the Women's Voluntary Service:* Some children may try your patience by wetting their beds, but do not scold or punish; as this will only make matters worse.

Cecily Matthews *(now Mrs Poppy) left Thanet in 1940, destined never to return to her home in Margate:*

We left on 2nd June, 1940, and the small mining village of Boney Hay in Staffordshire was to be our destination. My mother kept the news of my evacuation from me until the morning of our departure. So with a few items in a small case and my gas mask over my shoulder, I was taken to the railway station where we all assembled. The train ran through the end of a recreation ground which was close to our house and my last glimpse of my family was them waving frantically from the recreation ground.

The journey seemed endless, but we finally arrived at Lichfield sometime in the evening. We all got off the train and there were hundreds of us standing about, waiting for buses to take us to our various destinations. Our bus arrived at Boney Hay and we all assembled in the village hall waiting for people to choose us. My friend Eileen and I insisted on staying together, which meant that we were among the last to be chosen.

Eventually a very young couple was persuaded to take us in. The man was a miner and was very kind to us, but his wife, who was only 22 years old and with a young baby, made it quite obvious that we were not wanted. She stayed in bed in the mornings and so for the first time in my life I got myself up, got breakfast and made the mile or so journey to the village school. The school work was very easy because we had covered the same work many months before in Thanet. They were very kind to us at the school and made great efforts to make us feel at home.

It was not such a happy life with our foster parents though, and I remember vividly being unable to sleep and sitting out on the landing crying very late at night. In the meanwhile, as my father was unable to find work in Kent, he came up to Coventry and managed to get a job in Rootes Aircraft Factory, staying in lodgings. Mother wasn't going to stay in Thanet either, so she, my sister and young brother moved in with my aunt in Rugby. My grandfather, who lived with us, moved in with his twin sister in Crewe. So our family was completely dispersed. Dad stayed in his 'digs' until mother found a large top floor flat in Leamington Spa when we all came together as a family again. The family, however, never returned to Margate to live.

I have visited Margate only once since the war and that was in 1949 while on my honeymoon, but I was unable to find any of my old friends during that week.

Summing up, I would say that, although done with the best of intentions, evacuation has had a detrimental effect on the whole of my life. I had three schools in two years which had a disastrous effect on my education and left me lacking confidence and drive. I have also had problems showing affection, even to my three daughters, and much prefer being with animals rather than people.

Evacuation for **Audrey Dennis** *(now Mrs Kember) proved to be a traumatic time:*

I was 11 years old when I was evacuated with St George's School, Ramsgate, in June of 1940. Our train journey took us to Stafford, in the Midlands. When we arrived, we were taken to a big market place and each given milk and a bun. Then from there we were taken by coaches to various surrounding villages.

I went with others to the village of Seighford where we assembled in the village hall to be selected by the locals. A friend and I were chosen by the local vicar – we were far from happy there; he got us watering his vast garden the first night we arrived! We were only there for two weeks and then we went to a billet in Stafford with a very nice family. They cared for us really well.

Our school, St George's, shared the premises of a Stafford school. We had to manage in the dining hall which was divided into various classes. It was quite chaotic because every day we had to move out in time for the school dinners to be served.

In January 1941 came the terrible news that my father had been killed in a bombing raid whilst working in Ramsgate. He was the manager of Dewhursts the butchers in the High Street. The war hardly reached us in Stafford, although I remember the time when German aircraft flew over the town and we all had to rush to the shelters nearby. I can also remember many Americans, who were stationed around the area, and the Italian prisoners of war who worked on the nearby farms.

After the tragic death of my father, my mother decided to join me in Stafford. I eventually left school and, after a period at secretarial college, I went to work for the town clerk in Stafford. Unfortunately, my mother was taken very ill and, because the air didn't suit her in Stafford, we returned to Ramsgate. By this time the war was virtually over, but we had to learn to manage without father.

(Author's note: At 14.40 hours on the 14th January 1941, a single Junkers 88 bomber dived out of low cloud over Ramsgate and dropped its bombs. Three shops received direct hits – Woolworths, a grocery store belonging to Messrs Saunders, and Dewhurst the butchers. Nineteen-year-old Edna Honess ran into the butcher's shop for safety. She was met at the door by the manager Albert Dennis. They had almost reached the large cabinet refrigerator when the bomb exploded. The massive door crushed Edna Honess and Albert Dennis was buried beneath the rubble. Rescuers later pulled him from the wreckage, but he died in hospital that same night.)

June Davis *was evacuated from St Peter's, Broadstairs, in Thanet:*

I was twelve years old when my school was evacuated to Tamworth in Staffordshire. The train journey wasn't too bad and when we finally arrived at our destination we were taken to a large hall where we were allocated to our foster parents. I was taken by a middle-aged couple who had no children of their own. My billet was shared by two other evacuees who were sisters, but they only stayed a very short time before being taken back to St Peter's by their mother. That left me on my own.

The Sunday after we had all arrived, our foster parents took us for a walk around the town; I was amazed to see so many young evacuees from back home, sitting on pub door steps with a packet of chips and a bottle of lemonade. I suspect that their parents would have been horrified if they had known!

My father was an electrician by trade, but also a great gardener, with a garden full of vegetables during the war. He used to send parcels of fresh vegetables to my foster parents to help out with the rations. He even used to 'pod' the peas to get more in the parcel; yet, on coming home from school one day extremely hungry, I asked my foster mother if I could have a slice of bread and jam and was told, 'No! You've had your jam ration for the week!' It was all these little things that mounted up to make the evacuees feel so unwelcome. I came from a family with the most wonderful caring parents.

I remember when we attended the senior school in Tamworth, the local girls used to wait for us evacuees at the school gate in the mornings and, as we walked through, we were thumped on the back and told, 'Go home you evacuee kids!' I wrote to my father and told him how unhappy I was. At the time Thanet was receiving many air raids. My father wrote back explaining how dangerous it was and that if I came home I would have to spend the nights in the air raid shelter. That sounded like heaven compared to where I was staying. Shortly afterwards I was taken home, back to St Peter's. It was wonderful to see my own home again – air raids or no air raids!

George Emptage's evacuation was not easy and he had to contend with tragedy after he returned home to Margate:

My parents decided that my sister Rose and I should go. I was eight and Rose was eleven. A few weeks later, on Sunday 2nd June, 1940, we set off from home with my parents and my other sisters, to walk to Drapers Mills School where all the children were examined by a nurse then given a label with our name printed on, which was either pinned to our jacket or hung around our necks. Outside the school, double-decker buses were waiting to take us to Margate railway station. There were a lot of tears as we said our goodbyes; some of the children didn't want to go and pleaded with their parents to take them home. Mr Bell, our teacher, was coming with us and it was he who counted us on to the bus.

Margate railway station was crowded with soldiers as well as hundreds of children. We walked in pairs to our special train, which was hissing and smoking, waiting to take us to some unknown destination. Suddenly we were on our way and people were waving and shouting to us; we waved and shouted back, then we settled down to face the journey ahead. We were then told that we were going to somewhere in the Midlands.

Once, we stopped opposite another train and people threw sweets to us and shouted, 'Good luck, kids!' Another time when we had to stop, we were told to be quiet as there was an air-raid going on.

It was late in the afternoon when we finally arrived at Lichfield Trent Valley station. It was still hot and sunny and we were feeling tired. We were all pleased to get off the train. We all assembled in a building close to the station, given something to eat and drink and were again examined by a nurse. Then about thirty of us left by bus with Mr Bell, to a village called Clifton Campville. I found out later that my sister Rose had gone to Chase Town, near Walsall.

When we arrived at Clifton we were told to sit on the grass near the village school, By this time I had paired up with a boy named Billy Dickenson. The people of the village came and looked us over and started to pick the children they wanted, but nobody seemed to want Billy and me; soon we were the only two left. We spent that first night at a farmhouse next to the school.

Broadstairs Railway Station and the station master's house after being bombed

The following day we had to report to the school where we met up with the other evacuees and the village children. Our teacher, Mr Bell, was there and we were found desks at one end of the largest of the two classrooms, and a curtain parted us from the village children.

At the end of the school day, Billy and I were told to stay at our desks and wait for the headteacher, Miss Culley, to speak to us. She told us both that we were going to live on a farm with a Mr and Mrs Brisco. Three of the village girls were asked to show us the way to the farm, which was about a mile from the village. They took us as far as the lane leading up to the farm, then ran off. Billy and I started to walk up this lane, which had high hedges on both sides, and when we came to a wood we were quite scared. As we went round a bend in the lane we saw a man driving a herd of cows towards farm buildings and he confirmed that it was Brisco's farm.

As we approached, dogs came running out barking, followed by a red faced lady wearing thick brown glasses and her grey hair tied up in a bun. She was dressed in old clothes with sack tied around her waist as an apron, and on her feet she wore wellington boots. To Billy and me she looked very frightening. She said, 'Are you the two evacuees? Where have you been? I was expecting you earlier!'

The house felt very cold and uninviting. The kitchen had bare blue bricks on the floor and the walls were white-washed. An old brown china sink stood under the window and a brick copper was in one corner. The towels that hung by the sink were made from sacks. In the living room was a small fire burning in a black-leaded grate. A large wooden table stood in the centre of the room with four wooden chairs and against one wall stood a huge grandfather clock.

Some time after our arrival, a red faced man came into the room and we were told that this was Mr Brisco. The woman continued by saying, 'If you stay here you must call us aunty and uncle. We have a son named Frank and if at any time we have to go out, you must do as Frank says.'

We were taken up to our room which contained an iron double bed, an old painted chest of drawers and a pegged rug on the bare wooden floor boards. A small window overlooked the enclosed farmyard – and we were told not to interfere with the curtains.

We settled into a routine, with aunty getting us up at half past six each day to do our jobs before breakfast, which was at eight o'clock after the animals had been fed and the milking was finished. After breakfast it was a quick wash in rain water which was collected in a large tank outside the back door, and then we would walk the mile or so to school with our gas masks slung over our shoulders. After school we had to hurry home, because we had more jobs to do before tea time, and we were always in bed by eight o'clock in the evening.

After we had been at the farm a few months, Billy became ill. They said he had TB. Aunty put a bolster down the centre of our bed and ordered us to stay on our own side. Billy's condition worsened and one day his father came and took him away. I never saw or heard of him again.

After Billy had gone, I was told that I had to do his jobs as well as my own, so I had to get up even earlier in the mornings – nobody ever had a lie in! On Saturdays I had to walk into the village to fetch a joint of meat and on Sundays I was sent to Sunday School and then on to church. For a while I was in the choir and then I had the job of pumping the church organ. Sunday afternoons I could please myself what I did – as long as I did not go off the farm. No other children were allowed on the farm.

Some weekends aunty would give me a pile of old crockery and I would sit in the barn and smash the crockery into tiny pieces to be used as grit for the chickens.

Aunty and uncle were very nervous about the war, although the war never came to Clifton, apart from a few incendiary bombs which the village Home Guard dealt with. But there were a few bombs dropped on other villages close by; once a German aircraft crashed in the next village of Lullington. Aunty would lie awake at night and at the first sound of a German plane on its way to bomb targets in the Midlands, she would get us all up and we would walk around the farm, well away from the buildings, and we would stay out until we heard the planes going home.

I remember one particular night when the skies in the direction of Coventry were bright red – like an early sunrise! There were a few nights when we stayed out so long, it was too late to go back to bed and it was on one of these nights when we came across a band of gypsies stealing a pen of young cockerels.

As the war progressed and we heard we were winning, some of the evacuees started to go back home. Our teacher, Mr Bell, was recalled to Thanet and, after he left, the curtain that had parted us in the classroom came down and those of us who were left were integrated with the village children.

When I reached the age of eleven it was time to leave Clifton School and go to Mercia Boys' Secondary Modern School in Tamworth. A Midland Red school bus left Clifton at 8.30 in the morning, picking up children in the villages on the way to Tamworth. When I started at the big school, aunty told me not to bother about exams as I would never be as clever as her son Frank who went to the grammar school. My time at Mercia Boys wasn't very happy. In the woodwork class everyone had to wear an apron. Aunty wouldn't get me one so I always had to stand outside the classroom. Neither would she buy me swimming trunks, so I never got any swimming lessons, instead I had to go to another classroom and sit in the corner and read.

Aunty would tell me that people who worked on farms didn't need much education. She more or less destroyed all my confidence at school and, when I did leave a few years later, I had no qualifications whatsoever.

Life went on and the war was coming to an end. All the other evacuees had left the village for home and the day finally came when I was to go. It was a cold January morning and a car came to the farm to pick me up. In a strange kind of way I didn't want to go. I think I had been brainwashed into thinking that this was the only life for me. That morning, for the first time ever, aunty and uncle kissed and cuddled me. I was eight and a half when I first arrived at the farm and I was thirteen when I left; in all that time nobody had kissed or cuddled me. I couldn't respond because I didn't know how, and even today in my late sixties, I still feel awkward when I have to do it outside my own family.

When I arrived back at Margate station, my father and sisters were waiting to meet me. My mother couldn't be there because she was ill and bedridden. As we walked through the streets of Margate I was shown the damage that had been done by the bombing and the shelling and when we reached our house I was amazed at how everything seemed so small. I had been used to a fifteen roomed farmhouse and 270 acres.

I entered the house to find my mother lying in bed in the downstairs parlour. How small and frail she was – we both cried our eyes out! During the weeks that followed I became very lonely and, in spite of everything I had gone through during my evacuation, I longed to be back at the farm. My poor mother was lying ill in bed and most of my friends that I knew before the war had left the area, or had made new lives for themselves.

In May 1945 my mother died. It was a very sad time for me because I hadn't really had time to get to know her again. The Brisco family had kept in touch and when I told them of my mother's death, they said I could go back to the farm and work for them. I left school at the age of fourteen with a very poor education and, as there seemed to be nothing for me in Margate anymore, I returned to the farm in Clifton Campville and started full-time work. I finally left the Brisco's a few years later and discovered that it was possible to have a social life. I made new friends and eventually married a local girl in the small village church at Hopwas, near Tamworth. We have had a wonderful life together and we have raised two fine sons. I regret not having a proper childhood with my mother and father, but I have never yearned to return to my home town of Margate.

We finish this chapter on a sombre note. Many, many World War II evacuees died for one reason or another while being separated from their natural parents. The following article is of one such incident. On 29th November, 1940, the Isle of Thanet Gazette *reported the tragic death of a young Margate evacuee:*

MARGATE EVACUEE DROWNED
Girl Disappears In River – A Fatal Paddle

The tragic news was received in Margate on Sunday (24th November) that a school-girl evacuated to Staffordshire in June had been drowned in the River Trent. The child was Eileen Hills, eight-years-old daughter of Mr and Mrs F. T. Hills, of Osborne Terrace, Margate, who previously attended Drapers Mills School, and was sent to King's Bromley, near Burton-on-Trent.

Up to Wednesday morning dragging operations had failed to find her body. It appears that on Saturday afternoon Eileen went out with two other girls and entered a field which was fenced and had barbed wire round. They reached the river which had overflowed its banks and Eileen, who had a pair of Wellington boots on, said she was going to paddle. As part of the field was under water the river bank could not be seen. Eileen took a few steps forward, lost her foothold, and slipped into several feet of water. The river had a good flow and she was quickly carried away.

Her companions ran back to their billet and very soon men were on the spot searching for any sign of the girl. They were followed by others, who commenced dragging operations. The river was running so strongly that the child's body was carried away quickly. It is considered doubtful whether an adult could have fought against the flow.

Mr J. C. Aspden, the director of education, and members of his staff went from Lichfield to the scene immediately they were informed of the tragedy and helped in the constant watch which was kept on the river for several days for signs of the girl.

The news was sent to Margate by telegram and Alderman W. C. Redman, chairman of the Education Committee, saw the parents. He arranged for the father, who is a local fisherman, to go to Staffordshire on Monday.

Author's note: It was also reported that Eileen Hills was the third evacuee to be drowned in the River Trent.

Chapter Six

PRIVATE EVACUATION

Not all families took advantage of the Government Evacuation Scheme. Some of those that did not, took it upon themselves either to send their children to a safer place, or in some circumstances, to evacuate the entire family.

Peter Rogers *was privately evacuated from the Thanet area in 1940. He recalls below some near disasters as the war seemed to follow him around:*

In 1939 I was twelve years old, attending St John's Secondary School and living with my parents who ran a boarding house in Margate. When the war started we had a number of soldiers billeted with us, as did many other households.

Following the evacuation of troops from Dunkirk in May and early June 1940, we were told that we would have to evacuate our premises as the town was soon to become a 'restricted area'. My school was evacuated to Staffordshire but my family

Peter Rogers, on the right, with his friend, Christopher Fright, at Margate in 1939

arranged to go and stay with relatives who lived in Sudbury Town, Middlesex, which up till then had not suffered any bombing. But the bombers eventually came! After one bombing raid at about 10.30pm, a gas main was fractured and the air raid warden, smelling the gas, instigated the gas alarm by the use of hand-held wooden rattles, causing everyone to don their gas masks. Unfortunately, when the cause of the smell was located, nobody thought to sound the all-clear, and we all sat around with our gas masks on until the general all-clear was sounded the next morning at 5.30am – seven hours we had sat there with our masks on!

After about five or six months we had the roof of our house blown off when a land mine came down in the next street – which meant we had to move to some other relatives in Eltham. Just three months later this house was destroyed after we had fled for safety into the Anderson shelter in the back garden.

It was this near-disaster that made my parents decide that I should be evacuated with the local school. My parents at this time were both engaged on war work and had to stay in London. Anyway, I ended up on Lady Lodge Farm about three miles outside Peterborough, where the farmer, Mr King, was most interested in my adventures and used to ask what a bomb sounded like coming down. There was no running water on the farm, or electricity! Lighting used to be by oil lamps and our water had to be pumped up by hand over a sink in the scullery. We bathed in a tin bath and the toilet was outside and was called an earth closet.

For a short while I went to school in the village public house, where I was told to look after the 7 to 8 year olds, as I was the oldest, being nearly 14. When I left school I worked on the farm which I really enjoyed because everyone was so good to me. When the ewes were having lambs in the spring, some of the lambs would be rejected by their mothers or became orphans. These lambs had to be bottle fed and this job was given to me. In time they became quite tame and would come running to me when I called them in from the field. When my mother came to visit me later on, she said she would like to see the lambs, so we went out to the paddock and I called them. When they came running, my mother was terrified because by then the lambs had grown into full size sheep – and mum had been expecting baby lambs!

Unfortunately, in 1942, a German bomber, assumed to be returning from a raid on the Midlands, jettisoned his stick of five bombs right across the farm house, causing considerable damage. Luckily nobody was really hurt. The only casualty was the other evacuee whose name was Ronnie. When I had helped the farmer to get his mother to safety, I went back to find Ronnie. When I got to his bedroom I found that an oak cupboard door had been sucked out of its frame and had landed across him, knocking him out, but we got him out safely. As I was getting out of the house I heard a loud ticking noise and, looking through what was left of the study window, I saw in the remains of the room, lying at an angle, what I took to be a delayed action bomb, upon which we all departed the area at very high speed!

As no one had heard of our predicament, I said I would run down to the nearest village and notify the air raid wardens. When I arrived at the village dressed in pyjamas and wellington boots, which incidentally were on the wrong feet, I met the warden on duty who happened to be the farm foreman. On telling him that we had been bombed out, he said that he didn't believe me and said that I had probably had a nightmare owing to my previous experiences in London. However, I convinced him that it had really happened because I was covered in soot and plaster, so he alerted the required services. When they arrived at the farm it was about 3.30am and still dark. I mentioned the unexploded bomb and everybody stayed well clear of the building until daylight. It was then that the fire chief took a careful look at the 'bomb'. It turned out to be a grandfather clock that had been blown over, losing its pendulum, but still rapidly ticking away!

Following this last attempt by 'Jerry' to get me, it was agreed that I would be just as safe in Margate, where I returned in 1942 to stay with an uncle even though my parents were still away on war work – my dad travelling around the factories of the Midlands and mum working in the War Office in Liverpool. From there I suppose my life progressed to being called up for service in the army where I spent four years, being 'demobbed' in 1949. I had left the family home when I was twelve years old, and I didn't return to it until ten long years later.

I returned to the Peterborough area years later, just for a visit, but unfortunately the farmer had passed away. The farm had been sold and the land was now a housing estate complete with shops! The actual farmhouse, however, was still there as a listed building and had become a heritage centre.

I must say that, despite being bombed out, I enjoyed my time staying with the King family at Lady Lodge Farm and, who knows, had things been different, I may well have stayed on in that area!

Colin Gardner *recalls the events early in the war and how he was destined not to return to his home town of Margate:*

One abiding memory of those early days in Margate is of soldiers with fixed bayonets at railway bridges, stopping everyone and asking to see identity cards, which was very frightening to a seven year old. At school, when the register was called, we had to state our identity card number.

When the schools were evacuated in 1940 my parents didn't want me to go. They wanted the whole family to stay together. As the school children were leaving, my best friend came to say goodbye and as a parting present he gave me a china rabbit. I still have that rabbit, and the price is still in pencil underneath – 1/9d!

When Dunkirk was evacuated in 1940, my mother and I went to Margate promenade, but were stopped when we reached the Nayland Rock Hotel and were told that civilians could go no further. The bay was full of every type of boat and soldiers were laid out all along the promenade. Some of the soldiers had clothes, but there were many who did not, so we went back home and collected all the spare clothes we could find and took them down to the soldiers.

After Dunkirk our family was ordered to leave. We were only allowed to take one case each. My parents decided to take us to Gloucester where both came from.

After a long journey we arrived at Gloucester, to be billeted on various relatives until we got a small condemned house – three rooms, a lean-to and a W.C. at the end of the garden. We finally ended up living with my grandparent.

Life in Gloucester was very different from what we had been used to. Nobody believed what we had seen back home in Margate.

After the war my parents decided not to return to Kent, so we settled in Gloucester.

In July 1995 I visited Margate for the first time in 55 years. Nothing seemed to have changed. Unfortunately I was unable to trace anybody I had known in 1940. I had always wanted to come back to Margate. Now that I have done so I am quite happy to have seen it. I do not think I will return.

June Peete *(now Mrs Durham) was privately evacuated to the Rhondda Valley, in South Wales, for most of the war period:*

In May 1940 I left my home in Ramsgate and was taken to relatives in Gilfach Goch in the Rhondda Valley. The following month I had my fifth birthday. Because I stayed with relations I was probably a lot more fortunate than many other evacuees.

My time in Wales was one of the most happiest periods of my life and my aunt, uncle and cousin were to have a great influence on my life. They were very poor but very loving. My uncle was a deacon of the local chapel and aunty was also involved in chapel work, so I was fortunate to have a Christian upbringing.

I had a good education at the local school and became well integrated with the Welsh education system. I remember that the winters seemed to be long and hard, with plenty of snow, and that the summers were always sunny. I can also remember the RAIN which seemed to persist for days and days!

I was a very sickly child in Wales but, after having my tonsils removed, my health improved greatly. The operation was carried out on the kitchen table one Sunday evening by a visiting surgeon. Imagine what the National Health Service would have to say about that today!

While I was in Wales, my grandmother, who was still living in Ramsgate, wrote a little poem for me which I treasure to this day. When I used to recite it I was aware of people dabbing their eyes, because it was all about 'The Little Evacuee' and about my father being a prisoner of war. It is reproduced below.

In January 1945 I finally returned home to Ramsgate. I was nine and a half years old and I had great difficulty in adjusting to a totally new life style. I used to return to Gilfach Goch every year and for many years spent all my summer holidays with my aunty and uncle. I shall never forget their love and kindness.

> I am only a little evacuee
>   And my name is June Peete.
> I live with kind friends over there
>   In Abercerdin Street.
>
> I've found a lot of little friends
>   Who share with me their toys.
> I'm happy when I'm playing
>   With these girls and boys.
>
> Our house is near a mountainside
>   And, when the day is good,
> We play amongst the hills and dales,
>   The bracken and the wood.

My mamma's working very hard
  To keep me safely here.
She still lives in a blitzed old town,
  But yet she knows no fear.

My daddy was a soldier,
  And fought so hard at Crete,
But they were all out-numbered
  And forced into retreat.

And then the Germans caught him
  And took him far away,
But God will send him back to me
  And that is what I pray.

I say my prayers each evening
  When I kneel at auntie's knee,
And remember all my dear ones
  In that town by the sea.

Nanny Peete.

Chapter Seven

THE SCHOOLS' PERSPECTIVE

We must not forget that, in the period leading up to and through the evacuation, the evacuating schools faced total disruption. At first some of them had to contend with the influx of young evacuees from other parts of Kent and London. Later, during the early months of 1940, the schools had to live with air raids and shelling as an almost daily occurrence. Air raid trenches and shelters had to be constructed in haste and the teaching of lessons became almost impossible. When their own evacuation was thrust upon them, most East Kent schools had just seven days in which to prepare.

We must also remember the fact that when the school children were evacuated, the family life of the teachers who accompanied them was also totally disrupted – and the teachers had the seemingly impossible task of finding school accommodation when the evacuees finally reached their destination. Teachers accompanying the children also found that they had new and additional responsibilities thrust upon them once they reached the reception areas. They took on the role of surrogate parents, to become in fact, *in loco parentis,* with the welfare of the children in their care high on their list of priorities.

Although records of many schools were lost during and after the war period, some are still available and this chapter will include some excerpts from school log books and admissions registers, and will also contain personal accounts and extracts from other school sources.

The following extract from the admissions register of **Minster C. E. Primary School,** *Isle of Thanet, shows a list of children from* **Rainham Junior School,** *Gillingham, who were evacuated to Minster. Date of admission to the school – 19th September 1939:*

Edith Hammond	David Payne	Maureen Lawrie
Gordon Moseling	Peter Baker	Julian Davies
Christine Fullager	Marie Knight	Audrey Beer
Alan Payne	Eileen Payne	Rosemary Long
Peter Milliner		

Eric Taylor and James Pawsey were admitted to the school on 25th September 1939.

Note written in admissions register: Children evacuated under the Government Scheme. Omitted from admissions register on instructions from area office 26th

September 1939.

Placed on register 29th September 1939 on instructions from Head Office. (Circular received 29th September 1939).

Other children evacuated to Minster included the following:

Keith Neville Fletcher, Stone C.E. School,

Brian Edward Fletcher, Dartford.

These two were admitted 3rd October 1939 under the Government Scheme (Expectant Mothers). All returned home by 3rd November 1939.

Barrymore Ross Offord – Central Park, East Ham, London, admitted 28th September 1939 – returned home 15th December 1939.

* * *

The following is an extract from the log book of **Minster C. E. Primary School** *for the war years:*

1939

17th Oct.	Air raid warning at 1.55. 'All clear' at 3.20.
30th Oct.	Air raid warning at 9.15. 'All clear' at 9.20.
9th Nov.	The ALO called with regard to transfer of Rainham teachers to Preston.

1940

1st Jan.	Mr A. W. M. Standidge, from Crayford Infants School reports for Special Duty at 11.30am.
1st Jan.	Major Howard took 11 shillings and 3d being school collections for War Comforts Fund.
12th Feb.	Heavy snowfall.
13th Feb.	Heavy snowfall.
22nd Feb.	Miss Babbage finished here today. Reports at Rainham on 26th inst.
21st May.	School finishes at 3.15 to enable Wartime Cooking Lectures to start at 3.30. Five present.
31st May.	No D.S. today. Broadstairs evacuating.
2nd June.	Meeting in Staff Room at 2.30 to get details of evacuation. Present: The Director, Mr Robson (Ministry of Health), Rev. McMichael, Mr Griggs (Dist. Secy. Deal), Miss Freeman, HM of Monkton, Miss Jobson, HM of Minster Infants, Mr Hitchcock, HM of St Nicolas, and Mr H. R. Cooke, HM of Minster. Detailed arrangements were given by the Director. Mr Robson arranges transport to East Grinstead or Horsham by bus.
28th June	Children who were registered for evacuation – 65. 57 remain in Minster, but some are evacuating privately. Medical inspection p.m. Dr. Lessey, Nurses Cheeseman and nurse from Womanswold.

Minster School closed today

Signed,
H. R. Cooke (HM)

(There were no further entries until 1942.)

1942
9th Mar.   I resumed duty today as Headmaster Minster C.E. School after leaving East Grinstead.

Signed,
H. R. Cooke.

12th Mar.   Mr E. Earl called to investigate a site for the additional shelter.
13th July.   Miss M. Bassett reported for duty today.
Full-time school was commenced for the senior children.
Class I – Headmaster
Class II – Mrs Butts
Miss Bassett Class IV in mornings and Class III afternoons.

1945
8th-9th May   V.E. Days.

* * *

The following is an extract from the school log book of **St Lawrence Girls' School,** *Ramsgate:*

1939
11.9.39   Owing to the outbreak of war on Sept 3rd no schools in the Borough are reopening today. We report each morning at 10.30am to await instructions. A few girls come up each morning to be given work to do at home.
Miss B. Dobinson, B.A. begins duty today. She reports daily at 10.30am.
20.10.39   All members of staff working daily at the Local Food Office.
26.10.39   Work at Food Office for staff finished.
10.11.39   School open for voluntary attendance of children.
Exceeding 50 per session. Great enthusiasm.

1940
Jan 8th   We reopened this morning, being the first official session since war began. Many children have left the town, chiefly owing to the fact that their fathers have been transferred elsewhere in connection with the RAF. No. on Roll = 122; Present = 114.
An air raid shelter has been built in the school playing field for use by this dept. though as it is incomplete we use the boys' trench this week. Air raid drill is receiving careful attention.
Jan 17th   Numbers attending very depleted owing to heavy snowfall last night.

Jan 29th	Same severe weather and consequently low attendance.
Feb 5th to Mar 11th	Low attendance due to German Measles epidemic.
Mar 21st	We close for the Easter vacation at noon. Four patchwork blankets, made from squares knitted by children, have been sent to the United Associations of Great Britain and France (Solidarity Committee). These are to be sent to the French refugees.
Apr 1st	Reopen 9am. No. on Roll 121. 10 children have left owing to removal etc.
Apr 20th	Examination of children for Free Place Scholarships at the Girls' County School. 21 girls from this dept. for the examination at Clarendon House. I accompanied them as it was requested that a member of staff from the larger supplying schools should be present on account of danger from air raids.
May 10th	Close for Whitsuntide vacation.
May 14th	Reopened under instructions from the B. of E. All staff present. 112 girls present. 122 girls on Roll.
May 22nd	An air raid warning was sounded last night at 10.35pm. The 'All Clear' went at 11.45pm. 106 girls were present out of a total roll of 120. All are calm and collected – we had a practice warning this morning.
May 24th	Empire Day celebrated in the hall by whole school. National songs, prayers – Empire message read – Hymn 165 – National Anthem. Miss Harradine has supplied a medical certificate for 'Nervous Debility', and has been ordered by her doctor to leave Ramsgate.
May 27th	Owing to the serious developments in the war, the Government has decided to evacuate the children in this area. Arrangements are in hand for the conveyance of all children whose parents so wish, to some place of greater safety.
June 1st	Attended morning session for final arrangements for evacuation. 75 girls are accompanying our school.
June 2nd	Assemble 10am. Proceed to station 11.15am. Train leaves for Uttoxeter at 11.40am.

(There are no entries in the school logbook for the period of the evacuation, the next entry being 1942 when the school in Ramsgate reopened in April as a Junior Mixed Department. In September 1942 the school reopened as a Junior Girls School with 72 girls on Roll. Air raids continued of course, with the children spending much of their time in the shelters, and this continued until the end of the war.)

* * *

The following is a list of most of the pupils from **Dame Janet Junior Mixed School**, *Newington Road, Ramsgate, who were evacuated in June 1940 to Stafford under the Government Evacuation Scheme:*

Norman Allen	Thomas Allen	Rosetta Arnold
Violet Arnold	Peter Ashby	John Attwell
Pat Baldwin	Joan Barlow	Derek Barlett
Ernest Bean	Douglas Beath	Alice Beddow
Nora Bell	Stella Bell	Hilda Birch
Peter Blackburn	Harry Blakemore	John Blewitt
Vera Booth	Olive Brown	Stephen Burns
June Card	Peter Carter	Urban Cartland
Derek Castle	Kenneth Castle	Wilfred Cavell
Joyce Chapman	Dorothy Clapson	Brenda Cobley
Pamela Cock	Roy Cocks	Terrence Cole
Margaret Colegate	Joan Collison	Betty Conway
Elsie Conway	Herbert Covus	Dorothy Cox
Pat Cox	Violet Cox	Daphne Dawkins
Frank Dunn	Joyce Dunn	Margaret Elen
Donald Ellender	Bruce Ellis	Stephen Elms
May Farrell	Margaret File	Bernard Flynn
Francis Flynn	John Foster	Jean Fuller
Roger Gifford	Edward Gill	Frank Gill
Peter Gilman	Harry Goodban	Joan Goodchild
Ronald Green	Ron Groombridge	Rita Guttridge
Peter Hall	Walter Hammond	Maurice Harding
Tony Harding	Frances Hardwick	Jean Hardwick
Muriel Harris	Anthony Henley	Donald Hill
Albert Hipwell	Ron Hipwell	Peter Homersham

Dame Janet County Junior School, Newington, Ramsgate, pictured in 1998

Mavis Hook	Margaret Hougham	Joseph Howard
Robert Howard	Sylvia Howells	Pauline Hughes
Thomas Hunter	Robert Hurst	Ronald Hudson
Norman Hulme	Anthony Jakes	Eric James
Monica James	Robert James	Beryl Johnson
May Johnson	Richard Johnson	Robert Johnson
Maureen Jones	Irene Jump	Kenneth Keeler
Thelma Kemp	Kathleen Knibbs	Ena Mabel Langton
Raymond Larkin	Winifred Larkin	Eileen Lednor
Eric Lodge	Agnes Longstaff	Harrison Marsh
Vera Marsh	Barbara Matthews	Dyllys May
John May	Ray McColl	Malcolm Middlemiss
Albert Mills	George Mills	Jean Mills
Eric Mirams	Marguerite Moody	Edward Munday
John Newing	Sylvia Newman	Peter Nixon
Gilbert Olive	Ray Osbourne	Evelyn Peakall
Ethel Pearce	Donald Pearce	Fred Pearce
Stephen Penny	David Perkins	Rosalind Phillips
Derek Philpott	Beryl Pitcher	John Pitcher
Alice Pollard	Victor Pollard	Alan Reford
Julia Richardson	Derek Rickwood	Phylis Rickwood
Sylvia Robson	Pamela Ruskin	June Sawtell
Mary Searle	Edward Setterfield	June Slesson
Don Smith	Hazel Smith	Ian Smith
John Smith	Peter Smith	Roy Smith
Pat Stupples	Enid Sturgess	Barbara Tilbrook
Joan Tilbrook	Dennis Thorpe	Ken Toombes
Ruth Upcher	Ronald Walker	Joan Webb
Brenda White	Derek White	Margaret Williams
Leslie Woodward		

Other pupils from **Dame Janet Mixed Junior School** *who were evacuated privately: include the following:*

Jill Easte – to Norfolk
Raymond James – to Surrey
Winnie Pott – to Essex
William Harrison – to Durham
Kathleen Limburn – to Worthing
Barbara Preston – to Worcester

* * *

The following are extracts from the school log book of **Holy Trinity CE Primary School, Ramsgate:**

1939
11 Sep   All teachers instructed by LEA to report at school each day at 10.30am. Schools remaining closed owing to the outbreak of war.

1940

8 Jan	School reopened for the first time since war started on September 3rd 1939. Hours of attendance 9–11.45am and 1.15pm – 3.15pm. Five staff at school. Time was spent in air-raid drill.
9 Jan	Gas masks inspection and drill.
16 Jan	Severe blizzard started about 3pm.
22 Jan	The blizzard has continued throughout the week, and is still blowing. Snow several feet deep. Number present this a.m. 85 ie 45%.
10 May	Gas mask drill held today. Roll 197. Average attendance 181.7 ie 92.2%. ARP officials visited and changed padlock on school air-raid shelter in order to make tunnel available to public during the weekends. School closed this p.m. for the Whitsun holiday of 1 week.
14 May	School reopened today (Tuesday) by order of the Government, owing to the war situation. As a result of this short notice and poor railway facilities, Mr L. H. Tombs, Miss M. E. Hubbard and Miss D. Ewell were unable to return in time.
20 May	Attendance down today owing possibly to a very disturbed weekend – gunfire! Air-raid drill held today.
27 May	Evacuation for Ramsgate was ordered in weekend. Owing to this and the air-raid on Saturday night, many have already left. Evacuation forms were sent out this morning to all on the school roll. As a result of the clerical work involved in Evacuation, the timetable will be modified this week.
28 May	An air-raid warning was given this morning at 11.50am. The school proceeded to the tunnel and remained there until 12.45pm. One boy (V. Fox) lost his head and ran home. Apart from this everything went according to plan.
31 May	Roll 176. Today school closed as Evacuation is planned for Sunday
2 June	School will be opened on Saturday for Evacuation Purposes. According to instructions, all registers, stock books, log books and keys are to be sent to the office.

(The next entry in the log book is not until 1942)

1942

13 April	School reopened today for Junior Scholars only. 73 children were admitted. Staff: Mr L. H. Tombs and Miss L. Geary. Air-raid alerts: 11.40am – 12 Noon and 3.10pm – 3.55pm
20 April	Admitted 30 more children today. Number on roll is now 108. My limit is 110.

(Shell warnings and air-raid alerts continued throughout 1942, 1943 and 1944, affecting attendance)

1945

1 May	Mrs E. J. Crosbie returned from evacuation in Stafford to the staff of this school today. She is to take the Infants Class.
8 May	V.E. DAY. – After assembly the school proceeded to church for a service of thanksgiving. The school then closed until Friday.

* * *

The following are extracts from the log book of **St Mildred's C P Infants' School, Broadstairs:**

1939

Aug 4th	School closed for Summer Holiday.
Aug 16th	Teachers recalled owing to serious international situation.
Sept 3rd	War declared.
Sept 19th	Owing to the war, school opened for only 60 children each session (a.m. and p.m.) today.
Oct 11th	Air Raid Shelters measured out etc by Grummant Bros. Work begun.
Oct 17th	Raid warning. Children living close sent home, others accommodated in cloak-rooms.
Nov 20th	Head teacher visited Wellesley House School with Mr Hutcherson with a view to its being used as a schoolroom for the infants.
Dec 4th	Wellesley House taken over by the military!
Dec 22nd	School closed for one week's holiday.

1940

Jan 8th	School open full time for all children 7+.
Jan 12th	Mr Martin HMI visited – stayed about half an hour.
Jan 18th	School closed owing to bad weather. Deep snow and no conveyances. Lavs frozen.
Jan 23rd	Only 40 children present . . . owing to continued snow.
Jan 30th	Lavatories still frozen. Fifty children at school in morning. School closed p.m.
Feb 13th	Lavatories again unusable owing to frost. School closed.
Mar 20th	School closed for Easter Holiday.
Apr 24th	Miss Little gave the first of a series of lecture-demonstrations on Cooking and Feeding in War Time. Nine people present.
May 10th	School closed for Whitsun Holiday.
May 14th	School reopened owing to war emergency.
May 31st	School closed. Children to be evacuated under the Government Scheme War emergency Act on Sunday June 2nd.

(The next log book entry is not until November 1940)

Nov 27th	The head teacher returned after filling a temporary headship at Lodge

Hill School, Welling, Kent from Sept 30th to Nov 25th. Miss Browne also returned from a temporary post at Eythorne.

The school to be used as a centre for the supply of milk to school children, for medical supervision etc. from Nov 27th 1940.

1942

Jan 5th	School reopened for compulsory full time education for all girls and infants 5-14 years. Roll 68. Head and one assistant in charge.
Mar 2nd	Miss Wallace resumed duty here on her return from Tamworth.
Oct 26th	Miss Rouse returned to duty here from Tamworth.
Nov 23rd	The Public Assistance Committee having vacated the School Hall, the top class is now being accommodated there.

1943

Apr 20th	School closed for the afternoon. Concert given by children in aid of Prisoners of War Fund. £14.3s collected.
Oct 1st	Attendance fell to 59% owing to measles epidemic.

1944

Feb 20th	Miss F. Browne retired after working 26 years at this school.
June 12th	School opened after Whitsun Holiday. Class II now using the end room on the girls' side (vacated by British Restaurant)
July 10th	Miss Wallace ill after bombing last night.

1945

May 8th – 10th	V.E. Day celebrated by two days holiday and Ascension Day.

* * *

The following selected log book excerpts are from **Ellington Boys School, Ramsgate:**

1940

May	The school's war efforts – saving paper and rag collection. The boys also collected £1.3s.0d for cigarettes for forces overseas.
May 27	Evacuation of school children from this area announced on wireless news at 9pm last evening. Forms distributed for return not later than Wednesday 1pm.
May 28	Air Raid warning at 11.50am. Children went to shelter quite orderly. All Clear sounded at 12.25pm. Afternoon attendance not adversely affected.
May 29	Evacuation list closed today. 125 children from this school are being evacuated; of the remaining 54, 14 are decidedly 'NO', no reply 18, and voluntary evacuees number 22. Two children have 'tacked' to our roll, one from a private school and the other a compassionate transfer. Contex filters were fitted to gas masks this morning.

May 31	School closed today. Evacuation to ? is on Sunday June 2nd and the evacuees from this school were told to meet at school tomorrow (Saturday) with their younger brothers and sisters so that the party could be checked and final instructions given. Younger brother evacuees in this dept. will assemble with parties containing the eldest child.	
June 1	The children duly assembled at 9am and were put in order for moving away at 11.45am tomorrow, Sunday June 2nd. 202 assembled, several being absent. Instructions given.	
June 2nd	EVACUATION DAY. Children and helpers assembled at 11.45am. Train to leave at 1pm. In charge: myself. Helpers: the staff, 4 teachers' wives and one parent, Mrs Palmer. Number of children: 201.	

(There were no further entries in the school log book until the following entry written in 1943):

EVACUATION: The Ellington Senior Boys' party consisting of the staff and children (with the younger brothers and sisters) of the school went to Stafford on Sunday June 2nd (1940). The children were sent to the following schools: Stafford Senior Boys' School, Walton C of E School, Gayton C of E School. Relatives of boys sent to Stafford Senior Boys' School were sent to Holmcroft Infants' School, Stone Road Infants' School and Corporation Street Junior School. Education re-started in Ramsgate, August 25th 1941. Miss Dexter had charge of the children attending the Ellington Centre. The return of evacuees finally led to the re-opening of all the schools in the Borough and this department returned to its pre-war function on April 1st 1943.

Signed, J Hartley.

* * *

The following lists represent some of those children who were evacuated with **Ellington Boys' School, Ramsgate,** *to Stafford in June 1940:*

John Atkinson	Derek Attwell	Alfred Bailey
Donald Bartrum	Reginald Baverstock	Donald Beard
George Blake	William Bodley	Dennis Booth
Leslie Bridger	Frank Burrill	Dennis Bushell
Ronald Carter	Ernest Cavell	John Chambers
Stanley Chapman	Geoffrey Cleaver	Eric Cole
Ronald Conway	Raymond Cook	Leonard Corns
Gordon Crompton	Leslie Curris	Sidney Dalton
Donald Dean	Cyril Dines	John Dorrington
Howard Dunn	Harold Farnham	Albert Farrell
Kenneth Fisher	Edward Friend	George Fuller
Kenneth Gapper	Vernon Gapper	James Gifford
Melvyn Giles	Norman Gillman	Leslie Green
Peter Greenstreet	Sydney Goldsmith	David Griggs

John Hall	Raymond Hall	George Hamilton
Sidney Hamilton	Gordon Hammond	Thomas Heritage
Hubert Hitch	Melvin Hook	Jack Hougham
Derek Hurst	Albert Isaacs	John Isaacs
George Jenner	Leonard Jennings	Geoffrey Jones
Frank Keen	Deric King	James Lay
Dennis Lawless	Sidney Leman	Donald Lowe
David Maxted	Ernest Maxted	Patrick McLeary
Gordon Middlemiss	David Moon	Kenneth Moyles
Eric Oclee	Mervyn Palmer	Ronald Palmer
Derek Pardin	Ernest Penny	Peter Philpott
Ronald Pierce	Gerald Pointer	Samuel Prewett
Roland Redford	Harry Richardson	John Rippin
Robert Rogers	Paul Rowney	Charles Saunders
Dennis Sayer	Cecil Sheppard	Arthur Shiel
Leslie Silk	Fred Sinclair	Victor Skingle
John Skinner	Alfred Smith	Derek Smith
Stephan Spain	Bernard Stanner	Arthur Taft
Colin Tinkler	Reginald Voisey	Dennis Waghorn
Alfred Walker	Cyril Webb	Frank White
Albert Whitcombe	Colin Whitham	Dennis Williams
Ronald Williams	Stanley Williams	Cyril Wilkinson
John Wilkinson	George Yandle	Cyril Young

* * *

__Marjorie Friend__ (now Mrs Marshall) was a teacher in Thanet at the time of evacuation, and went with her school to Tamworth:

On the outbreak of the war I was teaching at St Peter's Primary School. Life went on much as usual with occasional trips to the dug-out shelters in the playground. It was June 2nd, 1940 that we were told to assemble for evacuation at Broadstairs railway station, to be taken to Tamworth in Staffordshire. I had lodgings in Broadstairs but, of course, I had gone home to Deal to pack my case and say cheerio. When I arrived at Deal station on the morning of the 2nd June to go to Broadstairs, each train was filled with soldiers who had been rescued from Dunkirk.

That was an experience! They were dirty, tired and bloody, and were given copious cups of tea from ladies on the platform. I sat there waiting and hoping for a train with a spot of room – and receiving more 'wolf whistles' than anyone could possibly have! In the end I gave up and went back home and found someone with some petrol to spare to take me to Broadstairs – just in time for the line-up. As far as I remember, no-one was very upset at leaving or losing their youngsters.

It was an adventure of course and we hadn't gone far before packed food was opened and devoured. We arrived in Tamworth early evening and assembled in a large one-storey building where the children were soon sorted and taken to their billets. The staff was left till last and, with a colleague, I was taken to a very imposing house. The interior was all dark oak, and very gloomy! The gentleman there made me feel uncomfortable and I was glad that no children had been taken there. Later, I moved to another family, the town's drapery shop owner with a young baby and I was really happy there. We had no worries as far as the children's accommodation was concerned, except for one thing.

We had with us a number of girls who lived in the Tait Home. They were there for a number of reasons – orphans, ill mothers, health matters, etc. They had been well disciplined in the home, but in Tamworth they were 'free' and were allowed to go out and wander in Tamworth when not in school. One of these youngsters was made so welcome in her new home, that the family wanted to adopt her, but that was not possible. The school in which we had to have lessons, made us welcome, but it must have been very difficult for them. Luckily the weather was good, so much of our time was spent outside.

Our headmaster and his wife, Mr and Mrs Bird, were able to rent a cottage called 'The Garden' and I remember Mrs Bird told me that she felt truly guilty at being so happy there. Gradually the children returned to Broadstairs and I came back in the September as fewer teachers were needed to stay with the evacuees. I was then sent to the village school in Rolvenden, where, oddly enough, there were evacuees from Plumstead.

A schools inspector came there and persuaded me to go back to Margate, where there were older girls who had not been evacuated or had returned home. I was then able to get back to Deal every night. The drive home was a bit frightening at times, especially the time when Calais was burning and planes were buzzing about. Finally, I was married a year to the day after evacuation, so 2nd June has a special meaning for me.

* * *

One of the first Thanet 'seats of learning' to be evacuated during the second world war was St Lawrence College in Ramsgate. The following article appeared in the Isle of Thanet Gazette *for Friday, 12th January 1940:*

RAMSGATE COLLEGE LEAVES
St Lawrence Wartime Move

St Lawrence College, founded in 1879, is to leave Ramsgate because of the war. It is being amalgamated with Seaford College, Sussex, and will reopen at Seaford at the beginning of the spring term. Founded by the South Eastern Clerical and Lay Alliance to give a public school education upon an evangelical religious basis, St Lawrence was first known as the South Eastern College.

It opened under the presidency of the Dean of Canterbury (the Very Revd R. Payne-Smith) at Dane Park, Ramsgate, in September of 1879. The Revd E. C. d'Auquier was headmaster and there were five pupils. The college soon prospered and at the end of two years there were 50 boys attending. By 1886 the number had reached well over 200. The Alliance administered the school until 1892 when it was incorporated as a public school under the Corporation of the South Eastern College.

In 1885 a junior school was opened and ten years later another block, known as the Hoare Memorial Wing, was erected. A further ten years elapsed and the two blocks were united by the building of the tower, which was opened in October, 1905 by the Archbishop of Canterbury, the late Lord Davidson. It was built in memory of the school's second president, Mr John Deacon.

THE FIRST EVACUATION

It was in the following year, 1906, that the college changed its name and took that of the parish in which it was situated. When the Great War came Ramsgate was bombarded from the sea and it was decided to evacuate the school. In 1916 the senior school moved to Chester and the junior school to Carmarthen.

Over 600 Old Lawrentians served with the forces during the Great War, and of that number 129 lost their lives. After the war the upper school returned in January, 1919, and the following term the juniors were reunited with the seniors at Ramsgate. In 1927 the War Memorial Chapel was erected and dedicated to the memory of those who had lost their lives. It cost £26,000. During the Revd B. V. F. Brackenbury's headmastership, a number of improvements were carried out, including the building of laboratories at a cost of £4,000. Half the cost was provided by the parents of two boys. A new wing was also added to the junior school.

Two years ago Mr Brackenbury left to become headmaster at Chatham House School and he was succeeded at St Lawrence by the Revd R. Perfect, himself an Old Lawrentian. Mr Perfect is to be vice-headmaster of St Lawrence and Seaford College. At a recent headmasters' conference at which St Lawrence was represented, it was recommended that where possible small public schools should amalgamate. The linking of St Lawrence and Seaford College is understood to be the first result of the recommendation.

*   *   *

*The following extracts from the **Lawrentian Centenary Magazine** shows, among other things, that the college's stay at Seaford was short-lived:*

THE EVENTS OF 1940 AND 1941

(The Lawrentian was not published in 1940. An account of the events surrounding the life of the college between the outbreak of war and August 1941 appeared in the magazine of that month.) There must be many who have heard little or nothing of our movements since the outbreak of war and have perhaps been wondering whether there still is a St Lawrence College. In the Christmas term of 1939, we held ourselves ready for immediate action. We might be given a day's warning of evacuation, otherwise the sound of the chapel bell meant zero hour. Rumours of possible destinations flitted round the school, but by the end of the Christmas term nothing had happened.

Then surprise came just after Christmas. A letter was sent round to say that we had amalgamated with Seaford College under their headmaster, W. L. Land Esq. Our first impression of Seaford was not a good one. We arrived after dark, in the deepest of that year's heavy snow, just as it began to thaw. But cramped as our quarters inevitably were, we spent two eventful terms there. Eventful? Two disastrous terms. Calamity dogged us.

Hardly had the snow left us when an epidemic of meningitis broke out. Most of us were promptly sent home and, as far as possible, infection was prevented. The five cases all recovered and we prepared to start afresh with an early and long summer term. The Sussex countryside proved far more interesting than that round Ramsgate. Seaford Head and the Seven Sisters were popular for climbing and cyclists toured the 'sights' from Eastbourne to Brighton and further. Spasmodic cricket was arranged. But the war clouded the peace of the country. Two nights were spent on the hard basement floor; the crash of an exploding mine became no longer an 'event'; we bathed in a sea thickened with flotsam.

And then, as we watched the war map on the wall, we heard that France had fallen. 'Dunkirk' came during half-term and those who lived near Thanet returned with tales of blood and horror. The tension grew; England was about to be invaded; there was nothing for it but a second evacuation; and again the term ended early. Where next? Late in the summer we heard that Major-General Sir Hereward Wake had rented to us his manor at Courteenhall, near Northampton, and St Lawrence was to reassemble there in September as a separate entity again. Hercules was again required, to transform Courteenhall into a school – and he did it. Masters had had to leave, owing to the uncertainty of the school's fortunes, and other masters were not at first forthcoming. We had fewer boys than we had at Ramsgate. Laboratories were non-existent. The Junior School had to share the building with us and at the same time keep their identity. There was nothing to do but to work, and work we did, from the headmaster downwards.

Privations at Courteenhall, 1942.

Perhaps the most drastic change is the number of tasks we now do which once we took for granted. We no longer have anyone to roll the pitches, to make our beds, to clean our shoes. Our latest innovation is sweeping our common rooms, while volunteers have been helping with the washing up. It is not pleasant pushing a heavy roller through the damp cold mist, or carrying a pile of porridge plates, but no one has questioned the necessity of it.

A war-time Headmaster at Courteenhall, 1943.

Three years at Courteenhall has revealed many astonishing things to the editor, but nothing more astonishing than the headmaster. The editor's memory took him back to pre-war days at Ramsgate, when a headmaster was an Olympian figure, secure and secluded from the haunts of small boys like himself. The editor reflected on the present by way of contrast, and on the diverse situations in which he had seen the headmaster's energies expend themselves. He had seen him, when occasion demanded, humping chairs, tables and beds; helping to mark our hockey and cricket pitches; teaching as full a time table as any assistant master; refereeing matches, coaching teams, and occasionally playing himself; all this, and more, on top of his normal work as headmaster. He remembered, too, the stimulating sermons in chapel, produced Sunday after Sunday.

An extract from a letter from an Old Lawrentian who visited the College buildings in Ramsgate in 1944:

'I proceeded up the drive. Everywhere was damp and deserted. Windows in the common room were broken, and the east window of the chapel was boarded up, with bomb splinter marks on the brickwork beneath. A small bomb crater was evident a few yards away. In front of the college the grass on the lawn – once sacred to prefects – was long and uncared for, and the clock had stopped, each of the faces showing a different hour. Inside there seemed to be little damage, but I felt sadness at the unnatural silence and emptiness, with the names on the honours boards and the team photographs reminding me of the friends I once knew.'

A FAREWELL FROM SIR HEREWARD WAKE, 1945, AT COURTEENHALL

We are grateful to Major-General Sir Hereward and Lady Wake, who invited the prefects over to dinner at the end of term. It was a most interesting evening and we heard tales from the Boer War, from the Great War and from all the wars in Christendom! One of us, much to his delight, found that he was sitting in an armchair looted from a Dutch Farm in South Africa! Fortunately Sir Hereward seems to have forgiven us the fact that some of his chickens were once poisoned by pecking up gravel which had been covered with prussic acid from the laboratory sinks!

THE RETURN TO RAMSGATE, 1946

We shall all remember the journey that took place on the afternoon of January 28th of this year. First, the gathering crowd of Lawrentians on Platform One at Victoria Station; the train journey, for which the Southern Railway very kindly put on the 'St Lawrence' engine to haul the train; the arrival at Ramsgate; the first sight of our rightful buildings, and the excitement of entering the place of which we had heard so much. The college as a whole is grateful to those whose industry has enabled us to return to Ramsgate so soon. In particular the headmaster, the bursar and his staff have earned our gratitude, for they sacrificed every free moment of their Christmas holidays to straighten out the confusion involved in large-scale removals. We are also grateful to the boys who voluntarily sacrificed a considerable part of the vacation to assist.

* * *

The following passages were supplied by **Clarendon House Grammar School,** *Ramsgate:*

As soon as the Second World War started about fifty girls left the school immediately. In the winter months, after war was declared, schooling was only on alternate days, and at this time the underground shelters were being opened up and bomb drills were frequent. During these winter months school also finished early, to allow girls to get home before dark, and morning school could be delayed if the sirens sounded and the trams stopped running.

Lessons would be punctuated by sirens and the occasional sound of machine-gun fire. Once when a group of girls was playing netball in the yard, shells came right across the pitch, but mercifully nobody was hurt. Mr Board, the caretaker, was always anxious when the girls were playing outside. Acting as an unofficial sentry he carried binoculars and shouted 'take cover' if firing started.

As things got worse more girls left the school and some of the younger mistresses volunteered for war work. In April 1940, when the Germans were obviously extending their frontier, there was more intensive bombing of Ramsgate Harbour and Manston Airport and the decision was taken to evacuate the elderly and the young. About two hundred Clarendon House girls were evacuated on 2nd June, 1940, having had only one week's notice and no clear indication of their destination, except that it was to be Staffordshire.

The motif of Clarendon House Grammar School for Girls

The evacuation was further complicated by the fact that RAF personnel were being moved to the Midlands from Manston, which had been badly bombed, and many of these men travelled to Stafford on the same day as the girls. Also the evacuation coincided with the Dunkirk operation.

Ramsgate and Margate hospitals were receiving large numbers of troop casualties and as the girls left Thanet they had to walk through men of all nationalities, crowded into the railway stations. As the evacuation trains went through London, people were putting up banners to welcome the men home from Dunkirk. Needless to say train services were very confused and delayed.

When the school arrived in Stafford the younger girls were billeted first. For some of the older girls and staff the experience was traumatic. Joyce Whitehead remembers that she was finally taken in at nine o'clock at night, by a lady cycling up the road who took pity on her. Many of the Stafford women preferred to take the airmen, who spent a good deal of their time on camp, and for whom they were better paid! Miss Whithead believes that it may well have been the staff who suffered most from the evacuation. Initially their books and equipment were late, because of dislocation of road and rail services. Schooling was irregular and billets were unwelcoming.

*Memories of **Marie Cowell**, Head Girl 1940-1941.*

In 1939, the year of the war declaration, we only attended school once a week to collect work to do at home and, later, when the shelters were ready we often had to work in them during an air raid warning before the evacuation on 2nd June 1940.

We didn't go to school on Mondays, but shared Stafford High School and Baswich House with the Stafford School on alternate days including Saturdays. At Baswich House the senior girls took turns at fire-watching with some members of staff. We had to stay in Stafford for the Christmas holidays so various 'activities' were arranged including a Christmas Eve party on Tuesday 24th December 1940.

We supplemented our school dinner rations with cocoa which we made in bulk during the dinner hour and doled it out to such as wanted it. After school we often went out collecting acorns for the local pig farmers, which served two purposes – it helped the war effort and gave yet another opportunity for a house competition!

* * *

Many of the **Clarendon House** *girls did their part for the war effort while they were in Stafford, as the following article shows:*

Several parcels of clothing knitted by members of the school have been despatched; one large packet, containing four grey pullovers, two helmets, six pairs of socks, two pairs of mittens, gloves and seaboot stockings, to the Seamen's Home in Hull; two parcels, with altogether 21 pairs of socks, to the Red Cross Depot, one to the Royal Naval Barracks at Chatham, with socks, seaboot stockings, helmets and gloves.

In 1941, parcels were sent to Mr Stewart, RAF chaplain in Stafford, the Chatham Royal Naval Barracks, and the port chaplain of the Missions to Seamen, Hull. LVa has knitted five balaclava helmets for a group of men guarding a vital point on the South Downs and has also collected money for cigarettes for them. Blankets knitted by Ruskin and Bronte houses, and by Upper Va and Vb have been sent to the WVS for evacuees. With money given by Mrs Kate Helm, Upper Vb bought wool and knitted a child's blanket with furry rabbits on the squares. It was sent to Eastbourne Hospital and is being used by a small Thanet evacuee.

* * *

Finally, towards the end of the war, **Clarendon House Grammar School** *returned to Ramsgate and the following article in the local press welcomed them back:*

HOME AGAIN
WELCOME TO CLARENDON HOUSE GIRLS

Ramsgate has regained something of its pre-war atmosphere by the return of the girls belonging to Clarendon House School. On Friday evening the Deputy Mayor (Councillor Percy Turner) attended at Ramsgate Railway Station and extended a welcome to a contingent which had made the journey back from Stafford. He knew, he said, they were glad to be back and Ramsgate was glad to see them.

A larger party made the journey home the previous day and the scholars were warmly greeted by parents and friends at the various Thanet railway stations. Before they left Stafford the girls received a visit at the Stafford High School from the Mayor of Stafford (Councillor H. Wallace Copeland), who was accompanied by the town clerk and Mrs Broughton Nowell, and Miss Rees, the billeting officer. The headmistress, Miss I. E. Helm, M.A., welcomed the mayor. She spoke briefly on the significance of the evacuation period in the life of the school and commented with satisfaction that the school was able to return home as a whole.

She said she had been much touched and pleased by the offer made by Mr and Mrs Bird, parents of two pupils of the school, of an old painting of Cannock Chase, the work of Mrs Bird's uncle, an exhibitor at the Royal Academy and Paris Salon. This gift would recall many happy memories to all who loved the Chase, and had learnt to know it, during the four-and-a-half years spent in the town.

Miss Helm spoke warmly of the people of Stafford and of the grateful remembrance which the school would cherish. So much, she said, had been done for the school that could not be stated in words: appreciation could not be expressed in words; it could

21 MAYVILLE RD
ST. PETERS
BROADSTAIRS
KENT
C.T.10. 3.E.T

9.2.01

Dear Audrey,
    I would like to thank you very much for your surprise letter received last week. Enclosed please find a copy of the book in question for you to read and keep, or donate it to your local historian at the library in Tamworth, as you say its full of memories.
    Cilla and I hope to be in the West Midlands some time in April, but no date agreed at this time, I will contact you when known, perhaps a meal in town with REV. and M^rs REV.
    I am told by Stella that Dorothy and Gerald are coming down to see her in July, so she won't be with us on this trip. With regards to the weather we are experiencing the best of the country divide, in our little corner

we had a small layer of snow before Christmas with a hard frost for a few days then milder weather, since then plenty of rain and gales, not good for my days out on the golf course, as you say roll on spring.

Stella and Lilla send their best regards and like me hope that you are enjoying the best of health, please also give my regards to Mick and Margaret the next time you see them.

Hope to meet you all in the near future. All best wishes

Robert Edward

X FOR YOU.

only be felt, and would be long remembered. The mayor stressed the fact that in caring for the school, and by sharing buildings and homes, the town had made a real contribution to the war effort. He congratulated the girls on their good behaviour and the high reputation of the school, and concluded by wishing them success and happiness in the future.

There was some criticism when lorries laden with earth were allowed to drive through the Great West Door of Canterbury Cathedral (Photo by courtesy of the Kent Messenger Group)

Chapter Eight

THE CANTERBURY CHAPTER

DURING THE PERIOD SEPTEMBER 1939 TO SEPTEMBER 1940, Canterbury had gone from being a reception area, to a neutral area and finally to an evacuation area as the war with Germany worsened. As early as 1938, evacuation was a subject brought to the attention of Canterbury school teachers: the Director of Education for Canterbury called all elementary and secondary school teachers to meet him urgently in the main hall of St John's Council School in Northgate, Canterbury. The date was Tuesday, 27th September 1938.

Earlier, the Town Clerk, Mr G. W. Marks, had received a letter from the Home Office (Air Raid Precautions Department) calling for immediate details of the plan for evacuating school children from areas designated as being most likely to be bombed if war should be declared. This presented the Town Clerk with a problem and he brought it to the teachers' meeting on that afternoon.

'Where can I find enough people to carry out such a task at short notice?' was the question Mr Marks asked when he began his address. Up to this time the teachers had rarely come together in one group. They had their union meetings, but these did not attract large attendances.

When Mr L. W. Myers, headmaster of the Simon Langton Boys' School, rose to suggest that all were willing to take on the work, every teacher present approved his motion at once. It was no easy task the 94 teachers of Canterbury had so readily accepted, to visit every place where children might be billeted. Some householders were ready and willing to participate, but many thought it was very silly when war was so unlikely here in England!

But no teacher had time to argue that day, ensuring all forms were returned so that the Town Clerk could tell the Home Office on 30th September that the necessary details had been gathered in. The reports showed that the teachers had found accommodation for 3,000 children. (Mr G. W. Marks, the town clerk, was later to be killed in an air raid on Canterbury.)

In March 1939, the then MP for Canterbury made an extraordinary statement that Canterbury would not be an 'air objective' for German bombers in the event of war. Just over three years later in June 1942, the so-called Baedeker (or 'guidebook') raids on Canterbury devastated large areas of the city!

The following article appeared in the Kentish Gazette and Canterbury Press *for 11th March, 1939:*

Canterbury Not an 'Air Objective'.
Sir William Wayland and 'Bomb-proof' Shelters.

Sir William Wayland, M.P. for Canterbury, gave an interesting address on the international situation and current politics, at the Foresters' Hall, Canterbury, on Friday. Mr Vaughan Page presided, supported by Miss A. Collard and Mr C. S. Streatfield, Conservative Agent. Sir William said that election time was drawing near and the enemies of the government were working hard. One of their favourite attacks was on the question of unemployment. But no Government could avoid unemployment. In winter, when bad weather stopped work, hundreds of thousands of men had to stay at home. The total number of men in employment now, however, was greater than it had ever been.

The only permanent way to reduce unemployment was to foster trade. The reason why international trade had been so bad in the U.S.A. and other countries was due to the restriction on export trade. Each country had been trying to provide for itself.

'Stupidly Generous'

They had always been noted for being stupidly generous, but it was time they did something about it. One of the members of the government had been saying that a fairer dealing between the nations they bought from and the nations to whom they sold, was wanted (applause).

Touching on the question of A.R.P., Sir William said some people in Canterbury thought the city would be in a danger zone, but this was not the case. They might have thought that it would be safer to 'pop down into an underground passage', but it would cost them, as well as the country, a considerable amount of money. The speaker had received several letters in the past few months on the subject of deep bomb-proof shelters. He thought these would be unnecessary and that they would be quite satisfied with the splinter-proof shelters the government was providing. Certainly a town like Canterbury would never be made an objective.

The speaker had replied to the letters he had received regarding the shelters, to the effect that he did not believe that any shelter would be proof against bombs weighing a ton and a half.

'The Barrel of Gunpowder'

With regard to the international situation, Sir William said he believed that they could be easier in their minds than they had been for the last five or six months. Looking round the world today, they saw that the match was further away from the barrel of gunpowder, although the barrel was still there. Now that the world had recognised General Franco as victor, the speaker was confident that he was not going to give Hitler or Mussolini any territorial advantages whatsoever. Italy had said that they were not out for any territorial aggrandisement in Spain, and we had to accept their word until that word was proved false.

The speaker said that it was their bounden duty, as Nationalists, to do their utmost to support Mr Chamberlain, so that he could continue his life's work for the peace of the world.

A vote of thanks to the speaker was proposed by Mr R. F. Balls, who mentioned that although their member was a very hard-working man, he always found the time to come and address them. Miss A. Collard seconded and the vote was heartily accorded.

*   *   *

Extracts from an extensive article which appeared in the Kentish Gazette and Canterbury Press *for 22nd April 1939 gave advice on air raid shelters:*

SIMPLE COVERED TRENCH

The Home Office Air Raid Precautions Department have issued a pamphlet on Garden Trenches, which can be obtained from the A.R.P. Information Bureau, St Margaret's Street [Canterbury], price 1d. Detail plans are given, and I can recommend it as a real cheap pennyworth. The drawings in the pamphlet show a complete trench of simple construction to accommodate six persons.

The bottom of the trench is 6ft. below ground level, and the width is 3ft. 6ins. at the bottom of the trench and 4ft. 6ins. at the top. It is divided into three sections: (1) A shelter, 10ft. long, in which the occupants sit on a seat along one side; (2) A covered entrance, 3ft. long, with a sloping gas curtain resting against a wooden frame; (3) An entrance 3ft. long, giving access to the shelter from the outside by means of a ladder.

Over the entrance is a wooden cover or trap in order to exclude rain and gas-laden air. The bottom of this entrance should be lower than the floor of the trench, to collect any water leaking into the trench. The trench is lined, to prevent the sides falling in. The drawings show how this can be done by using corrugated iron sheets held in place by wooden frames.

Canterbury Cathedral shortly after the outbreak of war, when thousands of tons of earth were deposited in the Nave to protect the interior
Photo by courtesy of the Kent Messenger Group

STEEL SHELTERS

The Government has produced a standard steel shelter, which

is at present being delivered free to householders in vulnerable areas, but not in Canterbury. This design is now obtainable from local merchants, and is made from 18-gauge galvanised corrugated sheets. The standard shelter is 6ft. long x 4ft. 6ins. wide x 6ft. high, with a top curved to a 2ft. 3ins. radius and lapped 6ins. Each sheet is punched for easy bolting together. The shelter is intended to hold six people. The price of the shelter, complete with the instructions for erecting it, is, I understand, £7.10s There are many other types of steel shelters obtainable.

PILL-BOX SHELTERS

The Cement and Concrete Association has issued a pamphlet describing concrete shelters to be erected above the surface of the ground. These are particularly useful where the trenches cannot be excavated in waterlogged ground. The walls are designed to be 12ins. in thickness and properly reinforced. The inside measurements of the small type shelter are 6ft. x 6ft. x 6ft. high. It is suggested that such an erection could be used for dual purposes.

* * *

The Kentish Gazette and Canterbury Press for 9th September 1939 reported the arrival of evacuees into the Canterbury area:

EVACUEES' WONDERFUL WELCOME.
RUSH TO OFFER BILLETS.
MEDWAY AND ERITH EXILES.

As briefly reported last week, Friday saw the beginning of the reception of evacuees in Canterbury and district and the arrivals continued until Tuesday evening. On Friday, Saturday and Monday the trains brought exiles from the Medway area. The first train brought children from Troy Town and St Peter's Schools, Rochester. The kiddies carried an assortment of luggage and each child had a label with his or her name, sewn on the coat, and carried gas masks.

They were loaded on the buses for the rural area. Before this they were issued with the rations. The second train brought children from Gillingham (Napier Road Senior School) and the four subsequent trains provided similar scenes.

The total number of children – considerably less than was anticipated – was nearly 1,600. The other schools represented were Rochester Mathematical School, University School, St Peter's, Woodland, Rochester Girls' Grammar School, Borstal Infants, Skinner Street, St Mary's R.C. and the R.E. Garrison. Of these the numbers sent into the district were: Bekesbourne 16, Bishopsbourne 15, Harbledown 23, Hollow Lane 67, Bridge 49, Sturry 102, Barham 72, Blean 100, Chislet 39, Lyminge 57 Stanford, 32, Littlebourne 36 and Selling 58. The remainder, including secondary school and Roman Catholic children were billeted in the city.

All the children took the journey as something of a great adventure. Credit for their high spirits is due to their teachers. Throughout the day there was a fine spirit of willingness on the part of all the helpers who spared no efforts to help the teachers and to carry their luggage. Some arrived with cases nearly as big as themselves.

A Kindly Welcome

At the station, the children destined for the countryside were given their rations and departed in East Kent coaches. At each village reception committees were waiting and billeting officers took charge of small parties and conducted them to their new homes where they received kindly welcomes from their new guardians.

They soon settled down and, we hear, have since been feasting on the ample supplies of fruit. The children for the city were taken to the Simon Langton Schools – headquarters of the Reception Committee – where they drew rations and were then taken in charge by billeting officers in the same way. The welcome afforded the kiddies by the citizens of Canterbury was no less hearty and sincere than that of the villagers.

Mothers and Babies

Saturday was chiefly mothers' and children's day, although the six trains brought also a number of aged, crippled and blind folk. The mothers were accompanied by a fleet of prams which required a good deal of ingenuity in some cases to fix on the private cars by which they were taken into the city. As the mothers and other folk waited for conveyances, S.J.A.B. men and other helpers held the babies while tea was served at the expense of the Mayor (Councillor Mrs Williamson). who was present for long periods on both days.

The response to the appeal for cars was magnificent. Among the volunteer drivers we noticed the Bishop of Dover. The procedure was similar to that on the previous day. The evacuees for the country received rations and were sent off by coaches to their new homes, while those to be billeted in Canterbury were taken by cars to the Simon Langton Schools for rations and the services of the billeting officers.

An emergency such as this provides many strange and, at times, humorous sights, not the least of which was that of senior Langton boys acting as nursemaids – nursing babies in arms! The mothers and others received just as hearty a welcome everywhere as did the children on the previous day.

First Babies of War

Among those who came on Saturday were about 50 expectant mothers, who were found accommodation suitable to their case. More urgent cases were sent to the Dane John Maternity Hostel and to nursing homes. Two babies have already arrived at the Maternity Hostel – a girl shortly after arrival to Mrs Lester, of Gillingham, and a boy on Sunday morning, during the 'air raid', to Mrs Lane, of Gillingham. Both are doing very well under the devoted care of the Matron (Miss Maycock) and her staff.

The Youth Hostel in All Saints Lane was reserved for elderly people, including one dear old lady of 94. Here there is a very happy party with domestic science teachers in charge of the cooking. Of the nearly 700 who arrived on Saturday about 300 were billeted in the city and the remainder distributed as follows: Bekesbourne 15, Bishopsbourne 16, Harbledown 18, Elham 22, Barham 64, Blean 37, Lyminge 27, Stanford 43, Chartham 10, Hythe 2, Wickhambreux 26, Lower Hardres 17, Selling 44.

They were all extremely grateful for the kindness shown them and for the efficiency of the organisation. Incidentally the Mayor arranged for the opening of the schoolroom beneath the Presbyterian Church, so that all evacuees and helpers might be provided with tea.

Enquiry Bureau

An enquiry bureau has been established at the Simon Langton Schools, where the names and old and new addresses of all evacuees have been indexed, so that mothers arriving on Saturday could, upon application, be put in touch with their children who arrived the previous day. Sunday was spent in adjusting billets where necessary.

When all helpers did such splendid work it would be invidious to particularise, but perhaps just one tribute may be paid to the Simon Langton boys and girls who proved invaluable in numerous ways.

Two small parties from the Medway area arrived on Monday, including four expectant mothers and a helpless cripple. Of these 17 were sent to Barham and nine to Nackington, the remainder being billeted in the city.

The Erith Contingents.

There was another big influx of evacuees on Tuesday, three trains bringing schoolchildren and mothers and young children from the Erith area. The numbers were again less than expected and all were satisfactorily billeted, thanks to the splendid response to the broadcast appeal to householders to offer accommodation.

The procedure of reception and distribution in the city and villages was as on the previous days and again the mothers were very grateful for the kindness shown them and for all the efforts on their behalf. A feature was a successful effort to locate parents near their children who had come with the school parties earlier in the day.

The first trains brought 267 girls, with the nuns, from St Joseph's Convent, 150 boys from Erith County School and 12 girls (resident in Erith) of Dartford County School.

All these were billeted in the city so that their secondary education might be easily continued. There were also 118 children of West Street and Picardy Schools, Erith, who were sent in coaches to Saltwood, 32 of St Fidelis School, who went to Lyminge – and 48 of West Street Junior School who were taken to Swingfield.

Blind Party

In the afternoon coaches which arrived at the Dane John car park brought 21 expectant mothers who were distributed in the Bridge-Blean area and 13 expectant mothers with seven young children who were taken on to Elham.

A party of 30 blind and infirm were accommodated in the Lattergate House of the King's School. It was a pathetic sight to see the blind folk being led away to their new home. A train late in the afternoon brought about 120 mothers and young children from Erith. Of these a mother and three children went to Lyminge, 19 to Ickham, 11 to Wickhambreux, 10 to Newington, 29 to Acrise, 14 to Swingfield and 26 to Elmstead.

Needless to add, everybody – health visitors, midwives, district nurses, home helps and all the rest of the volunteers – did all they could to ensure the comfort of the evacuees, while the volunteer car drivers again did splendid work in the way of transport.

*   *   *

The war had a terrible effect on some of those who were evacuated as the following article from the Kentish Gazette and Canterbury Press *for 9th September, 1939 shows:*

SHOCKING EVACUATION TRAGEDY
MOTHER KILLS SON AND HERSELF WORRIED BY THE WAR

A shocking double tragedy has marred the reception of the evacuees in the Canterbury district, a mother and her only son dying as a result of her mind giving way under the strain of the worry of the war. Having been prevented from killing the boy with a carving knife, she afterwards secured razors and cut both his and her own throats.

The tragedy took place on Wednesday at Elm Tree Farm, Grove, where they had arrived from Erith on Tuesday. The victims were Mrs Beryl Doreen Bull (31) and Brian George Bull (4), of 47 Sandcliff Road, Erith.

When the Deputy Coroner (Mr A. K. Mowll) held the inquest at the farm yesterday (Thursday), he said he was becoming very alarmed, as that was the fifth inquest attributable to the effects of war worry which he had held that week.

Albert V. Bull, house decorator, giving evidence of identification, said that he himself was working with the rescue and demolition squad. On Monday evening he did not know that his wife and child would be evacuated. They had made up their minds not to go. On Wednesday, however, while on duty, he received a note from his wife saying that she had suddenly made up her mind to leave as she thought the boy would have a better chance. She was terribly upset by the war, but she had never threatened to take her life. The letter promised to let him know as soon as possible where they were.

About 7.30pm on Wednesday he was informed of the tragedy by the police. He had been married eight years and the boy was their only child.

TOOK AWAY KNIFE

Mrs Mary W. Richardson, of 4 Crusoe Road, Erith, staying at Grove House, Grove, said that after Mrs Bull and Brian and she and her boy had been to Preston on Wednesday, they all went into Elm Tree Farm house. She went to the sink with the children to get a drink and Mrs Bull came behind her and said, 'I'm going to do him in.'

Witness turned round and took a big knife away from her. As soon as witness had got her calmed down she told the farmer, Mr Harrison, what had happened, and gave the knife to the housekeeper. She afterwards sat with deceased in a field. After about 15 minutes she appeared calm and witness went to get her own dinner at Grove House.

Deceased said she was sorry and witness then thought she was all right. Witness had hardly got into dinner when she saw Mr Harrison tearing up. Witness raced across, guessing that deceased had done something. She met the housekeeper coming out and she told witness not to go in. Deceased had looked strange all day.

Lloyd Harrison of Elm Tree Farm, Grove, said Mrs Bull and the boy arrived on Tuesday and he met them about 8.30pm. She seemed rather perturbed and upset about the war. He saw her again about 8.30am on Wednesday, when she said she could not sleep at all. She did not hear the air raid siren and they did not tell her about it in case it should upset her. During breakfast he did his best to cheer her up.

FARMER'S GRAPHIC STORY

After they had arrived back from Preston, Mrs Richardson came to him in the farmyard and said, 'I've just taken a carving knife from Mrs Bull.' Witness phoned for the police after the knife incident. Witness continued: 'As I turned to go into the scullery, I met the boy Brian, who came running from the yard with his throat cut.

I said to my housekeeper, 'Just look after him. I'll go and see where his mother is.' I could not see her about the yard, so I looked in the road. My first thought was then for the doctor, so I went to Mr Lilliott's and asked them to phone. I ran back and as I got to the front gate, Mrs North, the housekeeper, told me the mother had done herself in. I saw them both lying in the passage. The boy was apparently dead, lying on his side, and his mother was beside him lying on her back and still breathing. Dr Mercer and the policeman arrived within a few minutes.'

Mrs Kathleen North, the housekeeper, said she was present when Mrs Bull and the boy arrived on Tuesday in a private car driven by the billeting officer, Mrs Goodson. Mrs Bull seemed very distressed and worried and started saying that our government had turned Fascist and that Mr Chamberlain and Hitler were firm friends and had simply worked that war on them to create a panic. She said she had read a lot of literature about it and also that she had not slept for a fortnight.

SHOCK FOR HOUSEKEEPER

When witness took her a cup of tea about 6.45 next morning deceased said she had not slept at all. When they returned from Preston, and while witness had her back turned, she heard Mrs Bull open the drawer where the knives and forks were kept. She thought she was going to lay the table and did not even look round. She then heard shouting and Mrs Richardson telling Mrs Bull not to be a fool. She saw that Mrs Richardson had taken a carving knife away from Mrs Bull.

Witness went into the garden with the other two women and stayed for about ten minutes until deceased seemed much more composed. The next she knew was that after speaking to Mr Harrison about some small matter, he suddenly turned and called, 'Look out! I'm going for the doctor.' She guessed that something had happened and went to the cupboard in the passage for rags and then saw the boy lying on the floor.

Mrs Bull rushed through the door as witness was moving from the cupboard. Her throat was cut and she collapsed on her back by the boy. After that, witness said, she could not say what had happened, except that she remembered rushing along the road and meeting Mrs Richardson and stopping her from going in. Witness added that Mr Harrison kept his razors on a small shelf by the scullery sink.

P.C. Thurlow, of Littlebourne, said he arrived at the house about 12.30pm with Dr. Mercer. He found the blood-stained razor produced and a set of false teeth behind a shed. There was a small trail of blood across the yard through the dairy and scullery to the passage. A damaged razor was on the floor near the scullery sink. The boy was dead and the woman still alive. She had also her left hand practically severed at the wrist. She died within a few minutes.

Dr. E. B Mercer, of Littlebourne, said the boy had a large lacerated wound of the throat which had severed the windpipe and arteries, the cause of death being haemorrhage and shock. The mother was still alive, bleeding badly from a large wound in the throat and a large wound in the left wrist. He tried to stop the haemorrhage, but it was hopeless.

'A LOT OF NONSENSE'

The Coroner said it was one of the saddest cases he had taken for some years. The woman was apparently normal until she became worried about the war. She came down to that beautiful spot and had every chance to get rid of her worries. No doubt, however, she was beside herself. There was no earthly reason why she should take the life of her only child and of herself, but apparently she had been reading a lot of nonsense about the Prime Minister of this country and Herr Hitler having engineered that dreadful war. If the war was going to worry anybody, then the best thing was not to read about it.

He thought the dangers by which they were surrounded had been very greatly exaggerated. 'We come from a fine race,' said Mr Mowll, 'and let us be worthy of the race.'

The jury returned a verdict of murder against the mother in the case of the boy's death, and of suicide while temporarily insane in her own case. Asking the jury to join with him in sympathy with the husband, the Coroner said that while doing his duty on A.R.P. work, he had at one blow lost his wife and only child, and one could hardly imagine a greater blow befalling any man who loved his wife and child.

* * *

Schools evacuated into the Canterbury area express their appreciation as shown in this Kentish Gazette and Canterbury Press *article for 16th September 1939:*

EVACUATED SCHOOL CHILDREN

To the Editor:

May we, the Head Teachers of the schools which have been evacuated from the Medway area and whose schools are now in the City of Canterbury, through your columns express our grateful thanks to the citizens of Canterbury for the warm welcome given to us in this time of national crisis. The willingness with which everyone in this City has endeavoured to 'do their bit' in accepting into their homes and helping our evacuee school children is most gratefully acknowledged.

We should also like to express our thanks to all officials of the Education Department, head teachers, assistant teachers and helpers for the efficient and speedy way in which the problem of carrying out this huge task of evacuation was accomplished.

(Signed)   Miss M. Butterfield (Rochester Grammar School)
Mr E. Pattenden (Acting Head, Rochester Mathematical School)
Mr G. H. R. Newth (Erith County School for Boys)
Mother St. Hilda (St Joseph's Convent, Erith)
Mr Ponton (St Mary's R.C. School, Gillingham)
Miss Cork (Borstal Infants' School)
Miss Morgan (University School, Rochester).

* * *

A further depressing tragedy occurred as reported in the Kentish Gazette *and*

Canterbury Press *for 30th September 1939:*

CHILD EVACUEE TRAGEDY STRUCK ON HEAD BY SWING
FATHER'S GENEROUS TRIBUTE

The father of a child evacuee who lost her life as the result of being struck on the head by a swing from which she fell at the Millers' Field, Canterbury, on Tuesday, paid a generous tribute to the kindness which his daughter had received in Canterbury and exonerated anybody from blame when the inquest was held at the Kent and Canterbury Hospital yesterday (Thursday) by the City Coroner (Mr C. A. Gardner).

The victim was 11-year-old Eileen McGill, a St Joseph's Convent girl, who came from Woolwich. Mr R. H. Stevens represented the Canterbury Education Authority. Patrick R. McGill, an Experimental Q.M.S. in the Royal Artillery, of 10, A Block, Artillery Place, Woolwich, said his daughter was evacuated from Woolwich and was billeted with Mr and Mrs Barr, of 'Otranto,' St Stephen's Road, Canterbury. Her general health was good.

Eileen Rose Renaut, now billeted at 127, Sturry Road, Canterbury, said that at the time she was living at 'Otranto'. On Tuesday morning she went with Eileen McGill to the Millers' Field. At about 11am Eileen was sitting on the swing on which were six or seven children. Two were standing, holding the ropes on either side, and the others sitting. While they were swinging, deceased and another girl fell off just underneath the swing.

As she tried to get up, the swing, coming back, hit Eileen on the head, there being still four or five on the swing. Deceased sat down for a little while on a seat then she started crying and they took her home.

OVERBALANCED SIDEWAYS

Monica Teresa Payne, billeted at Wilmea, St Stephen's Road, Canterbury, said that on Tuesday she was playing with the others in Millers' Field and was sitting on the swing with Eileen McGill behind her. They were sitting sideways on the plank watching the soldiers when Eileen Renaut at one end and another girl at the other, started the swing, and after the swing had gone up three times, Eileen McGill overbalanced sideways and fell off and underneath in a crawling position. As the swing came back it struck her head. Witness overbalanced but did not fall off.

Deceased did not want the other children to see she was crying and she got up herself and went and sat on a seat. She said the swing had bumped her head.

Mrs Susannah Barr, of 'Otranto,' St Stephen's Road, Canterbury, said the child was billeted at her house and with her knowledge went out to play on Tuesday morning. She returned at about 11.50am and said she had fallen off the swing and hurt her head. Witness bathed it and she went and sat in the sitting room. She had a little dinner but only toyed with it and then lay down all that afternoon. Afterwards she became very ill and witness immediately sent for the doctor, who ordered her removal to hospital.

Dr I. B. Morris, pathologist at the Kent and Canterbury Hospital, who carried out a post mortem examination, said he found that the cause of death to be concussion of the brain due to a ruptured artery caused by a fracture of the skull. She died about ten minutes after admission to the hospital.

OVERCROWDING RISKY

The Coroner thought it did seem risky that so many children should get on the swing at the same time. It appeared rather due to overcrowding that the child slipped off. Mr Stevens, who said there was nobody in charge of the playground during the day, said the swing, a sort of boat, was provided by the Markets and Parks Committee. The Coroner said he had no doubt the Corporation would take notice of what had happened, and Mr Stevens agreed that they would be very concerned about it.

The Coroner recorded a verdict of accidental death and joined with Mr Stevens in expressing the greatest sympathy with the parents, the latter remarking that all concerned with the reception and billeting of evacuated children in Canterbury had been much distressed by that little girl's tragic death. Q.M.S. McGill said he would like to thank the Canterbury Education Committee for all they had done and to express his appreciation for all the kindness which Eileen had received since she had been in Canterbury. Personally he exonerated anybody from blame. What had happened was just as likely to have happened at Woolwich and had he been living at 'Otranto' he would have allowed Eileen to go out to play in the same way.

* * *

Some of the children who were not evacuated run from a bus to a shelter during an air raid on Canterbury
Photo by courtesy of the Kent Messenger Group

By February 1940 there was a real possibility of further evacuation to areas in East Kent. Many of the rural areas had neither the resources or accommodation to take a further influx of evacuees. The following extract from the Kentish Express, *dated 23rd February, 1940, is an indication of the problems these rural areas could foresee:*

ELHAM DISTRICT AND EVACUEES
COUNCILLORS SAY 'WE CAN TAKE NO MORE'

The new evacuation scheme, to be put into operation in the event of indiscriminate bombing of towns, led members of the Elham R.D.C. to say on Wednesday that they would be unable to accommodate the 500 children which the scheme proposes should be sent to their district.

The point of objection agreed upon by the majority of members was put by Mr E. J. Hutchence when he said that while they were most willing to do all they could, there was the point that theirs was a very poor agricultural district which has been very hard hit by the losses of poultry farmers and yet the Government expected an agricultural labourer earning only 38 shillings a week to house evacuees for 10 shillings or less a week.

'It cannot be done,' he said, 'for they have in many cases, to provide not only food and lodging, but clothing as well.' Mr Hutchence mentioned that recently an evacuee child in the district had worn out his own rubber boots as well as those of his 'foster-mother', and when she wrote to the boy's father he replied that if the boy had no boots he should stay away from school.

The Clerk (Mr D. Harrison) suggested that the return of persons willing to take further evacuees would provide the district's own answer. He thought the majority would decline. It was decided to wait for the result of the canvass of householders before putting the Council's case before the Ministry of Health.

* * *

In May 1940, with the British expeditionary force trapped at Dunkirk, and with the real threat of invasion a distinct possibility, the decision was taken to remove to safer areas, the evacuees who had come to East Kent in 1939. The following article appeared in the Kentish Express *for 24th May, 1940:*

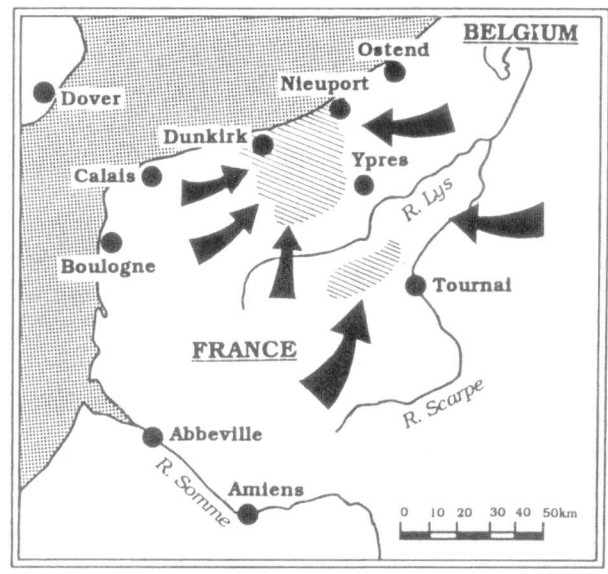

A map showing the British and allied troops trapped in the area around Dunkirk and surrounded by the Germans in May 1940

EVACUEES DEPART
LEAVE EAST KENT FOR WALES

Between 2,000 and 3,000 children who were evacuated from towns in North-West Kent to areas in eastern parts of the county last September have gone to new 'homes' in South Wales. They left by train early on Sunday morning and received a great welcome on arrival.

Crowds of foster parents and newly made young friends saw them off and pressed parting gifts on the kiddies whom they had come to regard almost as their own, or as brothers and sisters. All the children were greatly excited at the start of their long journey and as the trains left there were shrill cheers. They left behind some tears and a real sense of loss.

At Canterbury one Rochester Mathematical School boy was seen off by three girls! The departing guests were seen off by billeting officers, members of education committees and school teachers. The children were given food, fruit and sweets to eat on the journey.

In round figures the numbers who left the different towns were: Canterbury 400, Whitstable 300, Sittingbourne 300, Faversham 300, Folkestone 800. They also left from Deal and Sandwich.

* * *

By September 1940, with the Battle of Britain in full swing, the authorities deemed Canterbury to be an evacuation area and soon it was to be the Canterbury children to be evacuated. The following article appeared in the Kentish Gazette *for 14th September 1940:*

EVACUATION OF CHILDREN
REGISTER THEM AT ONCE

Parents who wish to evacuate their children to a safer area should apply immediately to the respective schools to-day (Friday). It is obvious that in this time of emergency, the children should not be subjected to the strain of air raids which may take place. Personally, we feel that any child should be given this better chance of safety and that it is the duty of parents to take advantage of the evacuation scheme.

Special trains yesterday (Thursday) took some 600 children from various schools to, it is believed, somewhere in Berkshire. The whole operation was carried out methodically and, as the trains steamed out, there were long lines of hands waving goodbye to the parents who had come to see them

A battalion of Canterbury's Home Guard marching through the Westgate Towers

off. A percentage of the teachers of the various schools were in charge of the children, each of whom carried a meal and a change of underclothes.

*   *   *

The following extract is from the school history of Simon Langton Girls' School, Canterbury, which was compiled for their Centenary Year in 1981. It covers the period 1936 to 1942, and gives an excellent indication of how many of the Canterbury schools must have coped with evacuation and the war:

In 1936, a party of German girls from Halle, near Leipzig, spent part of their four weeks' stay with Canterbury girls in camp in Dorset. The following year, an exchange was made, and Langton girls set off for Germany. For a month in the spring of 1937, an

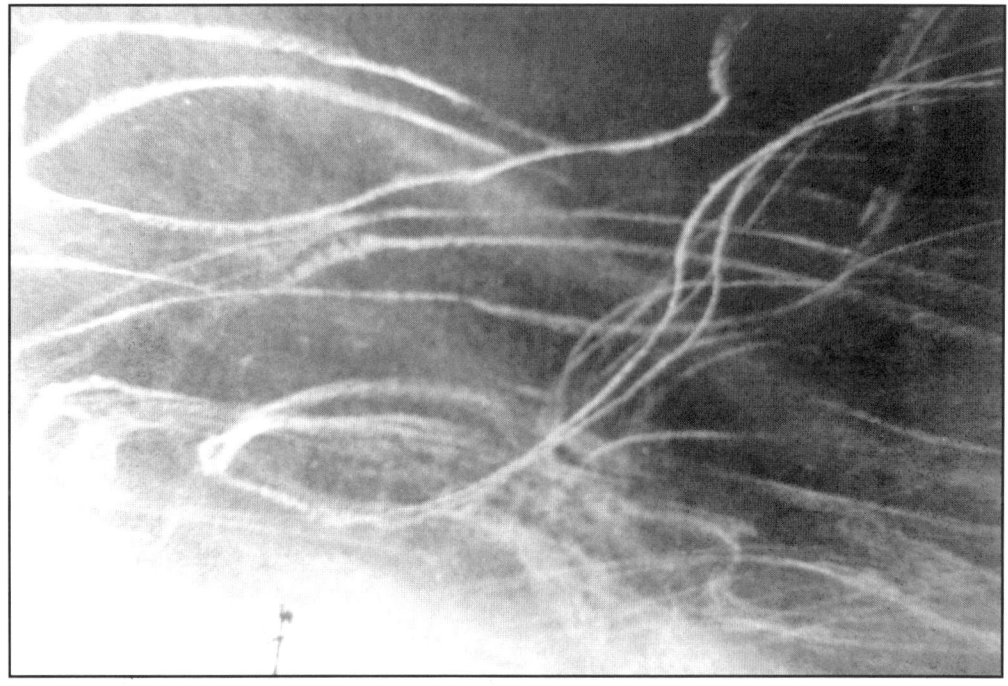

The sky over Kent during the Battle of Britain

'They were wonderful, weird, exciting days. Days when aircraft left beautiful curving vapour trails in the sky, days when some of our friends took off and never came back, when others came back maimed and burnt, never to fight again. Days when the Germans at their bases back in France must have sat and wondered, when their High Command must have been appalled at their growing losses, until at long last into the bullying German mind there came the realisation that they had lost their first battle – the Battle of Britain.'

Anonymous RAF Squadron Leader
Autumn 1940

extended tour took them to Koln, and thence to Halle, where they were received at the Town Hall, and where, later on, they attended a social evening. Tobogganing and tramping through the snow in the Hartz mountains, and sightseeing in Dresden and Potsdam, drove formalities from everyone's mind until the arrival in Berlin. There, a delegation from the school, Miss Campling, Miss Green, who had joined the Langton as a modern linguist three years before, and three girls, called at the Chancellory and was received by Dr Meissner, Secretary of State.

He accepted an etching of Canterbury Cathedral on behalf of the Fuehrer, who was away from Berlin that day. Margaret Rodgers presented the gift 'as a modest expression of our veneration for the German people and of our gratitude for the warm-hearted hospitality shown', and hoped that 'the idea of student-exchange be fostered'. The delegates returned to Halle with signed photographs of Hitler, the respective sizes of which nicely defined the importance of each recipient.

Nazi Germany was less hospitable to its Jewish subjects. When Eva Cohn arrived in England as a refugee, in May, 1939, she brought clothing and other personal property, but had been forbidden to take money or valuables out of Germany. Her 'adoption' by the school assured her of a home and tuition for the next four years. The girls made weekly contributions of one penny a head towards her fees. She became a prefect before she left, and won a reputation for working extremely hard. Her family was at last able to reunite in the U.S.A. Lisa Fuerth of Prague also joined the school. She, too, had been driven from home, owing to Hitler's policies.

The Second World War may have been unpleasant for the Langton, but at least it made a new building for the girls a necessity. By 1939, numbers had spilt over, despite the addition of a laboratory for physics and chemistry, a classroom and a cloakroom in

The then Dean of Canterbury, Dr Hewlett Johnson, had a narrow escape when a bomb damaged the Deanery in 1940
Photo by courtesy of the Kent Messenger Group

1936. Classes were held in the headmistress's house and in County Hall across the road, while Miss Southwood (later to become Mrs Shoner) taught her art classes over Eldonne's dress shop. 'Crocodiles' had to be escorted over a busy main street, if not to lessons, to go to dinner at Lefevre's restaurant, for there was still no school dining room. The bombing by German planes in June, 1942, was the most effective argument yet for new buildings.

Shops which had stood for centuries in Burgate, Canterbury, were badly damaged on 26th October 1940

A fire-fighting certificate and Red Cross certificate were necessary adjuncts of any teaching diploma in 1939. So, too, were a charmed tongue for use as a billeting officer, muscle for 'Digging for Victory', and a sympathetic ear for troubled evacuees. The staff showed remarkable adaptability to its various roles in the next six years, and considerable endurance in a period when fire-watching duties, beginning at 4.30pm succeeded a day's work, and ending at 9am the next morning, preceded another day's teaching.

The September (1939) term opened somewhat raggedly and, when the girls returned, obediently carrying their gas masks, they found the playground and gardens torn up by the mechanical excavator, to provide air raid shelters. Evacuees from St Joseph's Convent, Abbey Wood, moved to Canterbury which was designated a 'safe area'. By working in shifts – one half of the school had lessons in the morning, the other half in the afternoon – it was possible to share accommodation with them. Even so, more room was needed and classes were held in unlikely places, such as the Dean's Library, the Chapter House and Gaywood's rooms.

Life was comparatively quiet during the months of the 'phoney war'. The alert, rarely heard, sent girls scuttling to the shelters, but the greater discomforts of the winter were caused by bitter weather and by German measles. The Whit week-end of 1940 dispelled any thought of tranquillity in the future. An alert was treated with respect after Dunkirk and the fall of France and no one left the trenches until the 'All Clear' went, even if this meant staying long after school hours.

School and Higher Certificate examinations suffered many interruptions and candidates had to be separated from each other in the shelters by non-examinees. One School Certificate paper was completed at eight o'clock one evening by determined young candidates sustained on lemonade and buns. The status of Canterbury changed to being a 'neutral' area – not a particularly fitting title as August gave way to September and the Battle of Britain was getting to its height.

Apples and hops were picked that autumn, as an English mistress, Miss Gray, recalled, 'to the familiar drone of aeroplane engines, varied with the staccato rattle of machine guns . . . [while] the inevitable Junker or Dornier [was] to be seen somewhere in every walk, lying in the Kentish grass, or among the neglected plums'.

Tragedy came to the historic city of Canterbury on the 1st June 1942, when German aircraft rained high explosive and incendiary bombs on the city during the so-called Baedeker Raids
Photo by courtesy of the Kent Messenger Group

The City, shaken by sporadic bombs, and anticipating an invasion, became an 'evacuation' area in September. With less than thirty-six hours notice, 'while sirens wailed and windows shook, arrangements were made for half the school – the City half – to go – no one knew where at first . . .'

Mary Carlton *(now Mrs Sterling) remembers:*

On the morning of 12th September 1940 we assembled, with other Canterbury children, at the West Station, complete with gas masks, ration books, identity cards, one small suitcase and food. As a Sixth Former, I was put in charge of a compartment of unknown girls and young siblings. I was fifteen years old at the time! At about 1.30pm the train arrived at Reading. All the children were taken to a church hall and then to billets.

The school had fallen among friends, for Miss Campling knew the headmistress of the Abbey School from her own schooldays and was warmly invited by Miss Macdonald to share such amenities as there were. At Christmas a number of girls drifted home and during the spring there were so few left in Reading that they integrated with the Abbey School for the rest of their stay.

The subterranean existence forced on those in Canterbury slowly gave way to quieter conditions as 1941 merged into 1942. Downstairs classrooms were reinforced so that lessons continued even during an alert, unless 'Tugboat Annie' delivered her warning of imminent danger. With a school play, *The Rivals*, and Sports Day in prospect, the summer term began.

Then came, to quote Miss Gray, again, 'The Glorious First of June' – or 'Flaming June', what you will, and in a night old landmarks were no more, and the ancient City of Canterbury . . . was in considerable part destroyed by bombing. Rumours flew. There were tales that 'the Langton had gone', but six rooms remained to the girls, though furniture, books, equipment, precious examination notebooks were smouldering still. From the desolation of the playground it was possible to look across the rubble and have an uninterrupted view of the south side of the cathedral.

Miss Campling turned to meet the new crisis. Her second mistress, Miss Green, who had been appointed to this post in succession to Miss Snell in 1938, was a staunch aide. Together, they devised yet more timetables which, since the war began, had been tailored to every 'incredible chance and change'. Mr Myers generously assumed that the schools would pool resources, and with the boys' thirteen rooms it was possible to work a 'shift' system for the rest of the term. Thus, the boys and girls each had four hours of schooling every day. They laboured in dust and discomfort. A barrage balloon, anchored in the playground, screeched its complaint each time it was hoisted.

Yet many agreed, 'It was tiring, often frightening, but always interesting to live in South-East England in those days.' The boys made heavy, brotherly jokes when a home was found for the girls in the mental hospital up St Martin's Hill, where the day hospital now stands. In 1942 it was empty and bomb-damaged, but hard work made it habitable and in October 'the citizens of Canterbury saw a long line of girls leave White Friars and walk up the High Street, along Longport, and up St Martin's Hill to their new school at Stone House'. It was curiously named, since it was built of red brick, with a grey slate roof and it was still more curiously designed, with labyrinthine corridors and confusing entrances. Furniture, gleaned from surrounding schools, and equipment that had survived the blitz, were installed, but little could be done to create comfort. The heating was temperamental, torrential rain could cause flooding; ice rattled in the paint pots in the arctic conditions of the art room, but when summer came there were few who did not

A Ministry of Agriculture poster encouraging women to grow their own vegetables

NOT all the affairs of State are settled in Whitehall. There's a very busy woman at No. 16 with a War Office of her own. She runs a group—a Savings Group. She wants you to live like a warrior—to live tightly, to scrape and save every shilling you possibly can. Put that money into National Savings Certificates, either through her Savings Group or through the Post Office and Trustee Savings Banks. Savings Certificates cost 15/- each and they can also be bought by instalments with 6d., 2/6 and 5/- Savings Stamps.

BUY SAVINGS CERTIFICATES

Issued by the National Savings Committee

National Savings were most important on the home front during the war. This notice was issued in October 1942

revel in the spacious rooms and the beauty of the grounds.

Enemy activity abated and a more normal pattern of school life was possible. Although the blackout was restricting, the Arts Society and the Music, Geography and Dramatic Clubs were soon in business. Miss Alexander and Miss Wills, who in their different roles had fostered the music of the school for eighteen years, must have felt satisfaction at the reconstitution of the orchestra and choir. Lectures and concerts, a great feature in more peaceful days, were resumed, and so too were inter-form matches and competitions. Wartime bred new interests. Vegetables were grown by enthusiasts of the Gardening Club, and investments were made by members of the National Savings Group with an eye to a yield of another kind, but it was the adoption of two merchant navy ships through the Ship Adoption Society that had the most appeal to the imagination.

The association with S.S. *Gemstone* was brief; it was torpedoed – fortunately without loss of life – in 1942 by a German surface raider. Some contact was kept with the captain, E. Griffiths, who was interned in a P.O.W. camp near Bremen, until he was liberated. Meanwhile, letters, mittens, jigsaw puzzles, scarves, tobacco, pullovers, magazines, and seaboot stockings were sent with the greatest goodwill to a second ship, S.S. *Monkstone*, which was engaged in coastal trading in the North Sea, and a very happy relationship was established. Captain R. Williams visited the school for the first time in 1943, and then, with less formality, in February, 1944, when he brought the ship's dog, Silver, with him. Interest in the ship's company deepened into anxiety when there was no news; anxiety was replaced by relief and pride on hearing of the *Monkstone's* activities off the coast of Normandy on D-Day.

This war interrupted the careers of young men and young women alike, for both were subject at the age of seventeen and a half to registration and call-up, unless they were in reserved occupations. The variety of war-service for women may again be judged by 'Old Girls' News' in the magazines of the era. The Land Army attracted many girls who came of farming stock. Others went into the W.R.N.S,, W.A.A.F. or A.T.S., into munitions factories or the Auxiliary Fire Service, the Civil Service and Local Government.

* * *

The following short excerpt is taken from a history of the Payne-Smith School, Canterbury:

The advent of the Second World War inevitably interrupted the process of education, both from the human and organisational point of view. Before the actual declaration of hostilities a large proportion of children were evacuated from urban areas which it was expected would be the subject of enemy air attacks. Thus, in September 1939 the Payne-Smith School was obliged to accommodate evacuees; thirty-one were received under the government scheme and ten under private arrangements.

In September 1940 when the civilian evacuation of Canterbury was advised, forty of the Payne-Smith girls, together with two members of staff (Miss Holtrum and Miss Foord) went under the official scheme to Reading; they were accommodated at the George Palmer Secondary Girls' School. Besides this official evacuation, very many of the girls left Canterbury with their parents.

In October 1941, when the school reopened after the summer vacation, the school contained only fifty-four girls and three members of staff. This necessitated an entire re-grouping of the classes and, for eight weeks, the school operated on half-sessions only. To compensate for lost time a homework system was carried out. However, by the end of the eight weeks, the numbers had risen from fifty-four to one hundred and two. *The dramatic rise in numbers was presumably due to the drift back to Canterbury of evacuees.*

* * *

Evelyn Bonnick (*now Mrs Bissett*) *was first evacuated from Canterbury privately in 1939, and then again in 1940 under the official Government Evacuation Scheme:*

Sometime after war had been declared I left Canterbury and was sent to stay with my aunt and uncle in Coulsdon, Surrey. Although I became homesick, being with relatives and being loved helped. I quite enjoyed my stay until an enormous bomb dropped on the house next door, badly damaging it. We were all sent to the local church for safety. It just took one letter home and I was soon back in Canterbury! It wasn't long, however, I think it was in 1940, that I was on the move again.

I was nine years old and with hundreds of other school children from the Canterbury area, I can recall boarding a train – to goodness knows where, sobbing my farewells to devoted parents, and clutching my ration book, ghostly gas mask and a small case containing a few belongings. I can't remember much about the journey, but I know that my seven year old friend, Maureen White, and I ended up in Reading although I think some of the children went to Didcot.

Again I can't remember much about our reception, except that Maureen and I ended up in a snobbish doctor's home, where we had to live in the kitchen. We were most unhappy and cried to leave. Eventually, we went to stay with a widow and her son. Her name was Mrs Parker, and she was very kind to us – we quite enjoyed that! But we became very homesick and longed to see our parents. When my mother came up to see me, she was not informed where we were and had a very hard time finding out where we were. I think she went to every school in the area.

The locals were not very helpful, but eventually we were found. We then moved to a farm in Didcot. This was much better, but we hadn't been there long before Maureen's father came to take her back home, and I returned shortly afterwards. I cannot recall how long we were away, but it seemed like years! We returned only to encounter all the air raids on Canterbury – and it didn't seem worthwhile going away in the first place! I have never wanted to return to the Reading/Didcot area – and I never have! I think my evacuation has had a lasting effect on my life. Even on holiday I can't wait to get home!

The following is an excerpt taken from the December 1939 issue of The Langtonian, *the school magazine of the Simon Langton Boys' School, Canterbury, which again gives a good indication of how school life was severely disrupted during the first few months of the war:*

ON THE HOME FRONT

There were few, one may imagine, who, when the School dispersed at the end of July (1939), looked forward with assurance to the prospect of a holiday entirely undisturbed by some major event in international politics. During the whole of the school year then ending the possibility of an outbreak of war had protruded itself more and more forcibly, and had already caused a change of venue for the Easter trip and the abandonment of the projected visit to Alsace and the Black Forest in September. The mid-August 'black-out' came as a grim reminder of future possibilities, but in spite of this and other ominous events at home and abroad we clung to the hope that the alternative trip to North Wales might still be possible.

By the last week of the month, however, the situation had become so serious that steps were taken to recall the staff, and they, along with other teachers of the city, made their final preparations to deal with the expected evacuation. This was on Tuesday, 29th August (1939); by the Thursday the government had issued its orders, and the action commenced. The immense task of preparing rations was duly completed, and the complex organisation set in motion to secure the speedy billeting of our visitors.

Our own buildings had been chosen as the headquarters, and were a scene of great animation when on Friday, September 1st, the first evacuees arrived. It would take too long to describe in detail all that happened; it is sufficient to say that by the early evening, with the assistance of a large band of voluntary helpers (among whom were not a few of the senior pupils of both our schools), all the visitors had been found a home. The same procedure was followed for several days, and by the end of the following week over a thousand persons had been billeted in the city, in addition to a

Posters such as this urged women to join the war effort

further large number who were dealt with at the East Station and dispatched by bus to the outlying villages. A certain amount of adjustment was not unnaturally called for, and it was September 16th before the headquarters was transferred to the Education Office.

In the meantime, however, two events of more personal character had taken place. The Welsh trip had been finally abandoned, and the air raid trench system had been commenced. Whatever else happens, this last will inevitably leave its mark. The (Simon Langton) Girls' School playground and the lawn were its chief victims, and although at the time of writing the work has not yet been completed, it is reaching its last stages. At the outset, when the digging was done mostly by hand, quite a number of antique objects came to light, and won us a certain fame when a description appeared in the columns of *The Times*. Later a mechanical excavator was used, and portions of the old walls and a number of human bones were disclosed. Some of the finds have been deposited in the 'Beaney'.

On completion of the billeting, preparations were made for the re-opening of the school. From September 18th onwards forms were recalled one at a time, books distributed and classes commenced. At first their was only a skeleton programme for the Middle and Upper Schools, but as the trench accommodation grew, we were able, with the help of the rooms generously loaned us by Kent College and St Edmund's School, to provide part-time education for the whole school in addition to the evacuated section of Erith County School who had by this time been allocated to our buildings. A good deal of outdoor work was being done at this period and at frequent intervals during the day large parties were conducted by bus 'up the hill'.

There was, in fact, a constant coming and going and with the school so scattered it is surprising that there was any time left for actual teaching! A succession of provisional timetables made their appearance but by the middle of November the whole work had been once more concentrated upon our own premises and the amount of tuition considerably extended. Although at one stage it was found necessary to organise an eleven period day and to 'requisition' Wednesday and Saturday afternoons, the last weeks of the term have found the school approaching more and more closely to the normal method of working.

All (Erith) County boys now leave just before 3pm, so that they may reach their homes in daylight, while the descent of the blackout requires everyone else to be away shortly after 4pm. For the rest there is little to tell. Practically all school football has been suspended and school societies have had temporarily to lapse. Even house games have not, as yet, been held, but it is expected that some competitions on this basis may be arranged next term.

It will not be out of place here to mention the erection of a shelter, with the kind permission of Mr Mount, in the chalkpit at the grounds. Although our own boys have put in a little 'hard labour' on occasion in the interests of the general security, the greater part of the work has been carried out by Mr Leasor and the Erith boys, to whom all credit must be given for the substantial result of their efforts. To turn from construction to demolition, it is sad to record that the school canteen has been on the move again. Its former comparatively new and commodious premises adjoining the bicycle sheds had to be removed to make way for the trenches and it has lately found a temporary home in the old woodwork room.

Such, in brief, has been the course of our fortunes in this first term under war-time conditions, a term which has undoubtedly placed a great strain upon, and caused much personal inconvenience to boys and staff alike. As the routine becomes more familiar, however, it is expected that no one will find difficulty in adapting himself to the altered circumstances, and may in the end come to the conclusion that the great upheaval, with its accompanying restrictions, possessed after all some elements of benefit both to the individual and to the school.

To have come into such close association with Erith County School has afforded us great satisfaction. We have admired the dexterity with which they have carried on under strange conditions and in surroundings which are perhaps less palatial than those to which they are accustomed; and although the two schools have continued to exist as separate entities, those occasions which have called for mutual consultation have always produced perfect agreement. It would be inappropriate, not to say ambiguous, to express the wish that their stay with us will be a long one, but we can at any rate entertain the hope that it will have been pleasant, and not unprofitable for either school, to have worked together in conditions of such intimacy. *(Author's note: Erith County School was re-evacuated to a safer area in May 1940 as the international situation worsened.)*

*   *   *

The July 1940 edition of The Langtonian *included the following passage:*

The war situation is changing so rapidly that it is impossible to forecast what the future may have in store for us; but we may conclude with a reference to two possible developments. The first of these is the Overseas Evacuation Scheme, for which a number of applications have been sent in from the school. To any who may be fortunate enough to be selected we wish 'bon voyage'. That their reception in the

The cover picture of June 1941 issue of The Langtonian, *showing the old buildings of Simon Langton's Boys' School which succumbed to the bombing a year later*

dominions will be cordial goes without saying. The other is the agricultural work with which it is expected that some of us will be concerned in the coming months. Here is an opportunity for all who can to contribute towards the common effort, and we hope that we shall be in a position to satisfy all calls that may be made upon us.

* * *

It is interesting to note the reference in the last passage to the Overseas Evacuation Scheme. The following short article appeared in a September issue of the Kentish Gazette and Canterbury Press*:*

KENT CHILDREN IN SOUTH AFRICA

Thirty-seven boys and girls from Kent were among a party of 315 British schoolchildren who recently left for South Africa under the Children's Overseas Reception Scheme. The children will spend their first night ashore in South Africa at the country home of the Governor General, Sir Patrick Duncan, who has placed it at the disposal of the reception organisation. It will be used as a hostel from which to distribute the children to their new homes in Capetown, Pretoria, Johannesburg, Durban and Bloemfontein. Five hundred pounds worth of toys, books and games have been supplied by the South African Reception Committee.

* * *

Also in the same issue of the Kentish Gazette and Canterbury Press *appeared the following poem, which, ironically, mentions the 83 evacuees who perished when the* City of Benares *was sunk by enemy action:*

THE BATTLE OF BRITAIN

> We long for peace, but it must be
>   A peace that will not cast
> A shadow on our victory
>   Unworthy of the past.
>
> We glory in the days of old –
>   The battles fought and won;
> Our tale will presently be told,
>   When we our course have run.
>
> We dare not let our country down,
>   It is for Freedom's sake
> That every village, every town
>   Is now so wide awake.

The men and women of today
  They serve by day and night,
Not in the old familiar way
  When men alone would fight.

But, oh, the horror of it all,
  The children are not spared –
The nightly terrors that appal
  The little ones have shared.

And now we hear of eighty-three
  Young children being drowned –
Their ship torpedoed out at sea
  By cruelty profound.

Bad beyond measure are our foes –
  But we shall not forget,
And the Great God above us knows
  He will repay them yet.

                    S. Pagden
                    September, 1940.

*   *   *

September 1940 saw the evacuation of Simon Langton Boys' school to Wantage, Berkshire. The following passage appeared in June 1941 issue of The Langtonian*:*

AT WANTAGE

A section of the school has for some time been evacuated to Wantage, Berkshire, where they have found life, on the whole, very agreeable. Soon after their arrival independent accommodation was secured and school work was able to proceed on

Canterbury evacuees waiting at Canterbury East Railway Station to depart for Berkshire in 1940

normal lines. In addition, many out-of-school activities came into being to occupy the evening hours, and it is no exaggeration to say that 'The Club', a comprehensive title sanctioned by popular usage, has been most popular. Nor has the corporate life of the school ceased on Sundays, for it has met without interruption for its own morning service, at first in the chapel of King Alfred's School and latterly in the chapel of St Katherine's, for the use of which we wish to express our gratitude to the Sister Superior. *(For the first two weeks, the boys from Simon Langton's shared the buildings of King Alfred's School, but then moved to independent accommodation at St Katherine's Convent, Wantage.)*

*   *   *

Roy Arnold *was evacuated as a pupil of Simon Langton Boys' School, Canterbury:*
In September 1940 my parents, my sister and I made our way to Canterbury West Railway Station. Pupils living within the city boundary were to be evacuated – destination unknown as far as we were concerned. We all said our goodbyes, not knowing when we would be seeing each other again. I was 15 years old and my sister was 13. We were all with our friends which lessened the sadness of parting, but how my parents felt it is difficult to imagine.

Earlier in the year I had spent my summer holidays working on farms, harvesting at

A scene of devastation in the High Street, Canterbury, a few weeks after the Baedeker Raids of 1st June 1942
Photo by courtesy of the Kent Messenger Group

Adisham and fruit picking at Chilham. During these days I had seen the Battle of Britain being fought overhead, with planes crashing and parachutes floating down. The summer term had seen us in and out of the air raid shelters; normal lessons and learning became almost impossible. Strangely, the children living outside the city boundary were not evacuated.

Our train journey took us to Newbury and that night we were housed at various places in the district. I spent that first night at a large country estate on the outskirts of Newbury. My sister and her school, Simon Langton School for Girls, went to Reading.

The next day we were taken to Wantage and assembled in the playground of King Alfred's School. I remember local people arriving and selecting those of us they considered would fit into their homes. Our ages ranged from 11 to 17. My friend and I were chosen by a local estate agent and his wife, Mr and Mrs Morse, who were both probably in their sixties.

We were taken to their large house on the outskirts of Wantage. There was a long gravel drive leading up to the house and there were flower beds, a walled vegetable garden and an orchard at the rear. Mrs Morse's elderly mother also lived with them.

We were two very lucky boys. At the time of our arrival two young maids were employed at the house, but they soon disappeared and were replaced by a middle aged woman, who turned out to be the mother of one of our masters evacuated with us.

For a short time we shared the premises of King Alfred's School, but were soon found premises of our own in the annexe of a local convent. School life during the day then became very normal. In the evenings the premises became a sort of youth club and many activities were available – table tennis, chess, draughts, whist drives, community singing – or homework in the comparative quiet of the first floor rooms. Looking back at those times, I now appreciate the efforts of our masters and mistresses who did so much to make our lives as evacuees so enjoyable.

We were also able to indulge in outdoor sports and we played soccer against several local schools, in which we had a certain amount of success, but I remember we were severely thrashed by a local army team on a pitch which was more mud than grass! More than fifty years later I was surprised to learn that the four goals I scored in our 4-0 win against Wallingford Grammar School had been recorded in the history of my old school. Some of us joined the local fencing club, a sport which was completely new to us, and later in our stay we were able to play both cricket and tennis.

We were very well looked after at our new foster home. My friend and I shared a very comfortable double bedroom and we dined with the family and, when we were not at school, we were able to share the fireside. In addition to his estate business, Mr Morse had a small farm a few miles from Wantage, from which came a plentiful supply of milk, vegetables and fruit. They even cured their own bacon and there was always a large portion in the pantry.

The people of Wantage absorbed us into their community and as far as I know there were no serious problems concerning the evacuees. From time to time my parents sent me pocket money by means of a postal order. One of the pleasures of the day was, after some strenuous games of table tennis, to call at the local fish and chip shop on our way 'home' for a tuppenny bag of chips.

I must admit that my time at Wantage was very happy and comfortable due to the kindness of Mr and Mrs Morse, the efforts of our teachers and by the way we were accepted by the local community. At weekends, if not engaged in football or cricket, we explored the local countryside and made cycle excursions to Oxford and other nearby towns. It was during this period that I first became acquainted with the Ridgeway Path.

During our first term at Wantage my parents visited both my sister at Reading and me at Wantage. They found that my sister was billeted with a family with severe health problems, so my parents took my sister home with them. We remained at Wantage until June or July 1941 and those of us in my age group sat for the School Certificate examination. Some time before we left Wantage for home, Mr Morse became ill and was taken to hospital in Oxford. Before leaving for good, my friend and I cycled to Oxford to say goodbye to Mr and Mrs Morse and to thank them for their kindness. I remember that Mr Morse was on the verge of breaking down when we said our final farewells. He died shortly afterwards. I continued to keep in touch with Mrs Morse until she died in her early 90s.

I cannot remember any air raid or other wartime problems during our stay in Wantage so, apart from being away from home, our education continued without interruption. Those who decided upon Wantage as our temporary home chose wisely.

When I returned to Canterbury I found employment and within the first year was involved in firewatching duties at my work premises during the so-called Baedeker raids on the city in June 1942. A month or two later our home was made uninhabitable by a daylight hit and run raid. The following year I found myself in the Royal Navy and didn't see Canterbury again for a further three years.

I have returned to Wantage several times over the years and, even now, when I get the chance, I still visit for a nostalgic look round.

It seems that all the boys from Simon Langton School had returned home from Wantage by December 1942, as the following passage from the December 1942 issue of The Langtonian *indicates:*

EDITORIAL

During the eighteen months since the last issue of *The Langtonian*, the effect of the war on school life has become more and more widely felt. For a year enemy air activity was very slight. The return of the exiles from Wantage united us all under a single roof once more and we began to settle down to a steady life rather remote from the war. True, we felt its indirect effect in the growing scarcity of luxuries, but until June of this year we were not seriously affected.

Then, totally unexpected, came the enemy bombers. We, who had left the school quiet and peaceful in the evening, returned, next morning, to find part of it a smoking ruin. Buildings, which must have held a sentimental value for many, were now mere skeletons of brick and mortar. Slowly we recovered; our wounds healed and we set about the task of getting back to normal. We have worked to that end ever since. Interruptions and set-backs, such as the November (1942) blitz, have occurred, but at last the machinery of the school is working efficiently again. The sporting and social activities, so essential to the life of a school, have been, in some part, restored and are helping to keep alive our great traditions, so that we may look forward to a peace in which we may prosper once again.

The production of this magazine has been difficult and the space at our disposal has been very much restricted. By using small type throughout and omitting the Valete and Salvete (a change which we were very loth to make), we have managed to include, as in the past, some articles by boys. We hope that this Magazine may fulfil its purpose of giving the reader a true picture of our life and of enabling Old Boys to keep in touch with the School.

R. D. Haxby, P. S. Hayes

In the Chronicles section of the same 1942 issue of the school magazine appeared the following three articles:

JUNE, 1942. Two members of the staff were fire-watching on that memorable night. It was an exciting experience. Standing in the playground, about 1am, they watched blood-red flares dripping from the skies. A few minutes later, a low-flying Junkers let

Simon Langton Boys' School, Canterbury, gutted by incendiary bombs
Photo by courtesy of Kent Messenger Group

loose a shower of incendiaries. Dodging their way through the innumerable flaming patches, the fire watchers raced for the underground shelters. They stayed there for an hour or more, fanned by ripples of air as bomb after bomb burst up above. When they ventured forth, they found the playground littered with earth, masonry, and burnt-out incendiaries. Already part of the school was ablaze. They did what they could to check the fires and then salvaged records from the headmaster's study. On the roof, they used a stirrup pump and a crowbar to good effect, but the answer to a small boy's question: 'Please, sir, is it true you put out 400 incendiary bombs?' is definitely, NO!

* * *

Mrs Roosevelt paid a visit to Canterbury on the 31st October (1942). A party from the Junior School went to the Cathedral and to the West Station to welcome her. Some of them enjoyed the novel experience of waving the Stars and Stripes, and all of them were fascinated by the newsreel apparatus mounted on an American army car.

* * *

D. R. STIGGER. We much regret to announce the death in a recent air-raid on the city of D. R. Stigger, of Form IVc. We extend our sincere sympathy to his parents.

* * *

Mrs Jan M. Barber remembers the time when she and others of her family were privately evacuated from Canterbury to South Wales:

St Augustine's College, Canterbury was badly damaged during the air raids
Photo by courtesy of Kent Messenger Group

In 1940 mum took me, my brothers Bob and John, and younger sister Corrie, on a train journey to London and then on to South Wales as wartime evacuees. My father stayed behind because he was a Kent fireman. I can't remember the journey at all although I know it was dark when we arrived in Ferndale in the Rhondda Valley and I remember walking through darkened streets of this strange place, which was a bit frightening for a seven year old. We were boarded with Mr and Mrs White and their son John who was about my age. If Mr and Mrs White wished to speak 'privately', they would speak to each other in Welsh, which annoyed my mother a lot. The village was situated at the foot of a mountain and opposite our back gate was a flight of wide steps leading up to the next street.

I didn't enjoy school in Wales. I had trouble doing long division sums – because I had never been taught how to do them. For this I was punished by being given the cane on my hand. For a school medical examination I remember having to strip down to my knickers which made me very embarrassed.

When we were not at school we played in the river which ran through the centre of Ferndale. I suppose we spent most Saturdays playing and paddling in the water. Sundays were different. We were made to stay quietly indoors.

I remember the sheep would come down from the mountain and wander in the streets.

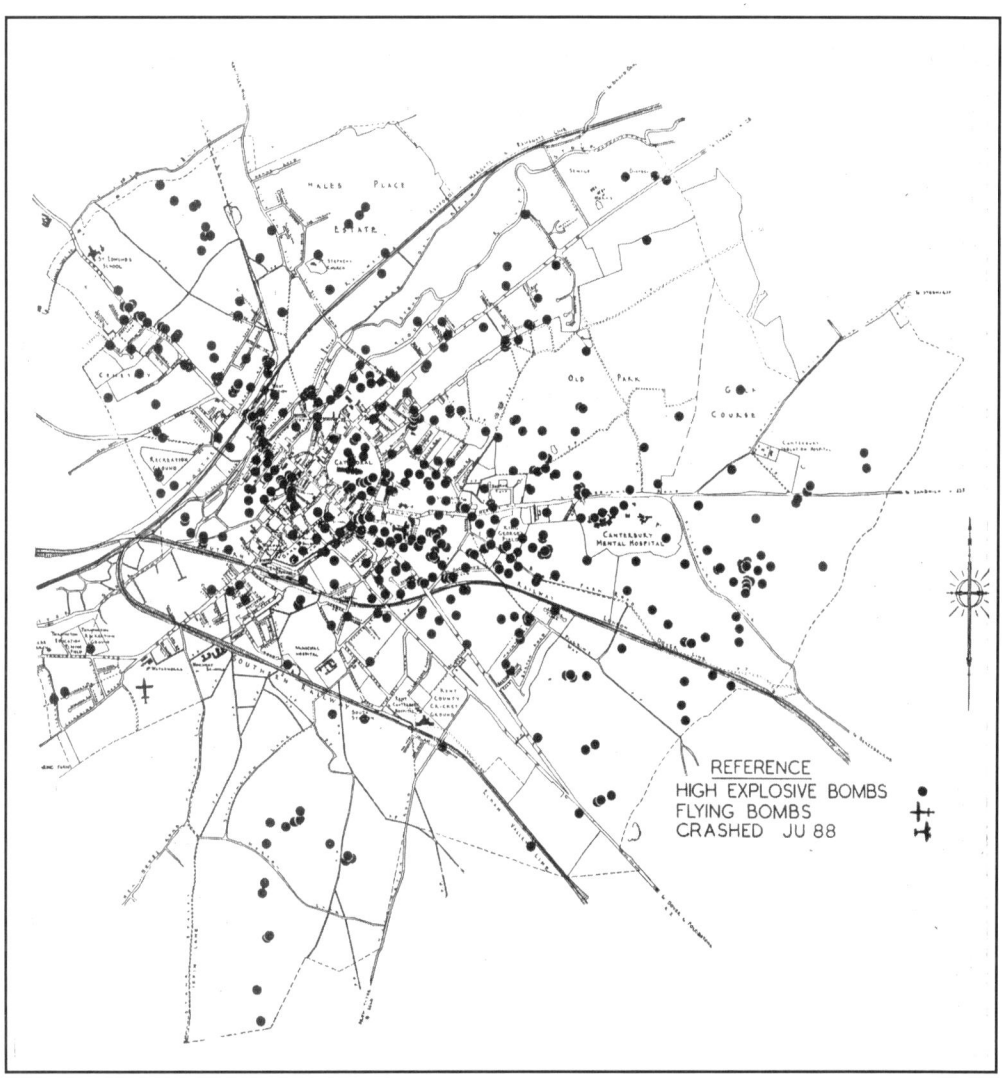

The City of Canterbury, showing the intensity of bombing that it received during the war

They would come into the gardens and knock over the dustbin and leave a terrible mess everywhere. I also remember the heavy rain and, when the wind blew very hard, tiles would come crashing down off the houses and into the street.

Happier memories of my time in South Wales include walking on the mountain on my own, picking pink and white heather to take home – and waiting for Sundays to come round so that we could have a drink of Tizer!

We returned to Kent in about 1942, but not to Canterbury. Father took the whole family to stay with friends in the village of Chislet and we were there when Canterbury was blitzed.

Sometime after we had returned to Kent, my mother told me how unhappy she had been in Wales. My mother was about 38 years old when she took us to Wales. She wore makeup, she was auburn and pretty. I remember her telling me that some of the spiteful Welsh women had called my mother names and said she was a hussy for walking out wearing lipstick. She cried when she told me this and I have never forgotten it.

And finally we end this Canterbury chapter with a short poem written in 1942 by a boy from the Simon Langton School:

VICTORY

When peace is won, and raids are done,
  How happy we shall be
To see our lads come home again –
  From air, and land, and sea.

The Victory bells will joyous ring,
  And everyone will gladly sing –
Thank God for hard-won victory:
  God save His Majesty the King!

K. R. Smith (Form Ib)

THIS PLAQUE WAS UNVEILED ON JUNE 1ST 1992 BY THE LORD MAYOR OF CANTERBURY TO COMMEMORATE THE 50TH ANNIVERSARY OF THE BAEDEKER RAID ON THIS CITY ON THE NIGHT OF JUNE 1ST 1942 AND IS PLACED AT THE CENTRE OF THE DEVASTATION

"THE DARKNESS HAS PASSED AWAY AND THE TRUE LIGHT IS ALREADY SHINING"
1 JOHN 28

A plaque with these words can be seen on the side of the tower which is all that is left of St George's Church in Canterbury High Street

Chapter Nine

THE ASHFORD CHAPTER

When the Government Evacuation Scheme was put into effect in September 1939, Ashford in Kent was a fairly quiet market town, and it was to Ashford and the surrounding rural area that many of the London evacuees came when war was imminent. Many of these evacuees, especially young mothers with children, found it hard to settle down in such quiet surroundings. Another problem that arose in the rural areas was the financial hardship most host families had to endure when taking in evacuees.

We start this chapter with an article from the local Ashford newspaper, The Kentish Express *for 1st of September, 1939:*

EVACUATION OF CHILDREN FROM DANGER ZONES BEGINS TODAY
THOUSANDS COMING INTO KENT PURELY AS A PRECAUTIONARY MEASURE – OFFICIAL

Purely as a precautionary measure, and this means that war is not inevitable, the government has ordered the evacuation of children and all priority classes, in all areas included in the evacuation scheme, to begin this morning.

The whole evacuation scheme will take several days to complete. Under the scheme, 136,000 children, teachers, mothers, invalids and blind persons will be moving into the reception areas in Kent.

The evacuation from the Medway Towns – Chatham, Gillingham and Rochester – will last two days. Today the older children will be evacuated and on Saturday the infants and their mothers.

The evacuation from London will last three days and the first day and a half will be devoted to the older children and the second day and a half to the infants and their mothers. Invalids and blind persons will be sent as the opportunity arises. There will be one teacher or helper for every ten children. Evacuation from London will begin at 5am and continue until late in the day.

Local authorities have all matters for receiving evacuees well in hand and will notify all those who have volunteered to help with dispersal when they will be wanted. No other person should go to a railway or bus station. If they do, they will only hinder organisation.

The Medway Towns children will go to the rural districts of Strood, Swale, Bridge-Blean, Elham, Eastry and Dover, the urban districts of Sittingbourne and Milton, Whitstable and Herne Bay, and the boroughs of Faversham, Canterbury City, and Sandwich. Deal Borough will receive London and Medway Towns children. The other reception areas of Kent will receive London children.

Except in the case of the evacuation of Medway Towns children to the Strood rural district, which will be done by motor coach, the evacuation will be carried out by special trains. The evacuated persons from Gravesend and Dartford are being sent to Norfolk and Suffolk.

Two thousand five hundred German Jew refugees at Richborough Camp have volunteered for National Service. Some were engaged yesterday in filling sandbags for protection in Sandwich.

The archives, pictures and panels in the Guildhall at Sandwich have been packed and will be sent away today for safe custody.

Throughout yesterday afternoon, housewives were volunteering at the Ashford Council Chamber to take children.

The Kentish Express is not stating the numbers of evacuees to be received into the various districts, for reasons that will be obvious to its readers.

* * *

Three weeks into the evacuation, The Kentish Express *produced a progress report on evacuees who had come to the Ashford area:*

TOWN CHILDREN IN THE COUNTRY
WHAT THEY THINK

The London children are settling down well in their new surroundings and, generally speaking, the billeting has been carried out satisfactorily. There have been a few misfits, but these are being rectified.

Every credit is due to the mothers for the way in which they have taken the children into their homes and made them 'one of the family'. In many cases this has not been an easy task, but with that wonderful gift of 'a mother's love' and patience, extraordinary results are being achieved.

These mothers have tackled their job and are making their contribution to National Service in a really wonderful manner, and it is seldom that one hears a grouse, although many are making considerable sacrifices to carry out their duty.

While not wishing to criticise the government allowance, there is certainly nothing to spare, after adequately feeding and caring for healthy, hungry children, and this leads up to the point of the children who have arrived with insufficient clothing.

In several cases children have no change of underclothing and housewives, already hard hit and struggling to make ends meet, have been forced to buy clothes for them, rather than see them suffer from the elements. Such a state of affairs should not exist and as one woman said, 'What can I do? I cannot see them go without, but I can do with every penny I get for my own home and children.'

Probably the most exasperating feature is that in some cases, where the parents of the evacuees have been relieved of the financial responsibility of their children and are thus better off, the mothers having no ties have gone out to work!

Compare this position with the mothers who are caring for the children. In some cases they are anxious to go out to work to help keep the home going, but are debarred by the responsibility of looking after another person's children.

On Sunday a lady arrived by car at a house in Maidstone to visit her son. She expressed pleasure that he was in such a nice home and then said:

'The house is so empty without him that I have gone out to work – an office job. There is no real need of course, as my husband is in a good position.' This was said to a mother who was struggling to make ends meet . . .

Various individual evacuee stories were also included in the same article:

. . . An amusing story comes from Great Chart, where a mother and her children were staying with a poultry farmer. One afternoon they returned with a large number of eggs. Suspicion suddenly dawning, the farmer asked them where they had gathered the eggs. They had been all over the field picking them up, and the farmer had no idea which were the new laid eggs, and which had been laid previously and not discovered.

. . . Two boy evacuees in the Bradbourne district visited a neighbouring farm and returned with what they said were two white rats they had killed in a hutch, thinking thereby they had helped the farmer. They had never seen white ferrets!

. . . Asked if they liked being in the country, a few evacuees admitted that, though it was very nice, they would rather be at home. One small boy was nursing an injured arm in a sling. He bashfully said that he had fallen from a tree, but excused himself by saying it was not an apple tree!

. . . A little tot, asked where her mother was, replied, 'Which one, I have got two mummies now.'

. . . Conversation piece in bus: Small boy, 'Ain't this blooming bus ever going?' Mother, exasperatedly, 'How many times have I got to tell you not to say "Ain't".'

* * *

As time went on, further stories of the evacuees to Kent appeared in local newspapers. The following appeared in The Kentish Express *for January 5th, 1940:*

EVACUEE'S HOME IN A PARK
BALLROOM FOR LESSONS
LONDON PLAYS SECOND FIDDLE TO COUNTRY

Some of the happiest evacuated children in Kent are those living with their teachers within the hospitable gates of Cale Hill Park, Little Chart, where their host is Mr Chester Beatty, and their home is a two-storeyed converted art gallery and ballroom of great size and convenience.

At the outbreak of the war Catford Central School for Girls made its journey to the country and it was divided into three sections. Two were housed at Bethersden and Smarden and the third, numbering fifty, with smaller brothers and sisters, were given the sanctuary of the gallery, under the guardianship of Miss McCallum, Mrs Bennett and Miss Lewis. At first fifty camp beds were provided and the teachers slept with their charges at the end of the lower hall. When it was decided that their stay be prolonged, the mistresses took immense pleasure in working hard to transform the building into a real home. They have succeeded admirably in blending the busy, absorbing atmosphere of school with the recreative one of hours out of lesson-time.

The huge main hall, the original ballroom with its beautiful oak floor, is divided into a spacious classroom and a dormitory. The upper hall, or art gallery, is curtained into sleeping and dressing cubicles. A covered way, built by Mr Beatty to ensure that no child is exposed to rain or cold, connects the whole with an orangery overlooking exquisitely planned gardens. Here are housed the younger children, from four to six, whose toys are to hand. The orangery extends to a nursery washroom and lavatory, perfectly fitted. The whole is warmed by a system of central heating.

In addition to the teachers there are helpers contributing to the care of the children. One sleeps at the North Lodge, which has been included in the zone of usefulness, three in the gallery and one in the orangery. They assist with cleaning and washing, and with serving meals, which are cooked by Mr Beatty's staff.

The school has the use of the servants' hall in Cale Hill mansion and it becomes both a dining room and a class room. Mr Beatty has provided school furniture and the children have his permission to use four tennis courts and a croquet lawn.

A gas-proof air-raid shelter, accommodating fifty children, is situated in a corner of the garden and an escape aperture is part of its measure for safety. Each child understands what it has to do in air-raid drill.

Among the practical and the artistic occupations followed in the school curriculum are those of dressmaking (the children's clever conversion of gifts of clothes into neatly fitting garments for themselves), out-of-door sketching, memory-drawing of scenes and animals about, nature walks and decorative art with cones, beech nuts, acorns and other fruits of the country.

A tribute to the watchfulness and unselfishness of the teachers is expressed by the children, none of whom wishes to be sent back to London. It is an actual fact that many other children have wanted to come to Cale Hill gallery to share life in such ideally restful and natural surroundings. Both Mr Chester Beatty and his son visit the 'school in the park'.

Lights are put out at 8.30pm for the children. Eleven of them, under supervision, sleep at North Lodge. The mid-day meal is served at the mansion to all. Unless parents object, the children attend one service on Sundays, in accordance with their faith. They are allowed to invite young friends from the village to play with them and a few private evacuees from Little Chart and neighbouring places go to the gallery school for tuition.

Christmas was a pantomime season from the children's viewpoint. They made festive decorations and performed their own version of *Cinderella* entirely by themselves.

*   *   *

By February 1940, some billeting officers in the Ashford area were experiencing difficulties in placing evacuees, as the following article shows:

BILLETING MAY BE COMPULSORY
West Ashford Evacuation Officer asks for Powers

Mr G. P. Lawrence, the evacuation officer of the West Ashford Rural Council spoke of the difficulties of billeting in his report to the council on Wednesday.

The chief difficulties arose, he said, from the exchanges that were necessary due to illness either in the families who had taken the children or among the evacuees themselves. He paid tribute to the cottagers and farmers who had voluntarily taken evacuees, but said that in certain cases owners and tenants of larger houses had been unwilling or refused to take children.

He asked for the compulsory powers which he was reluctant to use but if the second evacuation occurred they would be necessary in order to find further accommodation unless greater help was given by the public. This was agreed to and the Emergency Committee of the Council was given power to prosecute if necessary.

* * *

Gordon Brooks' *link with Kent is that he experienced a traumatic time when he was evacuated to Ashford from his home in Eltham, South London. But his evacuation experiences are classic examples of how some families were totally disrupted because of the war, which is why we have decided to include his full account. It is interesting to note that his final place of evacuation was Staffordshire – the area where most of the children from the Isle of Thanet were evacuated to:*

My evacuation began in the winter of 1939. I was not quite seven years old. My school, Kings Park Junior, had closed down after the Christmas holidays and was then to be used as a fire station, manned by the Auxiliary Fire Service. Hostilities in Europe made the likelihood of war very real although talks were still going on.

My father and his brother were working in munitions at Woolwich Arsenal and it wasn't long before my father's brother was sent to the munitions factory in Aycliff, near Chorley in Lancashire to teach new employees the skills of shell and bomb filling. It was rumoured that my father would follow, and, as there was no schooling for me and my brothers, my parents decided that my mother, my three brothers, my sister and myself should go to Lancashire to find accommodation – and a school!

We travelled north in early January 1939. Accommodation was in short supply because of the number of workers and their families drafted into the area to work in the factories, so we lodged with my uncle and his family. So there we were, three adults and seven children squeezed into a three-bedroomed semi-detached house.

We found a school, but no house. Things weren't ideal living with my uncle and his family. I didn't help matters by not getting on too well with my cousin Bob. This way of life went on for about a month until dad found out that he was not to be transferred after all, so we made our way back to London.

When we arrived back home we discovered that the black-out had started. All the important buildings were being protected by sand bags – and iron railings were being taken away to help with the war effort. All the lights were dimmed, signposts and road signs were taken away and railway stations had no names.

Once back home we found that my school had been evacuated to Ashford in Kent. My parents made enquiries at the local authorities and were told that if my parents took us kids to Ashford at their own expense, billets would be found for us. We travelled to

Ashford by coach and were met by the billeting officer. My mother insisted that we three boys were billeted together. I was seven, Bob was six and John was five.

There was only one billet that would take the three of us. Mr and Mrs Lucas were both approaching retiring age and they had a son in his forties living at home. He was a bus conductor on the Maidstone and District bus service. The billet was a three-bedroomed terraced house and my brothers and I slept in one bed, head to toe. Mrs Lucas had all the dealings with us. She gave us our food, our orders and our punishments. I don't remember Mr Lucas or his son ever speaking to us. Whatever Mrs Lucas said or did was law, and everybody obeyed, including her husband and son.

Every day we had porridge for breakfast and tea to drink. Our packed lunch for school was sandwiches, either jam, paste or Marmite. We were only allowed to wear our shoes on Sundays in order to make them last longer. We had to wear our wellington boots outside at all other times, and these caused sores on the backs of our legs, especially on John's. For tea after school we had sandwiches again, either jam, paste or Marmite. The only cooked meal we had was on Sunday lunchtimes.

'School' was a marquee on the local cricket field where we sat in rows, cross-legged on matting. We would leave school at three o'clock each day, arriving 'home' to find the house locked – everyone was out until four-thirty. If it rained it was 'too bad'. One day we decided to go round to the back entrance. I climbed the fence to let my two younger brothers in and we sat in the greenhouse until Mrs Lucas came home. She used the cane on all of us because I had left the back gate open – and because we were in the greenhouse where she had grapes growing.

The next day a tent had been erected in the garden for us to go into, with strict instructions to lock the back gate after us. Unfortunately, the tent wasn't waterproof so we got soaked anyway. There was an old table in the garden which we pushed inside the tent so we could sit underneath – it tore the tent so we got another caning!

I wrote home every day telling our parents everything that had happened. We seemed to get caned every day for one thing or another, wasting food by leaving a sandwich was good enough.

John's legs had started to bleed with the canings. Mrs Lucas must have felt bad about it because she got her son to bathe and cream the wound. I started to play truant from school and got caned for that, but I played truant again and again.

I was standing in front of a toyshop in Ashford one day when I felt a hand on my shoulder and a voice said, 'What are you doing here?' I looked up and saw it was my mother. The education authorities had been in touch with her. Before I could answer her, she had pulled me into the sunlight and was looking at my hair. I was 'running alive' with lice!

She took me back to the billet but, as there was nobody there, we went on to the school where my mother spoke to the headmaster. We then picked up my two brothers and went to see the billeting officer where she made a complaint and showed him our hair and our legs. Mother then left us with the education medical staff whilst she went to collect our belongings from the billet. By the evening my brothers and I were back home with mum and dad.

Back in Eltham our schooling consisted of one hour, three times a week in a lady's front room, where there were about ten of us. By September 1939 the Government was advising parents to send their children away because of the impending war situation.

Evacuation was not compulsory, but my parents agreed to send us away only if the L.E.A. promised that we would be well looked after. War was declared on 3rd September 1939. Dad had bought three rucksacks and these were packed with our clothing as per instruction sheet. Luggage labels were attached to us and our luggage, with our name, address and school written on them. Then we waited, complete with gas masks, outside Kings Park School for the transport that would take us away.

Eventually along came a convoy of London Transport double-decker buses. We said our goodbyes to our mother – dad had gone to work, I don't think he could face seeing us go. I felt bewildered and didn't quite know what was happening. Surely they weren't going to send us away after what had happened last time! I was crying and holding John's hand. He just had a puzzled look on his face. Bob held his other hand and we clambered on to the bus. I could no longer see mum. She had got lost in a sea of faces as all the mothers tried to get a last glimpse of their children, then we were off.

The buses took us to Well Hall station and we had passed lots of people waving to us on the way. We were bundled on to a train and told to keep our luggage on our laps – and were told not to eat any of the sandwiches or sweets that we had with us. We were not allowed to take drinks with us and there were no corridors or toilets on these trains.

Our train took us to Paddington station, London, where we transferred to another train bound for the west country. The journey was very slow and I remember the train being shunted into sidings, then going into reverse to get us on to the correct line.

We finally arrived at Staverton station just outside Totnes, South Devon. We were then ushered into a long, narrow hall. We were all very hungry, very tired and very lost. There were chairs and benches in the hall, but not enough for all of us. Those who couldn't find a seat sat in rows on the floor.

People began to come in to choose which children they would have. Farmers were obviously looking for the bigger and stronger-looking boys. I didn't have to wait long before my name was called out, along with another boy, Kenny Brimmer, who was two years older than me. This was unusual because everyone else was being sorted like cattle. A man appeared, took our luggage and in a very kind voice said, 'Follow me, me old 'andsome.' That was the last time I was to see my two brothers for fifteen months. We didn't even have enough time to say 'goodbye'.

We made our way to a car and the man took us to Coombe Farm, near Buckfastleigh, and by the time we arrived at the farm it was about nine-thirty in the evening. The farm nestled in a valley and the house was built entirely of grey slate. Waiting for us were Mr and Mrs Webber and Mrs Webber's mother and father, Mr and Mrs Bonathon, whom we were told to call 'granmere' and 'granfer'. Granfer was totally blind, but a really wonderful man, in fact the whole family were very kind to us.

That night I had my first introduction to home-made turnip soup, which is still my favourite and which was to become a regular meal every Saturday lunchtime before we went to the 'pictures' (cinema). After feasting and bathing for the very first time in a tin bath in front of a roaring kitchen range, we were taken to our bedroom – two very tired, very clean and very full boys!

Ken and I awoke the next morning to brilliant sunshine and the sound of machinery. Looking out of the window we saw a working water-wheel which pumped water to the reservoir on the hill which served the farms and surrounding cottages. After breakfast we went down into the farmyard to meet all the animals and collect eggs from the chickens, turkeys and geese, a rare experience for a 'townie'! There were pigs, cows, sheep, two ponies and one working horse, Masher, the biggest horse I have ever seen. There was also a Welsh collie named Fluff. In all, Harry, our foster father, farmed about 60 acres.

My stay at Coombe Farm was a boy's dream. Of course, I missed my parents but on the farm there was always something to do – apple picking, potato planting, kale cutting, hay and corn harvesting. We would also pick mushrooms off the ten-acre field for market, pick primroses and wild violets, making them into bunches for the markets at Totnes, Newton Abbott and Ashburton.

School was five miles away at Landscove. On the first day we were taken by car, but after that we walked there and back – until we learned to ride the ponies!

The second Christmas we were there the Germans bombed the naval dockyard at Plymouth. Our fighters chased them off and some of the bombers jettisoned their remaining bomb-load. One landmine fell, exploding on the hill above the farm, causing damage to the buildings on both sides of the valley. It missed us completely, the blast going above us, although we did find part of the casing in the meadow, not far from the water-wheel.

One of my jobs on the farm was to help granfer cut wood each day for the fire. He and I would walk down to the barn, he holding my arm, me leading the way. Inside the barn was a two-handed crosscut saw and a wooden horse where we would cut the logs up. For that he would give me one shilling pocket money for the pictures on Saturdays in Buckfastleigh – and some sweets from the provisions van which came around twice a week. One day granfer wasn't very well so I spent some time with him at his bedside. That was the last time I saw him. The funeral must have taken place whilst we were at school. I missed him very much.

The farmhouse had four very large bedrooms, so my parents or Ken's parents could stay whenever they visited. Downstairs there was a large sitting room which was only used on special occasions, such as Christmas or when we had visitors. There was a very large dining room, heated by a range, where we lived and ate. Kenny and I had jig-saw puzzles, toy cars and lorries, and toy soldiers to play with. Adjoining the kitchen was the dairy where Mrs Webber made cream, butter and cheese, and where she graded the eggs before they were sent to market. The toilet was outside in the yard.

During school holidays we were allowed to visit Newton Abbott market each Thursday, with all the produce which was sold to the market stall-holders. We would then visit the cattle market and were allowed to milk the cows so that buyers could see the milk yield. Unfortunately, this was all to end in early December 1942. My father had been transferred to a new munitions factory in Stone, Staffordshire. A new estate had been built to accommodate the workers and their families. Dad came down to the farm, stayed the night and then the following day he took my brothers and me back to Staffordshire. I'm afraid there were a lot of tears from me and my foster parents as we left. I really missed my life in Devon. The following June I received a letter saying that Fluff, the Welsh collie, had had a heart attack and died in the hayfield.

My brothers and I attended St Michael's Junior School in Stone and we fished in the Grand Union Canal. Our house was not far from the River Trent. At the age of eleven I left the junior school and went to Stone Senior School where my farm expertise came in handy. The local farmers used the older boys for potato picking and mangelwurzel cutting.

The war ended in my thirteenth year. There were bonfires, fireworks and street parties, and troops returning home from the war. I basked in reflected glory and with my 'best mate' went to meet his dad. I was proud just to be there and be part of the reception party.

Our family had increased by now to six boys and one girl. Dad took his severance pay and returned to London seeking other employment. He found a house and a job and so we all returned 'home' to join him.

The following letter was sent by **Gordon Brooks** *to his parents during his stay in Ashford, Kent, May-June 1939:*

Dear Mummy and Daddy,

I don't like it here 'cos Mrs Lucas hit me round the face and John shot a catapult at the bus conductor [Mrs Lucas' son!] and he smacked John round the face then I picked it up and punched him in the face. Then Mrs Lucas came in and the bus conductor went upstairs to get his bus conductor's hat and after that we had our dinner in the tent and after that we had our pudding.

From Gordon and Bobby and John

X X X X X

To Mummy and Daddy and Raymond and Sheila.

Another London evacuee, **Sheila Arnold** *(now Mrs Barnett), travelled with her school, the Mary Datchelor Girls' School, Camberwell, to the Ashford area on 1st September 1939, when she was aged 13:*

Most of us had been used to going regularly to church from early childhood, so it was quite natural for me to make my way up the hill to Kingsnorth Church on that first Sunday of evacuation (3rd September 1939). I had spent the previous two nights on a mattress on the floor of a bungalow owned by a young couple, Mr and Mrs Mills. My companion was a girl called Mary Rate. We did not mind in the least about this strange sleeping arrangement, but some days later, when my mother came to visit me and expressed her horror, I was soon removed to another billet – which was to be the second in a long line of billets until I left school in July 1943.

Once in church on that Sunday, I joined some of my school friends. The rector, Mr Swan, was conducting the service. About half way through the service, just as he had entered the pulpit to deliver his sermon, an ancient verger tottered up the aisle with a piece of paper in his hand, which he duly handed to Mr Swan. There was a moment's pause. Then the rector read aloud the grim message that war had just been declared on Germany.

In the silence that followed I became aware of someone weeping, and realised that one of the German refugee girls, who had joined our school in 1938, was probably thinking of members of her family, left behind in Germany.

Mr Swan then announced that he did not think it appropriate now that we should listen to his sermon, so we all sang 'O God, our help in ages past' and the national anthem, before returning to our billets.

We left the church to the loud wailing of the air-raid siren and feared that German bombers were already on their way, but this was a false alarm, and the 'all clear' followed almost immediately.

My next billet was also in Kingsnorth, at the home of Mr and Mrs Craig. I shared this with another girl, Joy Woods, who was in my form at school and we were both very happy there. Mrs Craig used to make wonderfully light fairy cakes which she put at our disposal, together with a tin of chocolate biscuits – a great weakness of mine! But alas, Mr Craig was soon 'called up', and so the couple moved to his base in Portsmouth.

Joy and I were then sent to live with Mrs Gibbs aged 65 and her sister, Miss Down, aged 72, in a very small bungalow in Stubbs Cross. Mrs Gibbs was deeply religious. There were framed texts on the walls and a bible in every room, including the lavatory! Joy did not stay long at this billet, as one day Mrs Gibbs saw her at the gate, talking to a young man. Fearing the worst, she soon dispatched poor Joy elsewhere. So the other side of the double bed, which we had occupied, and which Mrs Gibbs later on told us was where her husband had recently died, was now taken over by my friend, Margaret (Peggy) Flood, whom I had known since we were seven years old. Our mothers, who also knew each other well, had engineered this transfer. Peggy had been leading a frozen existence at Great Mumford Farm, where the snow, which fell down the chimney, or filtered into the house through ill-fitting window frames, remained in situ all day. Certainly, Mrs Gibbs' tiny bungalow was always warm and cosy, though we found that a bowl of mulligatawny soup for breakfast was rather a strange, albeit warming, way to start the day.

By this time it was January 1940 and we were experiencing an extremely severe winter. Several times the snow was so deep that the buses were not running, so we had to walk into Ashford with frozen toes and fingers. One of our teachers, the intrepid Miss Thompson, who lived in a billet in Hothfield, arrived at the county school on skis, causing some amusement among her pupils.

Schooling was very limited to start with. Because the air-raid shelters took time to complete, the school building was only allowed to accommodate up to 60 girls at any one time. This meant that everyone could have only one hour's tuition each day, followed by three hours homework back at our billets. Later on, when the air-raid shelters were completed, we attended for half-days: Mary Datchelor School in the mornings and Ashford County School in the afternoons.

With the coming of spring 1940, we discovered the delight of bluebells and primroses to be gathered in the woods: a new experience for London children. Time passed quickly, with such highlights as visits from parents; the school play, *The Barratts of Wimpole Street*; rides on our bicycles through the beautiful Kent countryside; a performance of *Messiah* in the Methodist Church; and many more activities.

The war seemed very distant. Then came Dunkirk and the wounded soldiers being given tea and sandwiches at Ashford station as they passed through. Suddenly, this part of Kent was no longer considered safe from enemy attack, so on 23rd June, 1940, we gathered at the railway station for the last time and departed for a safer place. As we left we were given a wonderful farewell from the people of Ashford. Both the station and forecourt were crowded. Everyone connected with our school seemed to be there to see us off: heads and staff of the several schools where we had worked, including

Miss Leary, headmistress of the county school; foster mothers from Ashford and the surrounding villages; and even a school governor, who had made a special journey from London to wish us well.

We travelled all day and finally arrived at our destination – Llanelli, in industrial South Wales. Here, the local population gathered at one end of a large hall, while we assembled at the other. We were then 'chosen', according to how attractive or otherwise we appeared. But that is another story . . .

Olive Chapman, *also from the Mary Datchelor Girls' School, Camberwell, recalls her time in the Ashford area:*

When I arrived with the school in Ashford, I was billeted for short time with three other girls at an estate worker's house at the approved school for boys in Kingsnorth. We all shared one room where a great deal of nail varnishing, hair-curling and general titillating went on. After a few days, when one of our girls had already established 'friendly relations' with the Big Boys over the fence, an open car appeared carrying Miss Baker and Miss Morton, who were out hunting for stray Datchelor girls. We were all invited to appear at school in Ashford the next day, and in a very short time we were all whisked away from the delights of the boys' reformatory to billets in the farthest parts of the village!

I was then billeted with Mr and Mrs Relf in their farmworker's cottage. It had no facilities. There was a privvy in the corner of a dark shed and I took my weekly bath at the house where my foster mother cleaned. But I led an idyllic life – there was a warm range in the living room where we all sat down in the evenings. Mr Relf would sit nursing the cat, and I would do my homework by the light of a polished oil lamp. The cottage had a sweet smelling apple-lined loft above the two bedrooms, and outside there was a cottage garden from which all the fruit and vegetables came. Eggs, butter and cream came from the farm.

I was totally spoilt there. I think of the porridge and cream for breakfast, of the chocolate cake made especially for me every week, I think of sun and snow, of blackberries and spindleberries, primroses, and glow-worms along our lane at night.

Almost daily I used to hop over the stile out of our garden and cross two fields to call for Stella Harvey at the Rectory's back door. I was forbidden the front door because when I once went to tea at the Rectory, I had been found wanting! I had scandalously put butter and jam and cream on my bread! Poor Stella had such a difficult time, while I was treated with such affection in our little cottage.

On the 4th September 1999, we revisited Kingsnorth during our school's 60th anniversary reunion in Ashford. We set off together to find the footpath and the stile from the Rectory. It was still there, as was the second stile – and beyond that was the cottage! What memories!

Rachel Rich *(now Mrs Dennyss) also records her evacuation experiences in the Ashford area:*

In 1938 we had prepared for evacuation. Then Neville Chamberlain came back from Munich with the promise of 'Peace in our Time'. But a year later the war clouds gathered again as Hitler continued to occupy countries on Germany's borders. On September 1st, 1939, Germany invaded Poland and two days later war was declared.

Meanwhile in anticipation of air raids on London and other large cities, thousands of children were evacuated to the country. On the 1st September, 1939, a large group of girls from my school in Camberwell, marched up Denmark Hill to entrain for an unknown destination – which turned out to be Charing Railway Station, near Ashford in Kent. From there we were transported by bus to various villages. At about the same time my parents went to Chatteris in Cambridgeshire, with my father's school. My brother went to Great Bookham in Surrey, and my eldest sister started college at the Royal Holloway in Egham.

I was 13 years old and my sister was 15, and we were initially billeted with an elderly couple at No. 1 Ivy Cottage, a small cottage in Great Chart, one and a half miles from Ashford. The cottage still stands. It has a preservation order on it and is over 500 years old.

Our school life was disrupted, but somehow we still managed to learn in spite of shortened school hours. We shared Ashford High School with the local girls, and I made a lifelong friend as a result of living in the village. This friend I made in 1939 still keeps in contact with me, and each time I visit England from my home in New Zealand, we renew this very precious friendship we forged during our evacuation. We both had sisters to share our enforced exile.

Our foster parents in Great Chart, though they were kind and fed us well, were really too old to look after children, so we spent many hours on walks, made interesting for us by the fact that we 'acquired' two dogs – the pets of our foster mother's employer. We were never allowed to have dogs indoors, so we used to walk these dogs, Boys and Bogles, for miles around the Kent countryside.

After a while we were moved into Ashford as our foster parents found us too much of a handful! We were not naughty children, but the extra washing, cooking etc., became too much for them. Eventually of course, we were among the thousands of children who, in May and June 1940, were re-evacuated from Kent to locations in South Wales, the Midlands and the West Country, at the fall of Dunkirk when invasion seemed imminent.

I remember watching trainloads of weary soldiers standing in the carriages, half asleep, after their horrifying ordeal.

We were again marched to a station, this time Ashford Railway Station, where we embarked on a much longer journey. After many hours we arrived at Llanelli, a steel town eleven miles from Swansea in South Wales – which later suffered heavy bombing! My sister and I had one billet for the first night, then we were separated. My sister remained in her billet until she left school two years later, whilst it took me a few months to get suitably settled.

I finally went to stay with a very nice Welsh family who treated me very well, and I spent three very happy years there. I grew from a gawky school girl to a fairly presentable Sixth Former. We shared Llanelli Girls' High School – and Llanelli Boys' High School, with the local children. I joined the Girl Guides and did some pre-nursing at the local hospital. During my last year at the school I did a secretarial course and also obtained a credit in biology to add to my School Certificate in order to help me in my nursing career.

In 1999, sixty years on since I was evacuated to the Ashford area, I came over to England from my home in New Zealand to attend an Evacuees' Reunion. The village of Great Chart still remains the same to me after all those years and when I entered the church hall, a man said to me, 'You are Rachel – where is your sister?' He remembered me after all those years. He was a boy of nine in 1939! Sadly I had to tell him my sister had died.

Finally, I must mention the kindness and support we all had from our teachers, who not only looked after our minds, but were also on hand whenever life became difficult. Our teachers often worked very long hours looking after us, which was far beyond the call of duty. Evacuation taught us a lot of lessons and made us all learn to help others.

Another Mary Datchelor girl, **Stella Harvey***, evacuated to the Ashford area, relives her time at Kingsnorth Rectory:*

How shall I describe life in Kingsnorth Rectory? It was rather like being in a novel by Anthony Trollope! Looking back, there are many incidents that make me laugh now, but weren't particularly funny at the time. The fact that there were two of us there together made life bearable and Edna and I often let off steam in the privacy of our bedroom!

The rectory itself was a lovely old building, part of it 18th century or even earlier – not appreciated by us at the time! It was large and rambling inside. I found it rather gloomy and sinister at first, especially when I saw two very old ladies in black, creeping up the staircase that we were not allowed to use.

We discovered later that a few of the rooms were let as separate flats, presumably to augment the rector's income. In one of them lived Miss Strachan, a delightful retired headmistress, who became our friend and confidante when the rector's wife had been particularly annoying.

The rector was rather a pathetic little man, about half the size of his domineering

Girls from Ashford, photographed at Oxford whence they were evacuated during World War II

wife. She was given to sudden, inexplicable tantrums which caused her to flush deep red, rise from the table and lie on a couch by the fire, whereupon her long-suffering husband would also leave the table and sit beside her, making sympathetic noises.

Edna and I would be left to finish our meal in silence and make as quick a getaway as we could, muttering to each other about the rector's wife having another one of her 'turns'. With hindsight, I think is was probably a manifestation of the menopause, but we didn't know anything about that at the time.

Mornings at the rectory began with the rising bell, operated from the kitchen, followed later by another one for prayers in the rector's study. Except for the maid, who would be preparing breakfast, everyone in the house was expected to attend, including the rector's two sons when they were home for the holidays from Christ's Hospital. We would sit in a circle and the rector would read a passage from the bible, after which we would kneel with elbows on chairs and bottoms all facing into the centre! This was an agonising time for me, as we were all expected to say out loud a short prayer. I could never think of anything to say except 'God bless mummy and daddy.' The boys were well trained and always knew the right things to pray for.

After this we would all troop into breakfast and the ritual of serving the porridge began. A big dish of the grey, sloppy stuff was put in front of the rector, who ladled it out into bowls, often slopping it over the edge on to the table cloth, as he was very short-sighted. This always brought on giggling fits from Edna and me, which did not amuse the rector's wife! Long-awaited letters from home were also ritually handed out at the breakfast table, though of course, not to be opened until later – a terrible discipline for me!

Florrie, the maid, was rather simple (to put it politely) and was apt to bring in the meals wearing her maid's cap upside down (another cause for the giggles), or to leave her false teeth in a cup on the kitchen dresser, to be found by an irate rector's wife. We discovered that Florrie had a small wireless set in the kitchen and, with the excuse that we were going to help her with the washing up, we would dance round the kitchen to the sound of the popular tunes of the day. Normally, the only 'listening-in' we were allowed was the nine o'clock news just before we went to bed. However, this harmless entertainment didn't last long, as the rector's wife reminded us that she was responsible for our welfare, and she didn't think our parents would like us consorting with servants! Coming from a humble background myself, with no conception of class-consciousness, this seemed ridiculous to me, but was just another rule we had to put up with. At the time, I never realised how hypocritical she was – never hesitating to use our services when Florrie was ill or an extra hand was needed.

At Christmas, the rector's eldest son brought a friend home for the holidays, and the four of us decided to have a midnight feast in our bedroom, which was along the corridor, far from the boys' parents room. We made elaborate arrangements to exclude the other son, considering him too young to be trusted with a secret.

I think we managed to scrape together some lemonade and biscuits, and the boys crept along at the appointed hour. It was all perfectly innocent, but I think the 'excluded' son must have told his parents, because we suddenly heard footsteps along the corridor, and the rector appeared dramatically in the doorway and ordered the boys out.

The following morning the boys were called into the study and I can only imagine what was said to them. Nothing was ever said to us, but the atmosphere was rather strained for a while! Soon after that, the boys went back to school, and it wasn't long before we left Kent for Llanelli – probably not before time!!

Irene Enright *recalls memories of family life at Ashford, Kent, and her subsequent evacuation to Oxford:*

At the beginning of the war my father was the manager of Dixon's the ironmongers in Middle Row, Ashford, where he worked very long hours. The rest of his spare time was spent growing fruit and vegetables and raising chickens and rabbits in our huge garden. He was also an A.R.P. warden and spent many of his nights on A.R.P. duties.

Every summer mother would take my sister Ann and me hop picking on the outskirts of Ashford and several times during 1940 we were fired on by German aeroplanes. As we were returning on the bus one evening from the hop fields, my mother saw a huge sign on the side of our local pub 'The Fox', telling of evacuation.

Within a week or two we were packed and ready to go. My sister Ann was six years old and I was only four. We all left by train from Ashford station and I remember it was dark. The train was overcrowded with both civilians and military personnel and we stopped many times because of air raids. Some of the rail bridges had been bombed and our train had to be diverted.

My father came with us on the journey and I can remember being very worried because the handle on our big suitcase had broken and I didn't know how dad would manage to carry it. We arrived at our destination sometime during the night and were taken by bus to Lady Margaret Hall in Oxford, where we had to sleep on the floor.

The next morning we were given breakfast and then taken to our billets. My mother, my sister and I were taken to stay with Professor Entwhistle and his wife. They had a huge house with a low brick wall all around it. As soon as we were settled, my father returned home to Willesborough, Ashford.

Our billet was very comfortable. We had a bedroom and a lounge of our own, and we used to eat in a very large kitchen along with the two maids, Nancy and Eunice. They

The chapel of Lady Margaret Hall, Oxford, where some of the Ashford evacuees initially stayed on their arrival in 1940

were all very kind to us. My sister Ann started school in Oxford, but I was too young. I remember that there was a huge park with a large duck pond nearby where my mother used to take me for walks.

Professor Entwhistle used to invite Ann and myself into his study on occasions, to talk and to read books and, although I was very young, I can remember enjoying these visits. At other times we would go for walks across the fields nearby and one day an aeroplane crashed quite near to us – it was very frightening.

The following Christmas my father came to visit for a few days and brought with him two dolls cots which he had made himself. My mother had made all the covers and had dressed the dolls; my sister and I thought they were wonderful.

I don't know exactly when we returned to Kent and I can't remember anything at all about going home, which seems very strange. However, we did return and eventually had to face the 'doodlebugs', sleeping indoors in a Morrison Shelter – and having to have evacuees ourselves!

I don't think being evacuated did us any harm, although we did miss our father, and of course we were lucky in having mother with us all the time. My parents kept in touch with the two maids, Nancy and Eunice, for many years after the war had finished.

By November 1939 the first School Evacuation Camp in England was opened near Cranbrook. The Kentish Express *for 1st December 1939 gave the details:*

MODEL SCHOOL EVACUATION CAMP

The only School Evacuation Camp at present fully established and working in England is to be found in the rural district of the Weald at Coursehorn, Cranbrook, where 200 boys of Dulwich College Preparatory School have an encampment on the most modern and up-to-date lines on this 18 acres estate. The encampment is composed of 15 huts or what can more suitably be described as temporary wooden buildings. They are of various sizes ranging from the smaller domestic and dormitories to large and commodious halls. All are linked together by roofed in corridors, the sides of which are protected by tightly stretched hop netting of a narrow mesh which acts as an effective screen against wind and rain and admits a maximum amount of light and air, while it secures dry access to any part of the encampment independent of climatic conditions.

The buildings are electrically lighted and heated and are very cosy and comfortable. The whole of the encampment is linked by wireless so that announcements and any other communications can be given to each building by microphone. A large oast house has been converted into a reception room where the boys can occupy their leisure in billiards, ping-pong, etc, while one hut has been set apart for draughts and other table games.

Work is carried on at Cranbrook School where the boys attend daily and where separate accommodation has been provided. The purity of the country air has already had a beneficial effect on the boys which is shown by the high standard of health maintained by them during the several months they have been in their new quarters; the maximum amount of illness having been at the extremely low figure of 1 per cent, against 10 per cent for the same period of the year in London.

(Author's note: A similar camp, but this time completely self-contained, was opened at Wrens Warren in East Sussex by the National Camps Corporation, and was used primarily by evacuees from the City of Rochester.)

* * *

Mary Cramp *(now Mrs Augustus) was sent with her sister from Ashford to the City of Oxford for a short period in 1940:*

In 1940 I was 14 years old and attending the South Central Girls School in Ashford, Kent. My sister Edith was 16 and was the school secretary. I can't remember exactly when, but it was sometime during the autumn of 1940 that we were evacuated with our school to Oxford. I can't recall much of the journey except that we were shunted into a siding at Reading for a time. When we arrived at Oxford, the authorities were not expecting us. Apparently, we should have been expectant mothers! Not knowing what to do with us, we were taken to the town hall where we stayed for three days and nights, sleeping on the floor.

Girls from South Central School, Ashford, pictured shortly after arriving in Oxford in 1940

Eventually, my sister and I were taken to a fairly large house in Divinity Road, off the Cowley Road. We were billeted with a lady, her aged mother and two daughters who were school teachers. The lady and her daughters all gave music lessons.

Edith and I had to cook and clean, which we had never been used to, and we worked very hard. On the plus side, we were exposed to good music, and we did go to the theatre a

South Central School, Ashford, at the time of the evacuation in 1940

Mary Cramp posing with her steel helmet at her home in Kingsnorth Road in wartime Ashford after returning from Oxford

few times. It was also lovely living so close to the colleges and churches in Oxford. It was totally different from our own small market town of Ashford.

We attended school in a poor part of Oxford, which was quite a way from Divinity Road. Consequently, most of the money our parents sent us was spent on bus fares. The school building was old and badly in need of repair. The roof leaked when it rained and it was always cold. After about three months our parents took us back home to Ashford as they could tell we weren't very happy. Looking back, I am glad we had the experience of living in a city like Oxford, even if it was just for a short while.

Finally, the following interesting article appeared in The Kentish Express *for 17th November 1939, which gives a good indication of how evacuated mothers coped with living in the country around Ashford:*

HOW THE EVACUEES ARE FARING
MOST LOVE THE COUNTRY

In some of the villages a trek for home still goes on among the evacuated children but, on the whole, this tendency is considerably less than formerly.

Two mothers from a London dock district had made their minds up to return together. 'It seemed such a lot colder here in the wilds than in town,' they explained. Then they heard, on their hostesses' wireless, the talk by Miss Florence Horsburgh, Parliamentary Secretary to the Health Ministry, who spoke plainly both to evacuees and to householders.

'We thought it such a jolly sensible speech,' they admitted, 'that we decided to stay here after all.'

Miss Horsburgh put forward an array of facts showing where a selfish attitude on both sides could ruin every plan for safety. Mrs M., a Catford mother billeted in the Kentish Downs, was not complaining of her new quarters, but she said, 'It's all right here now, with all the berries on the hedges and that. What I want to know is what'll we do in the winter when there ain't nothing to look at?'

Tommy, Maggie and Phyllis from Eltham were quite content to remain with their foster mother and they were longing for Christmas-time. 'There's a real Christmas tree growing in the garden – a real 'un!' they exclaimed, as if almost unable to believe it.

A rather fatalistic parent, who missed the gossip of neighbours in her crowded home-district, declared that she was taking herself and her little girls away this weekend. 'Might as well all die together where there's a bit of life,' was her comment on the situation.

Mrs Barwick from Eltham found the country very lonely and quiet when she first arrived but since she has met several people and is shortly to share a house with another mother and her children, she has settled down and now prefers the country to the town. The expense of bus fares to the cinema, she said, is a drawback, but she and her two little boys have been much healthier since they arrived and are very fond of the country walks.

Not quite so contented with country life was Mrs Andrews of the same village. She is sharing a house with another family of five, having eight children of her own with her. Her husband is also there, out of work, and, although she gets up early to do her work to save using the light in the evening, the other family can afford to be less economical. 'If I am asked to pay half the bill when the time comes,' she said, 'I won't be able to do it. With healthy growing children and a husband suffering from a nervous breakdown it is impossible to live with people who do not have to count every penny.' Mrs Andrews is looking for a small empty billet where she can live with her family alone while her husband is looking for work in the country.

Apart from her financial affairs she appeared to be perfectly satisfied with country life although she has been unable to settle down. Mrs Dent is looking after her sister's three young children as well as her own four in part of a lovely old-world house. She is an expecting mother and finds that the three

During the period known as the phoney war, the temptation for mothers to bring home their evacuated children was immense. Government posters such as this one were prominently displayed in evacuated areas to try and stop the drift back home of the evacuees

rooms which she has to keep clean, with all the children, makes more work than her own home at Leigh, where her husband is still living. Only a few weeks before the evacuation the Dent family moved into a new home and Mrs Dent said she was anxious to return to settle her family in properly. Although she agreed that it was necessary for each evacuee to pay something towards his living, she said it was impossible to live on her husband's wage when the family was divided and since there was a considerable amount of country around her home, she had decided to return after October with her children.

There is no doubt that Mrs Turner, another evacuee, with her five children, is perfectly happy in the country in spite of the cold weather. She said she had never visited the country before leaving her home at New Cross, when war was declared. She settled down at the beginning and is perfectly contented, and she quite definitely has no intention of going away from the country which she likes quite as well as home.

'It is not fair on the government if we keep going home,' was the opinion of Mrs Edwards from Gillingham. Her husband is serving in the navy and she has settled down with her small son and seven-months-old baby, in the country, for as long as is necessary. Her opinion was, 'We ought to be thankful that something has been done for us. It must have cost a great deal of money.' When asked how she liked the country and if she had found it easy to settle down, Mrs Edwards replied that she was not the type to grumble; if it was necessary for her to live in the country she accepted it and lived there happily.

Chapter Ten

THE HOME FRONT

IN THEIR PLACE OF SAFETY the evacuated children must often have wondered what life was like for those back home. Many heard news from their home towns, or sampled life in Frontline Britain if they returned for visits or holidays.

Many of their friends remained behind to take their chances with Hitler's bombs and many more parents faced daily wartime dangers. This chapter gives an insight into life at home in Thanet while the evacuees were away.

However, we start with general wartime issues, such as air raid shelters, the Home Guard and rationing, mentioned in part by the evacuees themselves in their personal accounts. In the build up to war as tension increased and, prior to evacuation, homes in areas deemed to be at risk from enemy action, such as the Isle of Thanet, were issued with air-raid shelters. These shelters, known as Anderson shelters, were delivered in 'kit form' and had to be erected by the occupants of the house to which it was issued, as they braced themselves for the expected onslaught of bombing.

The following morale boosting article of 28th June, 1940, praises the effectiveness of these shelters, but stressed the need for them to be properly erected:

SAFETY IN STEEL SHELTERS
WHAT RECENT RAIDS HAVE PROVED

Reports from technical experts of the Ministry of Home Security who have visited the areas affected by the recent air raids, including those of last week, furnish striking testimony to the protective qualities of the Anderson steel garden shelters. Although many large bombs fell in close proximity to a number of these shelters, none of the occupants received any harm.

In one south-eastern town a heavy bomb,

Anderson shelters were issued to all those families who were considered at risk from enemy action. Erecting them was however the responsibility of the householder!

probably of 500lbs, fell in the back gardens of a group of small houses, most of which had Anderson shelters in their gardens. One of these shelters was only 30ft from the crater and contained a family of four persons, including two children. All were unharmed. The house from which the occupants of the shelter had come was badly damaged by bomb splinters.

Two other Anderson shelters close to the bomb were damaged owing to their having insufficient earth covering and, in one case, owing to the entrance, which was not covered by the house, not having an earth bank or similar protection for the entrance, as officially recommended. Neither of the damaged shelters was occupied.

In a south coast town the debris of a house fell on an Anderson shelter, but the occupants were unharmed. Another large bomb fell close to a public shelter, the occupants of which were unharmed. The reports confirm the necessity which has so often been stressed in official announcements that those who have Anderson shelters should see that they have proper earth covering which is fifteen inches of earth on the top and thirty inches at the back and sides.

If the entrance to the shelter does not face the house or a stout brick wall, or is more than fifteen feet from such protection, it must be guarded by an earth mound or boxes filled with earth not less than thirty inches thick, or half the thickness of brick or stone.

(What the article omitted to say was that an Anderson shelter would not survive a direct hit!)

Later, 'Morrison' shelters, named after Home Secretary Herbert Morrison, were issued for use indoors. These were of robust construction, made of steel in the form of a table and offered good protection against falling debris.

* * *

Air Raid Precautions
The Air Raid Warden was a key figure in the ARP. These men and women, mostly part-time volunteers, did much of the organisational work, not only with regard to the preparations for air raids, but also when the bombing did actually begin.

One of their duties was to check that the blackout was effective and being observed by all. "Put that light out' became one of the wardens' catch phrases. Another of the wardens'

How to Use the Shelter as a Table
FIGURE 8

The side and end panels must be in place and fastened with the hook and eye fastenings, when the shelter is in use as such. To use it as a table, or to make the bed, the panels can be removed.

The Morrison shelter for use indoors.
It could also be used as a table and a bed

SMALL CHILDREN'S RESPIRATOR
INSTRUCTIONS FOR PUTTING ON

To put the respirator on to a child:—
1. Stand the child in front of you with its back towards you so that its head rests against your body.
2. See that the hook and eye on the head harness straps are undone.
   Put your left thumb under the bottom and middle straps on the left side of the head harness, and your right thumb under the bottom and middle straps on the right side, and hang the respirator from your two thumbs.
3. Catch the chin of the respirator under the child's chin and then stretch the head harness over the head.
4. See that the respirator is straight on the child's face and that the chin is properly in position. Then join the hook and eye on the two bottom straps to secure the respirator in place.
   NOTE.—Most children quickly learn to put on the respirator themselves. They should be taught to do it in the way described above.

With the prospect of war on the horizon, the British Government expected widespread bombing of British cities and, as with the First World War, enemy use of gas as a weapon. Many leaflets and instructions on the use of gas masks were issued. A series of Wills's cigarette cards on the ARP included gas masks

responsibilities was to ensure that everyone had been issued with a gas mask – against the possibility of the use of poisonous gas by the Germans. Gas masks were far from popular with the general public. One ARP warden wrote in his report in 1939:

'One man was horribly sick after half a minute through the smell of rubber, and has been feeling nauseated since. Two colleagues were fitting masks and had a dreadful morning with toddlers crying and screaming. . . Elderly folk looked ill and expectant mothers fainted.'

* * *

The Home Guard
From the moment war began, Britain existed under the threat of invasion from Germany. With its miles of vulnerable beaches, the defence of the nation was top priority. That task was performed by the Home Guard.

In October 1939, Churchill, then First Lord of the Admiralty, had proposed that a 'Home Guard' should be formed, made up of 500,000 men, all over the age of 40. Seven months later, on 14th May 1940, the new

Recruitment poster for the ARP

In the years when our Country was in mortal danger

JAMES FREWIN

who served 23 January 1941 - 31 December 1944

gave generously of his time and powers to make himself ready for her defence by force of arms and with his life if need be.

George R.I.

THE HOME GUARD

An example of the certificate signed by the king and issued to those who served in the Home Guard during World War II

War Secretary, Anthony Eden, made this appeal on the radio:

'We want large numbers of men . . . men in Great Britain, who are British subjects between the ages of 17 and 65 . . . to come forward now and offer their services. . . The name of the new force which is now to be raised will be the Local Defence Volunteers. . . This is a part-time job, so there will be no need for any volunteer to abandon his present occupation. . . When on duty you will form part of the armed forces. . . You will not be paid, but you will receive a uniform and be armed. . .'

Within 24 hours of Anthony Eden's speech, a quarter of a million men had enrolled in the LDV and, by the summer of 1943, there were 1,100 Home Guard battalions – a total of 1,750,000 men. In its early days, the Home Guard's somewhat eccentric character gained it the affectionate nickname of 'Dad's Army'. Nevertheless, the volunteers took their jobs seriously. In reality the Home Guard was indispensable. Younger men could not be spared from active service for the crucial role of defence. And the bravery, loyalty and patriotism the men of the Home Guard showed as they performed their duty set an example to the whole nation.

The qualifications required for joining the Local Defence Volunteers (LDV) were minimal. There was no medical examination and recruits had only to be 'capable of free movement'. Experience with weapons was not essential, nor was the upper age limit of 65 strictly observed – the oldest member was well into his eighties! One of the first tasks of the Home Guard was to pull up signposts around the county so that, in the event of an invasion, enemy troops would not be able to find their way around.

In November 1944, with the end of the war in sight, the Home Guard was disbanded.

THE LAST WORD

It is suggested that the substance of this brief postscript be got by heart.

The main duties of the Home Guard are:
1. Guarding important points
2. Observation and reporting—prompt and precise.
3. Immediate attack against small, lightly armed parties of the enemy.
4. The defence of roads, villages, factories and vital points in towns to block enemy movements.

Every L.D.V. should know:
1. The whole of the ground in his own district.
2. The personnel of his own detachment.
3. The Headquarters of the detachment and where he is to report for duty in the event of an alarm.
4. What the alarm signal is.
5. The form of reports concerning enemy landings or approaches, what the reports should contain, and to whom they should be sent.

An extract from the Home Guard Handbook, listing the main duties

Company advertisements supported wartime efforts

* * *

Rationing was first introduced in Britain in January 1940. Butter, sugar, bacon and ham were the first items to go 'on the ration', followed by meat in March 1940. Offal, fish, potatoes and bread were left untouched, although white bread vanished in 1942 to be replaced by the lumpy and universally unpopular 'national wheatmeal loaf'.

Bread and potatoes became the principal bulk items in the national diet. Throwing away bread was strongly discouraged by the Ministry of Food whose anti-waste campaign led to some strange prosecutions. One woman was fined £10 for 'permitting bread to be wasted' – it was being fed to the birds in her garden!

Between the summers of 1940 and 1941 Britain lost much needed food on ships sunk at sea. But the arrival of the first American Lend-Lease goods in May 1941 provided the housewife with versatile canned meats, especially Spam, and other goods.

By November 1941 a points system was applied to canned fish and vegetables, enabling housewives to choose between a range of goods, each with a fixed points price. Under this system each person had 20 points which had to last for four weeks, a measure which did much to prevent hoarding by the better-off.

People could not pick and choose where they wanted to shop for their rationed foods. Each shopkeeper's supplies were tied to the number of his registered customers.

Women began to turn their flower gardens into vegetable patches as the government encouraged self-sufficiency in people's own back yard with the slogan

A Ministry of Food notice for June 1940

'DIG FOR VICTORY!' There was an endless supply of recipes and dietary information, from 'food flashes' shown between films in the cinemas to the five-minute 'Kitchen Front' radio programme broadcast daily at 8.15am. Carrots were seldom in short supply and were the subject of a flood of resistible suggestions from the Ministry of Food.

The wartime housewife wasted nothing. She was encouraged to place her salvage in four separate containers so that tins could be transformed into tanks and aircraft, boiled bones could be turned into glue or glycerine for explosives, kitchen waste could feed the pigs and paper could be recycled.

Women had to cope with immense difficulties as a result of war-time shortages. But a sense of optimism, enterprise, good housekeeping and humour always prevailed. Almost without exception every woman was committed to Britain's national survival and determination to make any sacrifice to help her country.

It has been said that the wartime generation ate a healthier diet than modern society consumes today, and that their improved health and long term life expectancy was increased by an enforced healthy, balanced diet. Environmentalists would also applaud the lack of waste and the high degree of salvage and recycling that was achieved during the war.

> **The Battle of the Atlantic is being lost!**
>
> *The reasons why:*
>
> 1. German U-boats, German bombers and the German fleet sink and seriously damage between them every month a total of 700 000 to 1 million tons of British and allied shipping.
> 2. All attempts at finding a satisfactory means of defence against the German U-boats or the German bombers have failed disastrously.
> 3. Even President Roosevelt has openly stated that for every five ships sunk by Germany, Britain and America between them can only build two new ones. All attempts to launch a larger shipbuilding programme in America have failed.
> 4. Britain is no longer in a position to secure her avenues of supply. The population of Britain has to do with about half the ration that the population of Germany gets. Britain, herself, can only support 40% of her population from her own resources in spite of the attempts made to increase the amount of land under cultivation. If the war is continued until 1942, 60% of the population of Britain will starve!
>
> All this means that starvation in Britain is not to be staved off. At the most it can be postponed, but whether starvation comes this year or at the beginning of next doesn't make a ha'porth of difference. Britain must starve because she is being cut off from her supplies.
>
> **Britain's losing the Battle of the Atlantic means Britain's losing the war!**

An example of the many propaganda leaflets dropped by the Germans during the war

*   *   *

The Women's Land Army
During the war the 'Grow Your Own' campaign contributed to Britain's food supplies, especially vegetables, but it was still the farms which provided most of the staple requirements like grain, potatoes, milk and meat. A serious problem arose by mid-1940. Conscription of young men into the armed forces created a shortage of 100,000 farm workers. The solution to this problem was to encourage women to join the Women's Land Army, and by 1944, it was 80,000 strong.

RATIONING
of Clothing, Cloth, Footwear
from June 1, 1941

Rationing has been introduced, not to deprive you of your real needs, but to make more certain that you get your share of the country's goods—to get fair shares with everybody else.

When the shops re-open you will be able to buy cloth, clothes, footwear and knitting wool *only if you bring your Food Ration Book with you.* The shopkeeper will detach the required number of coupons from the unused margarine page. Each margarine coupon counts as one coupon towards the purchase of clothing or footwear. You will have a total of 66 coupons to last you for a year; so go sparingly. You can buy where you like and when you like without registering.

NUMBER OF COUPONS NEEDED

Men and Boys	Adult	Child	Women and Girls	Adult	Child
Unlined mackintosh or cape	9	7	Lined mackintoshes or coats (over 28in. in length)	14	12
Other mackintoshes or raincoats or overcoat	16	12	Jacket, or short coat (under 28 in. in length)	12	8
Coat, or jacket, or blazer or like garment	13	8	Dress, or gown, or frock—woollen	12	8
Waistcoat, or pull-over, or cardigan, or jersey	5	3	Dress, or gown, or frock—other material	7	5
Trousers (other than fustian or corduroy)	8	6	Gym tunic or girl's skirt with bodice	8	6
Fustian or corduroy trousers	5	5	Blouse, or sports shirt, or cardigan, or jumper	5	3
Shorts	5	3	Skirt, or divided skirt	7	5
Overalls, or dungarees or like garment	6	4	Overalls, or dungarees or like garment	6	4
Dressing gown, or bathing gown	8	6	Apron, or pinafore	3	2
Night-shirt, or pair of pyjamas	8	6	Pyjamas	8	6
Shirt, or combinations—woollen	8	6	Nightdress	6	5
Shirt, or combinations—other material	5	4	Petticoat, or slip, or combination, or cami-knickers	4	3
Pants, or vest, or bathing costume or child's blouse	4	3	Other undergarments, including corsets	3	2
Pair of socks or stockings	3	2	Pair of stockings	2	1
Collar, or tie, or pair of cuffs	2	2	Pair of socks (ankle length)	1	1
Two handkerchiefs	1	1	Collar, or tie, or pair of cuffs	1	1
Scarf, or pair of gloves or mittens	2	2	Two handkerchiefs	1	1
Pair of slippers or goloshes	4	2	Scarf, or pair of gloves or mittens or muff	2	2
Pair of boots or shoes	7	3	Pair of slippers, boots or shoes	5	3
Pair of leggings, gaiters, or spats	3	2			

CLOTH. Coupons needed per yard depend on the width. For example, a yard of woollen cloth 36 inches wide requires 3 coupons. The same amount of cotton or other cloth needs 2 coupons.

KNITTING WOOL. 1 coupon for 2 ounces.

THESE GOODS MAY BE BOUGHT *WITHOUT* COUPONS:

*Children's clothing of sizes generally suitable for infants less than 4 years old. *Boiler suits and workmen's bib and brace overalls. *Hats and caps. *Sewing thread. *Mending wool and mending silk. *Boot and shoe laces. *Tapes, braids, ribbons and other fabrics of 3 inches or less in width. *Elastic. *Lace and lace net. *Sanitary towels. * Braces, suspenders and garters. *Hard haberdashery. *Clogs. *Black-out cloth dyed black. *All second-hand articles.

Glamorous recruitment posters to join the WLA hid the fact that the work was extremely hard and that the hours were long! But it was largely through these women's efforts that the food production in Britain was kept up.

* * *

After the evacuation of 2nd June 1940, local authorities in the Isle of Thanet recognised a growing problem in the towns – the problem of those children who had remained behind, known in some quarters as 'The Dead End Kids'. This problem was further aggravated by some parents bringing their evacuated siblings back to Thanet. With all schools closed or taken over by the forces or civil defence organisations, and with teachers exiled to Staffordshire with those children that left under the Government Evacuation Scheme, authorities in Thanet had no ready solution to this problem. One local official even wanted evacuation for children to become compulsory, as the following *Isle of Thanet Gazette* article for 6th December, 1940, shows:

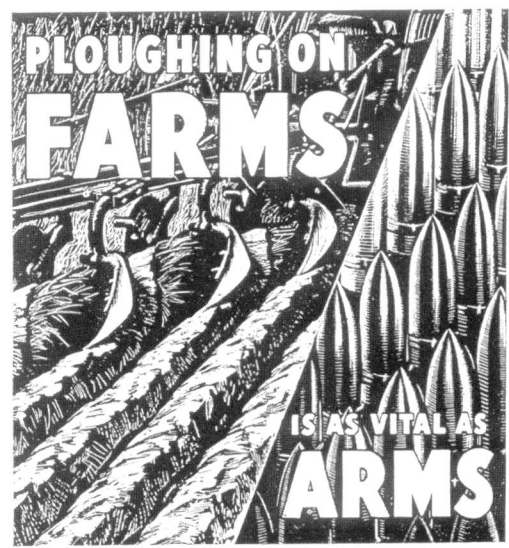

One of many advertisements to encourage farmers to intensify their efforts

CHILDREN WITHOUT SCHOOLS
RUNNING THE STREETS OF MARGATE
COMPULSORY EVACUATION WANTED — PARENTS' 'SELFISHNESS'

Parents who bring their children back to Margate were accused of being selfish by Alderman W. C. Redman, C.C., at a meeting of the Education Committee on Friday afternoon, when he referred to the many children running about the streets who were not receiving any education.

He expressed the view that it was contrary to the regulations of the Board of Education to reopen schools in the evacuation area, and said steps were being taken at the request of the Regional Commissioner to send children away. 'I wish the Government would make it compulsory for children to go away,' he exclaimed.

An appeal was made to parents not to bring their children home from Staffordshire for the Christmas holiday, it being pointed out that if they did they would probably lose the billets in which they had settled down after six months of evacuation.

In acknowledging his re-election as chairman of the committee, Alderman Redman said that it was little short of tragedy that, because of the doings of a maniac, there should be such an upheaval in the educational system, which for older children was bound to have a detrimental effect.

(The reader will note that there was little sympathy for the heartsearching undergone

by parents who did not want to be parted from their children.)

* * *

Pressure on non-conforming parents intensified, when, in January 1941, the Mayor of Margate was so concerned with the problem of children still in the town that he issued the following emotional appeal:

MAYOR'S APPEAL TO PARENTS
OF ALL CHILDREN OF SCHOOL AGE IN MARGATE

The recent census which was taken of the number of children in the borough gives me much concern, not only because of the possible intensification of enemy action in the air and the danger of threatened invasion, but more particularly because of the children themselves.

Margate is a 'DEFENCE AREA'. The possibilities of what can happen in the spring with such large numbers of children in our midst is an alarming outlook. Parents who from selfish motives have refused to allow their children to proceed to our Educational Centre are penalising them to an extent that may react in after years in a very serious manner.

Can you visualise the effect which the lack of education will have on the children if perchance the war continues over a lengthy period of years?

This is a serious matter and one that is causing much concern to me. I am constantly receiving reports from Staffordshire of the happiness of the pupils and of the progress they are making in their

THANET WAR WEAPONS WEEKS

OVER £250,000 SUBSCRIBED

FIGURES FOR FIRST FIVE DAYS

	MARGATE	BROADSTAIRS	RAMSGATE	WESTGATE (Included in Margate Total)	BIRCHINGTON
Saturday	£25,489	£35,955	£65,881	£2,382	£4,725
Monday	£23,486	£11,900	£12,776	£213	£1,077
Tuesday	£18,221	£3,420	£10,288	£656	£2,716
Wednesday	£21,505	£2,635	£11,796	£1,461	£1,154
Thursday	£27,587	£6,151	£10,750	£1,450	£2,763
Totals	£116,288	£60,063	£111,494	£6,165	£12,435
Aim	£150,000	£30,000	£75,000		£5,000

TOTAL FOR THANET, YESTERDAY (THURSDAY) EVENING

£287,845

TWO MORE DAYS TO GO

> GO TO IT, THANET
> EVERY PENNY MEANS ANOTHER
> BULLET FOR HITLER

Thanet War Weapons Week in May 1941 raised the astonishing amount of £393,756 despite the wartime population being only about 32,000. Ramsgate raised £165,626, Margate £157,122 and Broadstairs £71,008

studies. Are you doing your duty as parents by depriving your children of the enjoyment and benefits of the educational facilities which are readily being granted?

It will be my privilege in the early weeks of February to visit Staffordshire in company with the Mayoress so that I can pay my tribute, on behalf of the people of Margate, to all those who are so loyally looking after the welfare of the children.

Will you help at once by registering your children to take up their studies when schools reopen. Call at the Town Clerk's Office. It is your duty. Please respond. I appeal to you.

G. P. Hoare, Mayor,
Town Hall, Margate
7 January 1941

A milliner's model surveys the wreckage after a hit-and-run raid on the High Street, Margate

Despite these pressures and the happy propaganda images praising the experiences of the evacuees, the problem had seemingly worsened, as indicated in the Thanet Times *article for 8th March 1941:*

CHILDREN AT WAR

The minds of local authorities, on the south-eastern coast of England are much exercised as to the position of children of school age during the present period. In spite of repeated appeals, there are many parents who have either neglected to send their children away to a place of comparative safety or, having sent them away, have now brought them back again.

The result is that the towns which are subjected to the most direct attacks by the enemy are literally swarming with youngsters who, not being subjected to any form of education are running wild. Moreover, they are living under conditions which cannot be but detrimental to them, both physically and mentally. The numbers are staggering. It is estimated that at Ramsgate there are about 680 such children. Recently, Alderman W. C. Redman, Chairman of the Margate Education Committee, said that there were about 700 children still remaining in the town while at Dover the number is put at about 1,000. None of the authorities has been blind to the situation, and from time to time representations have been made to various government departments regarding the problem.

* * *

As 1939 gave way to 1940, the period known as the 'Phoney War' came to an end, and suddenly the Isle of Thanet was experiencing enemy action which was to increase from

The Dunbar Castle *was bound for Cape Town when she was sunk off Ramsgate early in 1940*

that point onwards: One prime target in Thanet, especially during the Battle of Britain, was the airfield at RAF Manston, which was attacked many times during the war. Other action included the following:

January 9th, 1940.
The 10,000 ton liner *Dunbar Castle*, was sunk by a German mine off Ramsgate on 9th January, 1940. The ship's back was broken in the explosion and 152 people died, including many children. The magnetic mine, dropped by parachute, was the first of Hitler's 'secret weapons'.

Ramsgate's Blackest Day.
August 24th, 1940 was the most tragic day in the history of wartime Ramsgate. On this day, RAF Manston was attacked at least three times by enemy bombers, but also on the same day, instead of attacking the airfield, one wave of enemy raiders turned their attention on the town and dropped 250 high explosive and incendiary bombs.

31 people were killed, 45 injured and 1,200 houses were destroyed. Streets in the town were blocked, water mains fractured and unexploded bombs littered the borough. Two auxiliary firemen, who were cycling to work when the raid began, were machine-gunned and badly injured. One of them, although severely wounded and weak from lack of blood, dragged his friend to a sheltered spot and then climbed over masonry and debris to a first aid post. His friend died but he was awarded the George Medal for his act of gallantry.

Most of those who died were in the town centre. Five pubs, the town's gasworks, lifeboat station and several shops were hit by bombs. The worst area was Camden Square where the Assembly Hall was demolished.

It could have been worse. Many of the town's 60,000 population were sheltering 70 feet below ground in the tunnels which ran for three miles under the town, and it was estimated that these tunnels saved up to 11,000 people.

It was Ramsgate's turn again on Saturday November 2nd, 1940. An air raid warning had sent people rushing for the shelters, but the 'all clear' quickly sounded and shoppers returned to the town centre. Without warning 25 aircraft swooped out of the clouds and released more than 60 bombs, sending hundreds of people scurrying for cover. One woman who survived the attack returned home to find her own mother and her two children dead in the ruins of her house.

In the dark days of 1940 when invasion seemed imminent, residents of Thanet still remaining in the area were aware that further evacuation was likely, although details of this scheme were kept secret. The Thanet coast was to be cleared of all non-essential civilians to allow troops freedom of movement in dealing with any enemy forces. 25,000 Thanet residents would have been entrained for Surrey and Hertfordshire in just 48 hours, leaving behind 3,000 Local Defence Volunteers, firemen, civil defence workers and officials.

*   *   *

We end this chapter with the text of a broadcast made by Her Royal Highness Princess Elizabeth, aged fourteen, on BBC Radio's Children's Hour on 13th October, 1940:

1943 – Holy Trinity Church, Margate, was badly damaged by a 'Bouncing Billy' bomb which fell near Fort Paragon, bounced over some cottages, landing in Canon Prior's Chapel, where it burst

In wishing you all good evening, I know that I am speaking to friends and companions who have shared with my sister and myself many a happy Children's Hour. Thousands of you in this country have had to leave your homes and be separated from your fathers and mothers. My sister Margaret Rose and I feel so much for you, as we know from experience what it means to be away from those we love most of all. To you living in new surroundings we send a message of true sympathy, and at the same time we would like to thank the kind people who have welcomed you to their homes in the country.

All of us children who are still at home think continually of our friends and relations who have gone overseas to find a wartime home and a kindly welcome in Canada, Australia, New Zealand, South Africa and the United States of America.

My sister and I feel we know quite a lot about these countries. Our father and mother have so often talked to us of their visits to different parts of the world, so it is not difficult for us to picture the sort of life you are all leading, and to think of all the new sights you must be seeing and the adventures you must be having, but I am sure that you too are often thinking of the old country. I know you won't forget us. It is just that we are not forgetting you, but want on behalf of all the children at home to send you our love and best wishes, to you and your kind hosts as well.

Before I finish, I can truthfully say to you all that we children at home are full of cheerfulness and courage. We are trying to do all we can to help our gallant sailors, soldiers and airmen. And we are trying, too, to bear our own share of the danger and sadness of war. We know, every one of us that, in the end, all will be well, for God will care for us and give us victory and peace. And though peace comes, remember, it will be for us, the children of today, to make the world of tomorrow a better and happier place.

My sister is by my side and we are both going to say goodnight to you. Come on Margaret . . .

Margaret: Good night children.

Elizabeth: Good night and good luck to you all.

Winston Churchill wore two hats – he was Prime Minister and Defence Minister. Here he exchanges his civilian hat for a 'Battle Bowler' during his visit to the Kent front line town of Ramsgate during July 1940

Chapter Eleven

EPILOGUE

By May 1945, after nearly six years the war in Europe was finally over. The air-raid sirens were silent. At last the population of Thanet could live without the daily fear of bombings or shelling, and people were now able to sleep safely in there own beds instead of using the often hated air-raid shelters.

The evacuees had been arriving back home to the Isle of Thanet in small groups for the past year, but now there was a sudden influx as the remaining boys and girls returned from Staffordshire. Their return marked the end of the government's official evacuation scheme and of an unprecedented episode in Britain's social history.

The Isle of Thanet's VE-Day celebrations on 8th May 1945 proved something of a

The headlines in one of Thanet's local newspapers for 8th May 1945

mixture. Ramsgate hailed Victory in Europe with ships' sirens, impromptu concerts, street parties, and a liberal display of bunting. Margate's celebrations, however, were somewhat slow to get started and at first there were few outward signs of jubilation. In fact, in many parts, it was a peaceful day more like an Easter bank holiday with people being far more restrained than their Ramsgate counterparts. Quite a number of people were on the sands, but the main indications of rejoicing came from the hotels and soldiers' billets where songs were sung with gusto and enthusiasm. Although one or two flags had been hoisted on public buildings and government offices, everyone began to wonder where the bunting was and the church bells remained silent. Nevertheless, on the following day, as news of victory began to sink in, hundreds of private houses and shops were gaily decorated with flags and streamers, and just about every kind of patriotic device which could be either found or made.

To mark the occasion all the schools were closed for the two days holiday and there was scarcely a child in any street without a red, white and blue emblem. Of course, in the evenings louder signs of revelry were heard from the public houses where a one hour extension had been granted. Only a few lights were visible, as restrictions in the coastal towns were still operative until 11th May 1945.

In Ramsgate, by contrast, there were scenes of excitement from the early afternoon. Soldiers, sailors and airmen formed a huge circle at the crossroads junction and gave a full performance of every known song in the British serviceman's repertoire. The audience at this impromptu concert extended into Harbour Street, High Street, Queen Street and King Street – even the church bells rang out with joy.

Although VE-Day was celebrated in various ways in Thanet, possibly the most popular, and successful, were the children's street parties. House to house collections were made to cope with the expenses of providing food and drink but, in spite of the fact that Britain had been at war for over five and a half years, there seemed to be no shortage of food for the celebrations. Brightly coloured flags and bunting hung from house fronts and stretched across the streets as well as decorating many of the heavily laden tables, the like of which, many of the youngsters had never before seen.

Peace at last meant that Sunday, 13th May, was observed throughout the country as a day of national thanksgiving and prayer. At Ramsgate a parade of over a thousand was organised to take place at the St Lawrence Cliffs bandstand in the afternoon.

Although Thanet's war was considered over, the police were to experience a new problem when the exiled children returned. The outlook of the returning evacuees was totally different to those youngsters who had remained behind. They had not been brought up in an atmosphere of bombs and shells exploding around them, the nightly excursions to the air-raid shelters or the tunnels. Few knew the daily observation of troops, airmen and naval personnel, the fascination engendered by the proximity of aircraft of every description flying overhead – identified by reference to the sixpenny booklets sold at the corner shop. Bomb sites became wonderful adventure playgrounds where wild flowers flourished, and where bomb craters filled with rain water, became homes for newts and frogs.

Top of the youngsters' list of priorities was collecting pieces of bomb casings and bits of crashed aircraft. Bullets, cannon shells, time-fuses, detonators, hand grenades, mortar-bombs, and 101 objects of war, filled garden sheds to overflowing. A police report described one shed crammed with war souvenirs as an Aladdin's Cave.

Adventure and celebrations aside, the end of the war brought some distressing family complications. Many evacuees returned to find their homes destroyed by enemy action, and some had even lost one or both their parents as a result of the war. The problem of orphaned children was to raise much public concern and heartache. But it was life within the family unit itself that had changed dramatically as a result of the war. Many of the evacuated children had left loving foster parents behind and had returned home to their own parents, who, in many cases, seemed like strangers to them. Some evacuees had a terrible time trying to readjust to 'normal' family life. In certain cases some children found it impossible to adjust, and eventually returned to their war time foster parents. The stress this placed on the family unit must have been enormous.

Another dramatic change to family life which had occurred during the war years, was that mothers, deprived of their evacuated children and, in most cases, their husbands, had learnt new skills and had had to become independent. Husbands, returning from the war and expecting things to carry on as before, found that family life was never to be the same again. The wives had suffered as much as the husbands and had learned to live without them, or worse still, had had extra-marital affairs in their absence. As a result, divorce rates rose eight-fold after the war, compared to figures for 1939, and most of these divorces were petitioned by the husbands!

So did anything good come out of the Government Evacuation Scheme? The scheme obviously saved many children's lives, but it also brought to the notice of the general public and to the government, the inequalities in family life, especially among the children. Indeed, today's modern welfare state can be attributed in part to the revelations brought about by the Government Evacuation Scheme and the different experiences of childhood that it highlighted.

By 1944, the evacuation had contributed to improvements in child care with the introduction of social workers and to proposals for a new local authority Children's Committee. But Parliament still needed to be persuaded to formulate a new policy regarding the children. Lady Allen, a stalwart of the children's cause, wrote her famous letter to *The Times*, which was published on 15th July 1944, and read as follows:

Sir,
Thoughtful consideration is being given to many fundamental problems, but in reconstruction plans one section of the community has, so far, been entirely forgotten.

I write of those children who, because of their family misfortune, find themselves under the guardianship of a government department or one of the many charitable organisations. The public are, for the most part, unaware that many thousands of these children are being brought up under repressive conditions that are generations out of date and are unworthy of our traditional care for children. Many who are orphaned, destitute or neglected still live under the chilly stigma of 'charity'; too often they form groups isolated from the main stream of life and education, and few of them know the comfort and security of individual affection. A letter does not allow space for detailed evidence.

In many 'homes', both charitable and public, the willing staff are, for the most part, overworked, underpaid, and untrained; indeed there is no recognized system of training. Inspection, for which the Ministry of Health, the Home Office, or the Board of Education may be nominally responsible, is totally inadequate, and few standards are established or expected. Because no one government department is fully responsible, the problem is more difficult to tackle.

A public enquiry, with full government support, is urgently needed to explore this largely uncivilised territory. Its mandate should be to ascertain whether the public and charitable organisations are, in fact, enabling these children to lead full and happy lives and to make recommendations how the community can compensate them for the family life they have lost. In particular, the enquiry should investigate what arrangements can be made (by regional reception centres or in other ways) for the careful consideration of the individual children before they are finally placed with foster-parents or otherwise provided for; how the use of large residential homes can be avoided; how staff can be appropriately trained and ensured adequate salaries and suitable conditions of work, and how central administrative responsibility can be set and can be maintained by adequate inspection.

The social upheaval caused by the war has not only increased this army of unhappy children, but presents the opportunity for transforming their conditions. The Education Bill and the White Paper on the Health Services have alike ignored the problem and the opportunity.

Yours sincerely,
Marjory Allen of Hurtwood.

The response to the letter was astonishing. *The Times* received more letters about child care than on any other subject (including the war!). One reason for the enormous public interest was that evacuation had made the issue of child care the concern of everybody.

The government was forced to take notice and conditions improved with the setting up of the welfare state in 1945 and, later, the Curtis and Clyde Reports were accepted by all political parties, and the Children's Act became law on 5th July 1948, ensuring future generations of children a better quality of life.

But what of the evacuees themselves? Did their experiences have any other lasting effect on them? The short answer is yes! Many found love, care and adventure, and the evacuation experience made many of the children more independent and able to cope with varying situations. For others, the experience of being wrenched from loving parents into abusive or neglectful foster homes was devastating and so traumatic that it has had a detrimental effect right into their adult lives. Others were so deeply affected that they are unable even to talk about their experiences.

I think that my own greatest regret, concerning my evacuation, is that I was deprived of the opportunity to grow up with my brother and three sisters during those formative years and that my father became a stranger to me. As we see people today in other lands being uprooted by war and ethnic hatred, let us pause and remember our own disrupted generation and pray that evacuation on the scale of the World War II episode, never happens to our children again.

* * *

The following list contains some of the interesting events leading up to and including the war years:

1933	
January	Hitler becomes German Chancellor.
1935	
March	Hitler ignores Treaty of Versailles and introduces compulsory military service.
1938	
12 March	Union between Germany and Austria.
September	Munich crisis – Britain and France agree to Hitler taking over the German-speaking parts of Czechoslovakia.
September	Mini evacuation of children in Britain.
	British Government starts stockpiling ration cards.
	The Auxiliary Territorial Service (ATS) is formed.
1939	
February	Anderson shelters issued.
March	Germany invades Czechoslovakia.
June	Women's Land Army formed.
August	'Lord Haw Haw' offers his services to Goebbels' Nazi Ministry of Propaganda.
	Trial black-out in London.
24 August	The King and Queen break off their holiday at Balmoral to return to London.
	Censorship imposed on overseas mail.
1 September	Germany invades Poland.
	Start of official evacuation of children from the cities.
3 September	France and Britain declare war on Germany.
	Air raid sirens first heard – a false alarm.
	Churchill appointed First Lord of the Admiralty.
September	British Ministry of Information formed.
	Identification cards issued.
19 September	First evening radio broadcast of ITMA.
October	British Expeditionary Force arrives in France.
	Beginning of 'Dig for Victory' campaign.
	Churchill proposes establishment of units of Local Defence Volunteers.
16 October	Sinking of battleship Royal Oak at Scapa Flow.
13 December	British victory in Battle of the River Plate.
15 December	Premiere of the film *Gone with the Wind*.
December	Many evacuees go home for Christmas.
1940	
1 January	Two million 19 to 27-year-olds called up.
January	BBC introduces the Forces Programme.
8 January	Food rationing begins (butter, bacon and sugar).
March	Meat rationed.
April	Vera Lynn voted British Expeditionary Forces' favourite singer.
9 April	Germany invades Denmark and Norway.

May	Germany invades Holland and Belgium and then France.
10 May	Churchill becomes Prime Minister.
14 May	War Secretary Anthony Eden appeals for men to join the Home Guard.
15 May	Home Guard begins patrolling.
27 May	Start of the evacuation of Dunkirk.
June	BBC begins broadcasting *Music while you Work*.
2 June	Evacuation of children from Kent coastal towns and Medway area.
4 June	Churchill promises to 'fight them on the beaches'.
10 June	Italy declares war on Britain and France.
22 June	Fall of France.
July	Ministry of Supply makes salvage collecting compulsory.
	Tea, margarine and other fats rationed.
	Free or cheap milk for mothers.
21 July	Hitler plans Operation Sea Lion – the invasion of Britain.
31 July	Aeroplane fighter production is 50% above target figure.
August	Icing banned on wedding cakes.
	Home Guard is affiliated to army county regiments.
15 August	Battle of Britain reaches its height.
7 September	Start of the blitz.
13 September	Buckingham Palace bombed.
15 September	RAF wins Battle of Britain.
September	Fresh wave of evacuation of children from cities.
13 October	Princesses Elizabeth and Margaret broadcast to evacuees on BBC Radio's Children's Hour.
14 November	Coventry heavily bombed.
December	Selling silk stockings becomes an offence.
1941	
February	Cosmetics rationing begins except for lipstick.
March	Lend-Lease Bill passed in America enabling Britain to receive US goods on deferred payment.
April	Germany launches North African offensive.
	Germany invades Yugoslavia and Greece.
	Women's services become part of Armed Forces.
	ITMA established as a huge hit.
	In Which We Serve released.
	BBC sets up Propaganda Unit for broadcasting.
	Battle of Atlantic: total allied loss at sea is 195 ships, weighing 687,000 tons.
May	First lend-lease supplies arrive from America.
10 May	Last and worst night of the Blitz.
June	Clothes rationing and utility scheme for retail goods begin.
	Venereal disease rate has increased by 70% in two years.
22 June	Germany invades Russia.
November	Points rationing on food introduced.
December	Vitamin welfare scheme for children introduced.
	Women conscripted for the first time – unmarried women aged 20 to

	30 subject to call-up.
7 December	Japan attacks Pearl Harbour and America enters the war.
1942	
26 January	First of GIs arrive in Britain.
February	Rationing extended.
	The fall of Singapore.
May	Introduction of utility clothing.
1 July	Churchill survives a vote of confidence in the House of Commons with a majority of 471.
12 August	Churchill meets Stalin in Moscow.
25 August	Duke of Kent killed in aeroplane crash in Scotland.
October	Battle of El Alamein.
	Ministry of Health launches a campaign to warn the public against VD.
November	Release of US film *Casablanca*.
8 November	British and American forces land in North Africa.
1 December	Beveridge Plan proposes far-reaching social reforms that form the basis of the modern welfare state.
December	Germans surrounded at Stalingrad.
	Points rationing extended.
19 December	British troops advance out of India, forcing Japanese back into Burma.
1943	
14-24 January	Churchill and Roosevelt meet in Casablanca and issue demand for the 'unconditional surrender' of Germany.
31 January	Germans surrender at Stalingrad.
3 March	Bethnal Green Tube Disaster – 173 people crushed to death.
5 March	Battle of the Ruhr begins: 443 RAF aeroplanes attack Essen.
April	Allies pull ahead in Battle of Atlantic with a loss of 18,000 tons of shipping compared to previous year's monthly average of 650,000.
May	Germany and Italy surrender in North Africa.
June	King George VI visits troops in North Africa, awards George Cross to Malta.
July	Age limit for conscription for women raised to 50, women with family responsibilities exempt.
August	Home Guard now numbers 1,100 regiments, consisting of 1.75 million men.
13 October	Italy turns against Hitler and declares war on Germany.
October	Completion of the Thai-Burma railway by POWs under Japanese command.
28 November	Churchill, Roosevelt and Stalin meet in Teheran.
1944	
January	Red Army breaks two-year siege on Leningrad.
3 March	RAF acknowledges use of new 12,000lb bombs in raids on German cities.
March	79 Allied airmen escape from Stalag Luft III camp.
March	Government announces a target of post-war house building at 300,000

	a year.
6 June	D-Day – Allies land in Normandy.
12 June	First V-1 flying-bombs dropped on London and the South-East.
25 August	Paris liberated.
September	Government releases details of demobilisation.
	V-2 attacks on Britain.
9-20 October	Churchill and Stalin meet in Moscow.
November	Home Guard disbands.

1945

4-11 February	Churchill, Roosevelt and Stalin meet at Yalta.
February	British forces clear the Reichwald of German troops.
13 February	RAF starts massive bombing raids on Dresden.
March	Princess Elizabeth joins ATS.
16 April	Roosevelt dies.
29 April	German forces in Italy surrender.
30 April	Russians take Berlin.
	Hitler commits suicide.
7 May	Germans surrender unconditionally.
8 May	VE-Day.
18 June	'Lord Haw Haw' put on trial for treason.
	Demobilisation begins.
5 July	Churchill meets with Truman and Stalin at Potsdam.
26 July	Election result announced. Churchill replaced by Labour leader Clement Attlee.
6 August	Atomic bomb dropped on Hiroshima.
8 August	Atomic bomb dropped on Nagasaki.
15 August	VJ-Day.
August	By the end of the war 100,000 British women have married Allied and Dominion servicemen. The total number of GI brides numbers 80,000. One in three newly-married women are aged under 21.
December	The divorce rate for the year soars to 25,000 compared with 8,000 in 1939. The number of illegitimate births rises from 26,500 in 1940 to 64,000 by 1945.

* * *

CASUALTIES

Casualty figures due to enemy action for the evacuation areas of Kent mentioned in this book:

		Killed	*Seriously wounded*	*Slightly hurt*	*By*
Ashford					
1940	17 July	3	1	10	Enemy bombing
	16 September	2	9		Enemy bombing
	26 September	7		2	Enemy bombing

	12 December	2	3	8	Enemy bombing
1942	26 October	11		16	Enemy bombing and machine gun fire
	27 November	1	2	2	Machine gun fire
	22 December	1	2	1	No information
1943	3 February	6	11	15	Enemy bombing
	24 March	50	77	79	Enemy bombing

Canterbury

1940	21 August	5	1	5	Enemy bombing
	9 September	9	6	7	Enemy bombing
	11 October	9	2	6	Enemy bombing
	14 October	2	1	25	Enemy bombing
1941	20 April	1		5	Enemy bombing
1942	1 June	43	40	41	Enemy bombing
	3 June	5	5	18	Enemy bombing
	7 June	1		2	Enemy bombing
	31 October	33	54	56	Enemy bombing

Margate

1940	19 October	3		2	Enemy bombing
	14 November	1	5	13	Enemy bombing
	16 November	2		3	Enemy bombing
1941	17 April	4	2	25	Enemy bombing
	8 July	3	3	9	Enemy bombing
	8 September	3	2	7	Enemy bombing
	9 November	3	1	2	Enemy bombing
1943	18 January	2			Enemy bombing
	30 January	4	3	11	Enemy bombing
	1 June	10	4	46	Enemy bombing

Broadstairs

1941	3 August	1		19	Enemy bombing
	16 August	5	1	10	Enemy bombing
1943	26 January	1		2	Enemy bombing

Ramsgate

1940	12 August	1	2	3	Enemy bombing
	24 August	31	11	47	Enemy bombing
	2 November	8	5	18	Enemy bombing
	11 November	1		8	Enemy bombing
1941	4 January	4	13	9	Enemy bombing
	11 January	2			Enemy bombing
	3 February	3		4	Enemy bombing
	3 March	3		2	Enemy bombing
	20 March	3	2	7	Enemy bombing

	Date				
	9 April	2			Enemy bombing
	14 June	4	1	11	Enemy bombing
	7 September	8	5	9	Enemy bombing
	9 November	1		5	Enemy bombing
1943	26 January	2	3	1	Enemy bombing
	28 June	1	1		Cross-channel shelling
	5 July	2	3		Cross-channel shelling
	16 August	1	2	3	Enemy bombing
	4 October	3	10	10	Cross-channel shelling
	3 November	2	1		Cross-channel shelling
1944	1 September	2	2	17	Cross-channel shelling

* * *

Readers might like to know that there is an evacuees' association with members nationwide and in Canada, Australia, New Zealand, South Africa and the USA. Those wishing to know more about the association should write to:

> The Evacuees' Reunion Association,
> Goodbody's Mill,
> Albert Road,
> Retford,
> Nottinghamshire DN22 6JD.

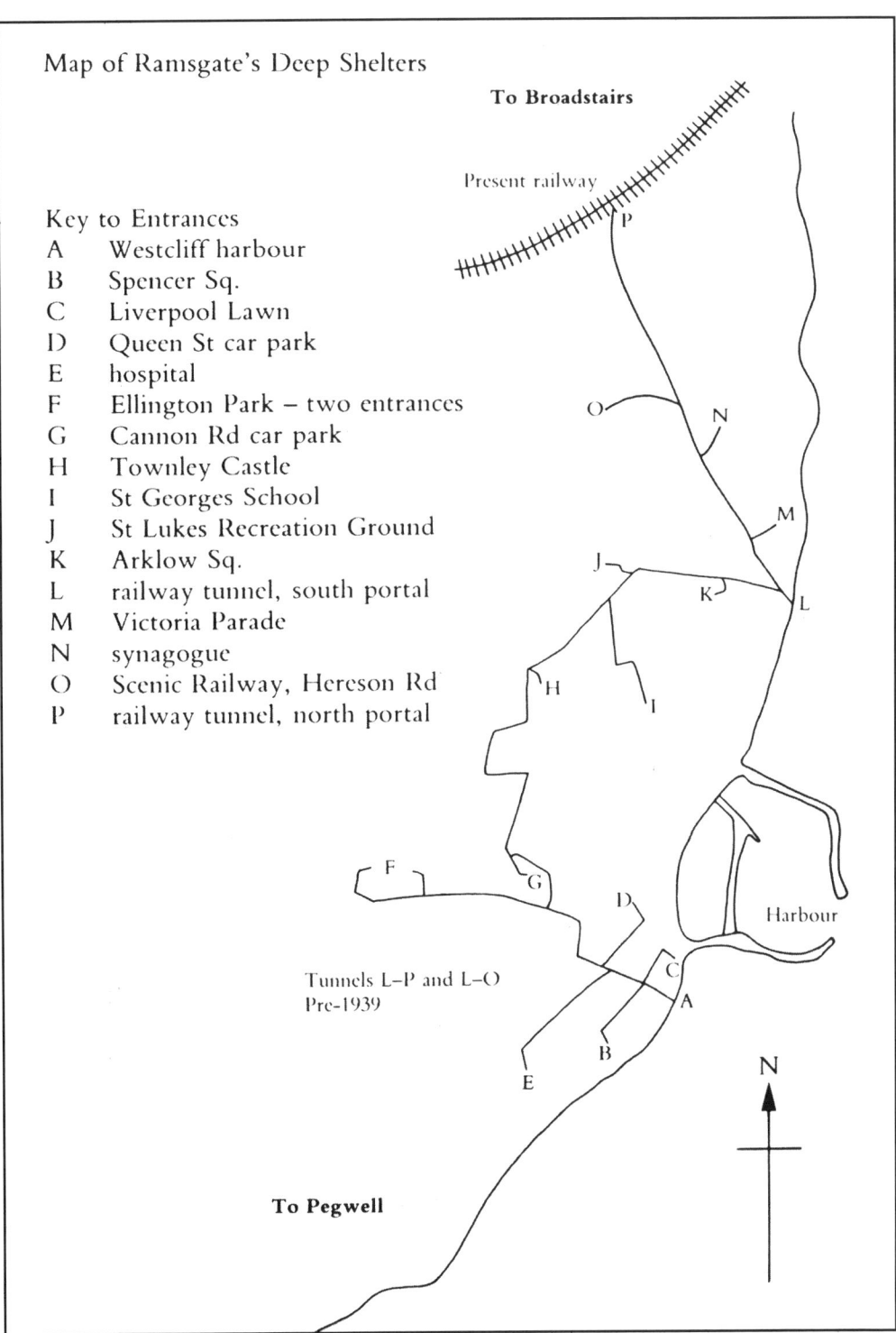

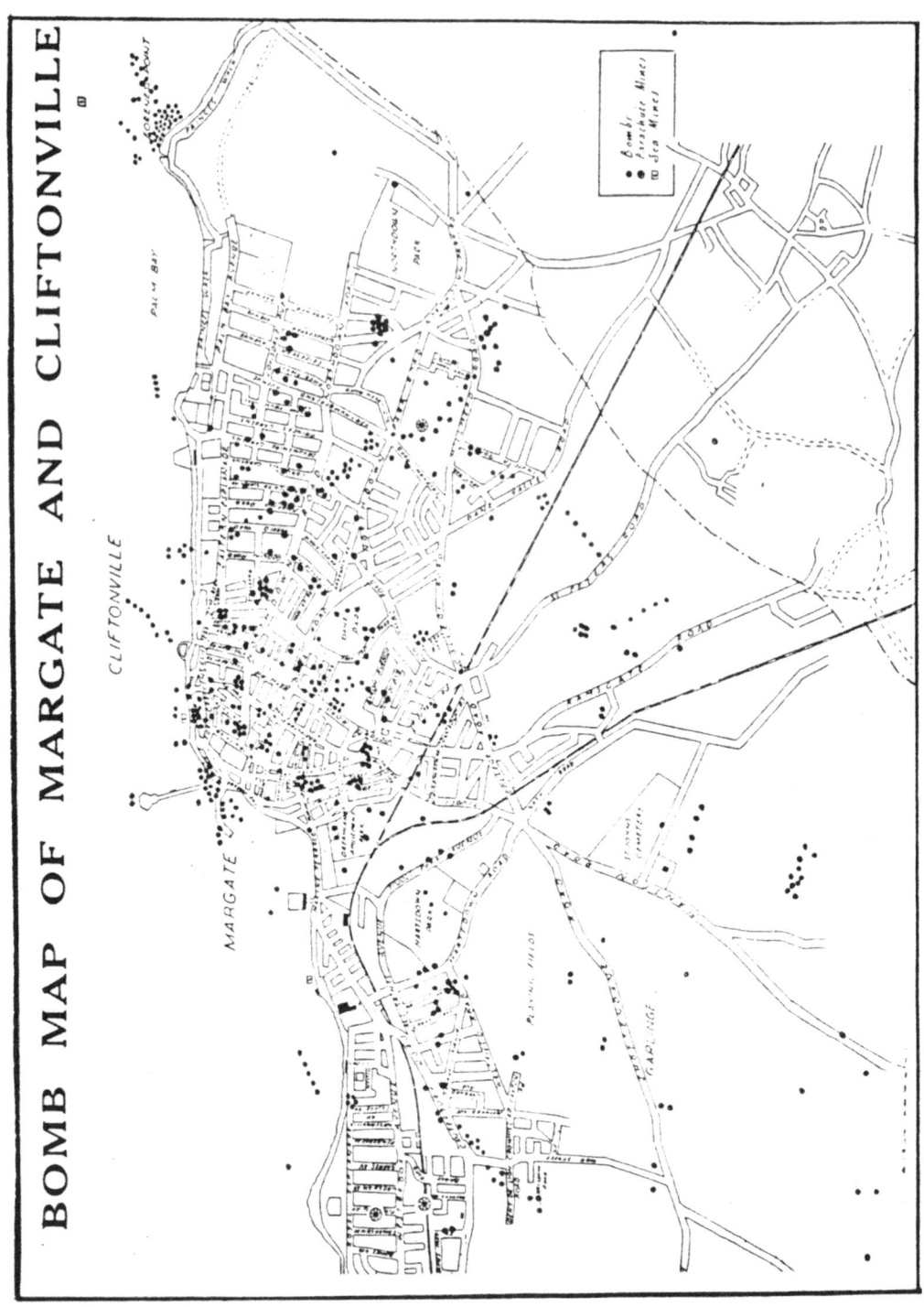

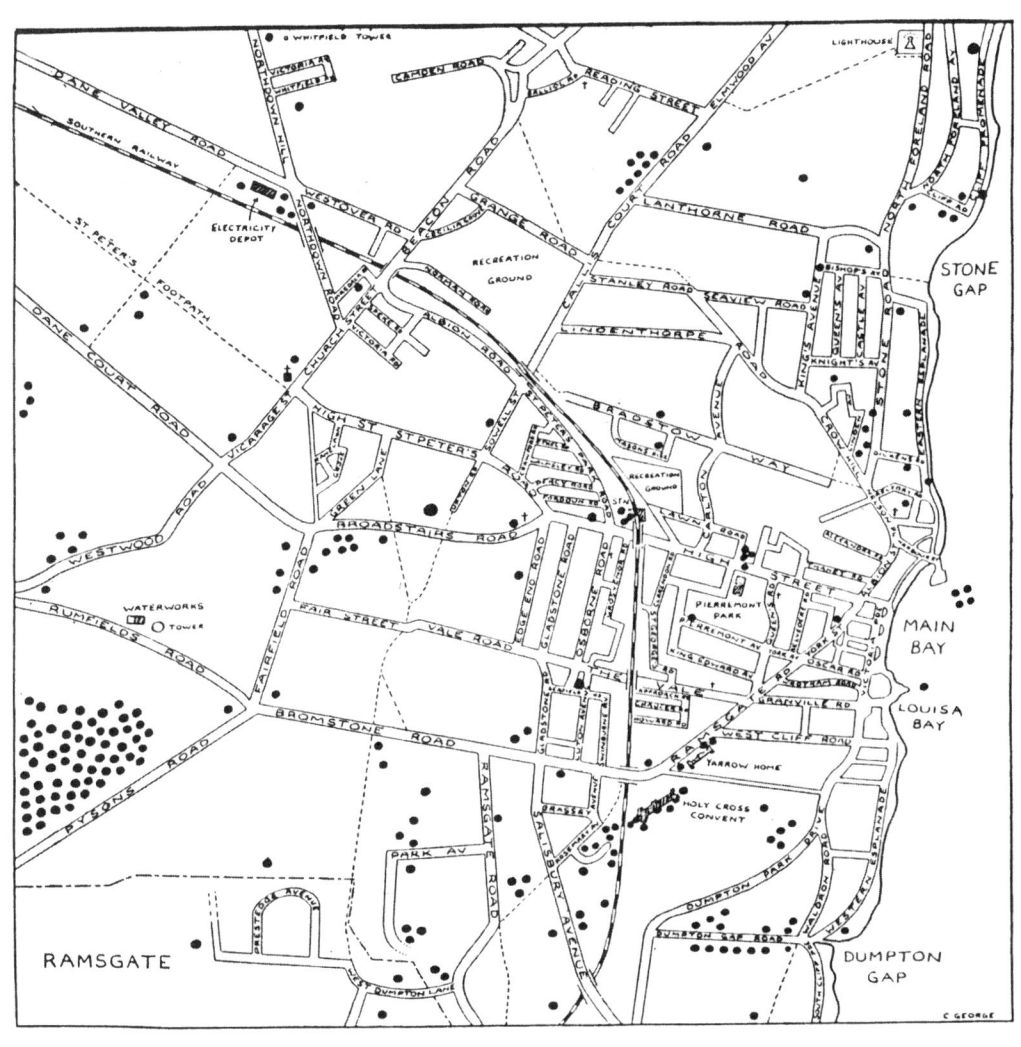

Bomb map of the Broadstairs area
The concentration of bombs to the left of the map shows the location
of a wartime airfield

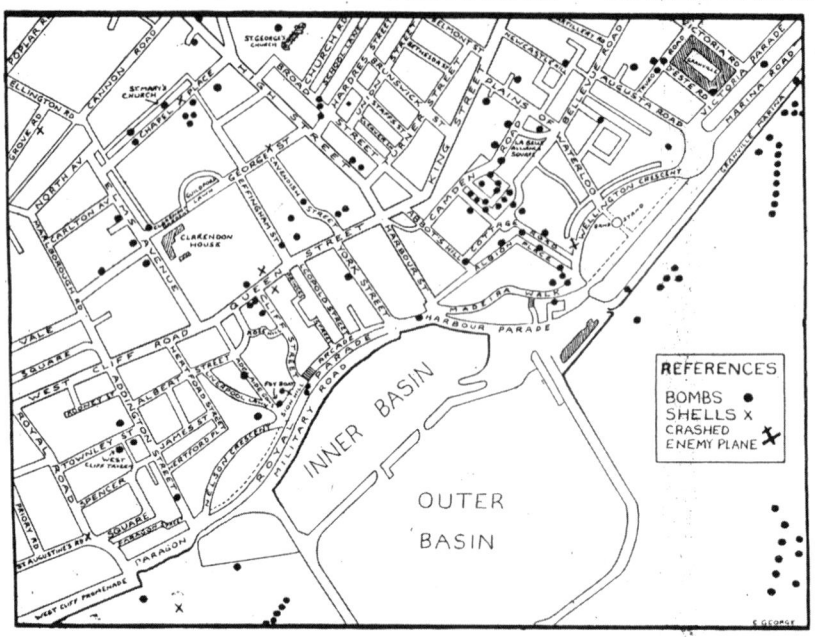

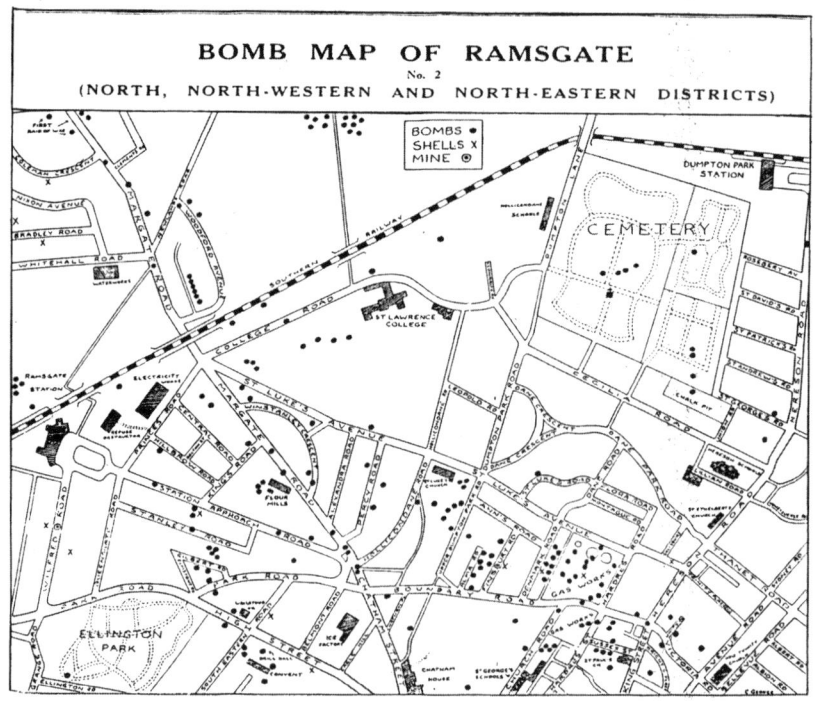

*Bomb maps of Ramsgate
(top) the town centre; (below) the northern part of the town*

8th June, 1946

To-day, as we celebrate victory, I send this personal message to you and all other boys and girls at school. For you have shared in the hardships and dangers of a total war and you have shared no less in the triumph of the Allied Nations.

I know you will always feel proud to belong to a country which was capable of such supreme effort; proud, too, of parents and elder brothers and sisters who by their courage, endurance and enterprise brought victory. May these qualities be yours as you grow up and join in the common effort to establish among the nations of the world unity and peace.

George R.I.

The Doodlebug map

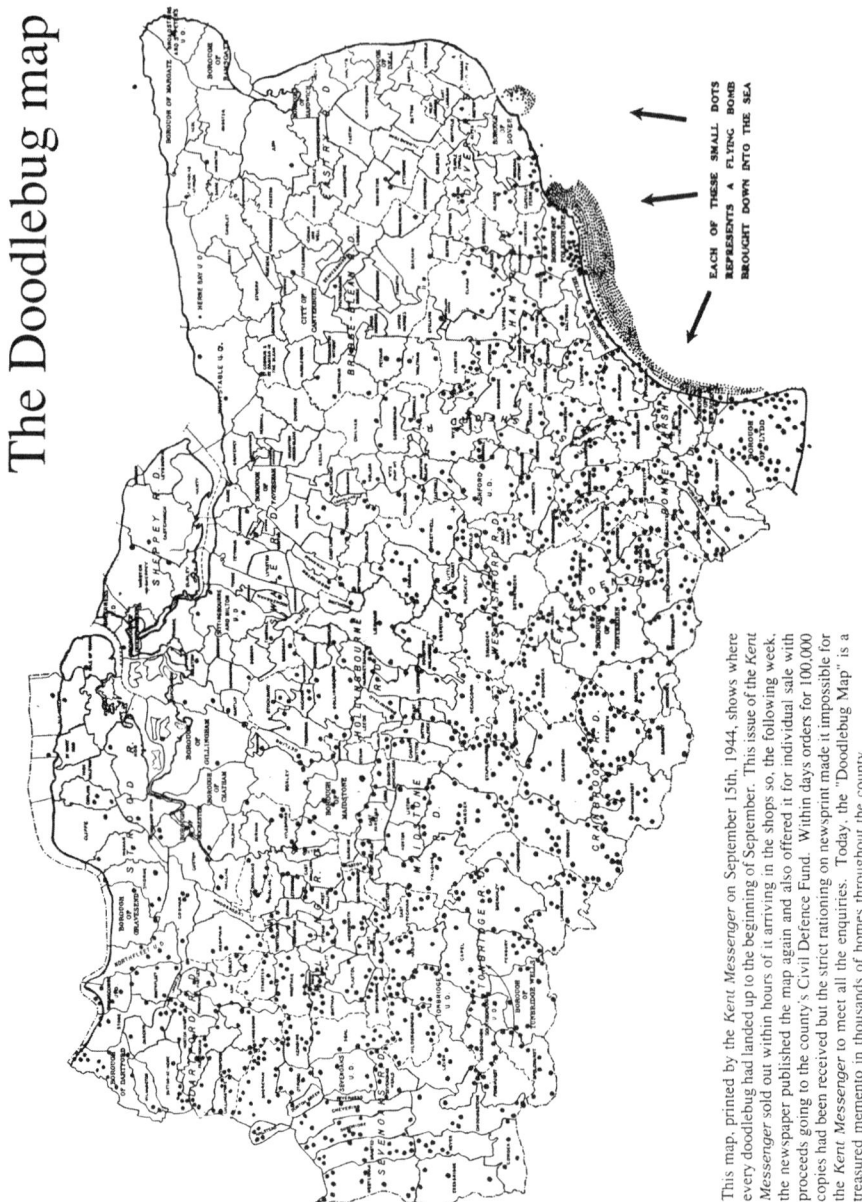

EACH OF THESE SMALL DOTS REPRESENTS A FLYING BOMB BROUGHT DOWN INTO THE SEA

This map, printed by the *Kent Messenger* on September 15th, 1944, shows where every doodlebug had landed up to the beginning of September. This issue of the *Kent Messenger* sold out within hours of it arriving in the shops so, the following week, the newspaper published the map again and also offered it for individual sale with proceeds going to the county's Civil Defence Fund. Within days orders for 100,000 copies had been received but the strict rationing on newsprint made it impossible for the *Kent Messenger* to meet all the enquiries. Today, the "Doodlebug Map" is a treasured memento in thousands of homes throughout the county.

ACKNOWLEDGEMENTS

As with *Children into Exile* and *For the Sake of the Children*, I am greatly indebted to all the contributors who are mentioned by name without whose co-operation this third book would not have been possible.

I am also most grateful to the following schools for allowing me to delve into their war-time log books and attendance registers, and who have helped me in other ways:

>Clarendon House Grammar School, Ramsgate;
>Dane Janet CP Junior School, Ramsgate;
>The Hereson School, Ramsgate;
>Minster CE Primary School, Nr. Ramsgate;
>Ramsgate Holy Trinity CE (Aided) Primary School;
>St Laurence in Thanet (Aided) Junior School, Ramsgate;
>St Lawrence College in Thanet, Ramsgate;
>St Mildred's CP School, Broadstairs.

I am also grateful to the editors of the following newspapers, for allowing me to quote from many wartime articles on the evacuees:

>*Isle of Thanet Gazette*
>*Thanet Times*
>*Kentish Gazette*
>*Kentish Express*

And to the *Kent Messenger Group* for allowing me to reproduce certain wartime photographs.

I am also grateful to the staff of the following libraries for their help during my research:

>Margate Reference Library
>Broadstairs Reference Library
>Canterbury Reference Library
>Ashford Reference Library

I must also thank the Evacuees' Reunion Association and BBC Radio Kent for their help in my search for material.

Finally, my grateful thanks go to my wife, Deborah, who has helped and encouraged me throughout the many years of research which have resulted in this 'trilogy' of Kent Evacuee books.

Every effort has been made to trace the copyright holders of certain photographic material in this book but we apologise if any copyright has inadvertently been breached.

INDEX OF PERSONAL NAMES

Arnold, Roy: 164
Arnold, Sheila: 179
Barber, Jan: 168
Bass, Jeanne: 29
Bonnick, Evelyn: 157
Booth, Vera: 100
Brooks, Gordon: 175
Campany, Arthur: 72
Carlton, Mary: 154
Chamberlain, Jean: 43
Chapman, Olive: 181
Cinderey, Anthony: 13
Collison, Audrey, 61
Cowell, Marie: 135
Cox, Betty: 95
Cox, Violet: 94
Cramp, Mary: 187
Davis, June: 108
Deacon, Peter: 18, 55
Degg, Olive: 78
Dennis, Audrey: 107
Doherty, Roy: 17, 83
Dorkings, William: 42
Edwards, June: 89
Elizabeth, Princess: 203
Emptage, George: 21, 109
Enright, Irene: 185
Friend, Marjorie: 130
Fuller, Jean: 98
Gardner, Colin: 117
Groombridge, John: 37
Harvey, Stella: 183
Heaton, Joan: 54
Hills, Eileen: 113
Holland, Joyceline: 23, 101

Horn, Joan: 67
Horn, Joyce: 87
Horn, Marjorie: 70
Horn, Peggy: 65
Jackson, Milly: 81
Johnson, Laurie: 86
Kentish, Betty: 60
Knight, Hazel: 84
Laker, Janet: 17, 81
Lawrence, M. A.: 19
Matthews, Cecily: 21, 107
McGill, Eileen: 147
Norris, Eileen: 76
Owen, Antony: 18, 63
Parker, Joan: 97
Peete, June: 118
Philpott, Douglas: 96
Price, Beryl: 19, 53
Rich, Rachel: 181
Rogers, Peter: 115
Sackett, Brian: 19, 64
Small, Janet: 18
Small, Joan: 57
Smith, K. R.: 170
Stigger, D. R.: 168
Sutton, Ivy: 102
Thornton, Irene: 17, 49
Tilbrook, Barbara: 91
Tipping, Edna: 104
Toole, Ron: 105
Walker, Eileen: 79
Wright, Don: 90